How to Be an Educational and Developmental Psychologist

Written in a clear and accessible style, this book presents a wealth of practical information to guide the next generation of educational and developmental psychologists in Australia and New Zealand in pursuing a career in the field.

There are over 800 educational and developmental psychologists in Australia, and over 200 educational psychologists in New Zealand, who represent a diverse workforce. Pathways to becoming an educational and developmental psychologist have seen rapid shifts with updated key competencies that prospective educational and developmental psychologists need to be aware of. This book gives the reader a comprehensive understanding of what makes an educational and developmental psychologist and outlines seven steps required to become an endorsed educational and developmental psychologist. Specifically, it offers guidance on understanding the role and its history, tertiary study requirements, registration requirements, professional competencies, skills and attributes needed, work experience, professional associations and member groups, endorsement and supervision requirements, finding work, and starting work. With a primary focus on Australia, each chapter also features a section on the career in New Zealand, with a variety of psychologists sharing their expertise and reflections from their experiences in New Zealand.

This resource is essential reading for students, provisional psychologists, and practising psychologists. At the same time, it provides insights for other educational and health professionals who may work multi-, inter-, or transdisciplinary with educational and developmental psychologists.

Kelly-Ann Allen is an Educational and Developmental Psychologist and Associate Professor in Educational Psychology and Counselling at Monash University, Clayton, Australia, and Principal Honorary Fellow at the University of Melbourne, Parkville, Australia.

Chelsea Hyde is an Educational and Developmental Psychologist, Senior Lecturer, and Course Coordinator of Educational and Developmental Psychology at the University of Melbourne, Parkville, Australia.

Emily Berger is an Educational and Developmental Psychologist and Senior Lecturer in Educational Psychology and Counselling at Monash University, Clayton, Australia.

Joe Coyne is an Educational and Developmental Psychologist and Course Coordinator of the Postgraduate Professional Training Programs at the School of Psychology and Counselling, Queensland University of Technology, Australia.

Simone Gindidis is an Educational and Developmental Psychologist and Private Practice Director of SavvyPsych, Melbourne, Australia.

Camelia Wilkinson is an Educational and Developmental Psychologist and Private Practice Director of CW Psychological Services, Melbourne, Australia. She is the current chair of the College of Educational and Developmental Psychologists.

Zoe A. Morris is an Educational and Developmental Psychologist, Course Leader of the Master of Educational and Developmental Psychology (Acting), and Lecturer in Educational Psychology and Counselling at Monash University, Clayton, Australia.

Gerald Wurf is an Educational and Developmental Psychologist and Senior Lecturer in Counselling and Educational Psychology at Monash University, Clayton, Australia.

How to Be a Practitioner Psychologist in Australia and New Zealand

The *How to Be a Practitioner Psychologist in Australia and New Zealand* series is aimed at providing a clear, accessible and reader-friendly guide to the routes available to becoming a practitioner psychologist in Australia and New Zealand. Each book covers key topics such as understanding the role of a practitioner psychologist, tertiary study, professional practice and registration requirements, skills and attributes, professional associations, finding work, and future directions.

Providing both information and advice, including testimonials from those recently qualified, this series will offer an invaluable introduction to anyone considering a career in this fascinating profession.

How to Be an Educational and Developmental Psychologist
From University Applications to Entering the Workforce
Kelly-Ann Allen, Chelsea Hyde, Emily Berger, Joe Coyne, Simone Gindidis, Camelia Wilkinson, Zoe A. Morris, and Gerald Wurf

How to Be an Educational and Developmental Psychologist

From University Applications to Entering the Workforce

Kelly-Ann Allen, Chelsea Hyde, Emily Berger, Joe Coyne, Simone Gindidis, Camelia Wilkinson, Zoe A. Morris, and Gerald Wurf

Cover artwork and Illustrations by Kathryn Kallady

Routledge
Taylor & Francis Group

LONDON AND NEW YORK

Cover Image: Cover artwork and Illustrations by Kathryn Kallady

First published 2023
by Routledge
4 Park Square, Milton Park, Abingdon, Oxon OX14 4RN

and by Routledge
605 Third Avenue, New York, NY 10158

Routledge is an imprint of the Taylor & Francis Group, an informa business

British Library Cataloguing-in-Publication Data
A catalogue record for this book is available from the British Library

Library of Congress Cataloging-in-Publication Data
Names: Allen, Kelly-Ann (Educational psychologist), author. |
    Hyde, Chelsea, author. | Berger, Emily, author.
Title: How to be an educational and developmental psychologist :
    from university applications to entering the workforce / Kelly-Ann Allen,
    Chelsea Hyde, Emily Berger, Joe Coyne, Simo4ne Gindidis, Camelia
    Wilkinson, Zoe A. Morris and Gerald Wurf.
Description: First edition. | New York : Routledge, 2023. |
    Series: How to be a practitioner psychologist in Australia and
    New Zealand | Includes bibliographical references and index.
Identifiers: LCCN 2022056676 (print) | LCCN 2022056677 (ebook) |
    ISBN 9781032362496 (hbk) | ISBN 9781032362489 (pbk) |
    ISBN 9781003330974 (ebk)
Subjects: LCSH: School psychologists—Training of—Australia. |
    School psychologists—Training of—New Zealand. |
    Educational psychology—Vocational guidance. | Developmental
    psychology—Vocational guidance.
Classification: LCC LB3013.6 .A4 2023 (print) | LCC LB3013.6 (ebook) |
    DDC 371.7/130994—dc23/eng/20230215
LC record available at https://lccn.loc.gov/2022056676
LC ebook record available at https://lccn.loc.gov/2022056677

ISBN: 978-1-032-36249-6 (hbk)
ISBN: 978-1-032-36248-9 (pbk)
ISBN: 978-1-003-33097-4 (ebk)

DOI: 10.4324/9781003330974

Typeset in Galliard
by Apex CoVantage, LLC

Contents

Contents

Acknowledgements

The authors would like to express great gratitude towards the generosity and kindness of Kathryn Kallady, who provided the original cover art and illustrations for *How to Be an Educational and Developmental Psychologist: From University Applications to Entering the Workforce*.

Acknowledgement and appreciation go out to our educational and developmental psychology community who have helped bring this book to fruition. In no particular order, we wish to thank Alan Hudson, Andrea Fairlie, Andrea Fernandez, Anna Jovanovic, Cameron Lee, Caroline Keating, Carrie Parratt, Cathlin Sheridan, Cheree Murrihy, Christine Grové, Cindy Hsiao, Claire Ting, Dianne Summers, Doug Scott, John Roodenburg, Nerelie Freeman, Pascale Paradis, Eileen Scott Stokes, Erica Frydenberg, Georgia Dawson, Grace Mackie, Hannah Yared, Helen Johansen, Jake Kraska, Jenna Miller, Jennah Alonso, Jesse Diggins, Jessica Carroll, Jessica Rodaughan, Jessica Smead, Kate Crosher, Keshini Niles, Kirsty Vondeling, Lauren Brabham, Linda Gilmore, Louise Laskey, Lydia Soh, Man Ching Esther Chan, Marianne Bishop, Melissa O'Halloran, Mervyn Jackson, Michael Bernard, Michelle Andrews Luke, Nicholas Gamble, Paul Bertoia, Paul Garon Lan, Louise Mclean, Rhys Mawson, Sally Kenney, Sarah Pearson, Shameema Saleem, Simon Finkelstein, Sophie Morris, Tamara Zafiropoulos, Tasma Dunn, Tim Hannan, Vicki Mckenzie, and Wendy McKenzie.

A special thanks to Monash University's Megan Lowe, Lara McKinley, and Hannah Machin for assisting to prepare some of the quotes from educational and developmental psychologists provided in the book.

An additional special thanks to Eileen Scott Stokes, who has been a tremendous help to this book and is soon to retire after an incredible 30 years of service to the profession. We are very grateful to Eileen, along with hundreds of other educational and developmental psychologists over the years.

Finally, a special mihi to our Kiwi colleagues and collaborators who offered their expertise and reflections from their experiences in Aotearoa New Zealand: Jean Annan, Rachel Drayton, Michele Blick, Sharnee Escott, and Robyn Stead. E mihi ana mātou ki ēnei māreikura e tautoko ana mai nei ki tēnei kaupapa. Tēnā koutou. Thank you to Greg Ratcliffe for his kindness and help, and Robyn Stead should be acknowledged for her remarkable networking and endless generosity. We are indebted to you.

In loving memory

This book is written in loving memory to our dear colleague and friend Janene Swalwell.

Edited photo of Janene Swalwell

Foreword
from Australia

Erica Fydenberg

You could almost say that I am an Educational Psychology veteran. In one form or another, I have been associated with the profession since 1970 without a break and without one minute of boredom or dissatisfaction. My levels of engagement, excitement, and learning have continued unabated since my first days in the field early in my career.

Having trained as a teacher and having had a short stint in the secondary school system in New South Wales, followed by three years in the role of Mental Welfare Officer in London with statutory responsibilities relating to mental health, I arrived in Melbourne as a novice school psychologist with little training and even less supervision. Over the past two decades, I had the joy and opportunity of working in multiple school settings as a counsellor, a consultant, a parent-educator, and general problem solver from preschool through to the high-pressured years of the School Certificate. The problems were many, as were the solutions, but there was always learning along the way, whether it was counselling skills, family therapy, or the newly emerging field of neuroscience. The profession was and remains truly diverse, ever changing in the skills required and the demands of the role.

Two decades followed as a curriculum developer and trainer of school psychologists, which complemented research to enhance both my own and my student's practice. We could not be complacent as circumstances changed and there was ever-increasing range of legislative requirements that needed to be understood and met. Along the way, there was active contribution to the major professional association representing psychologists, namely the Australian Psychological Society, with that contribution growing in the most recent decade.

Clearly, I am a fan of the profession in which I have had a most meaningful and fulfilling career and which I promote with enthusiasm to others so why is a book that tells us *How to Be an Educational Psychologist* needed?

While the profession may have been started by little known luminaries such as John Hall and others who returned from World War II with a lot of good will and a little psychology by today's standards, we muddled along as best as we could, most probably doing some good along the way. Now a 21st-century cohort of experienced practitioners is sharing their knowledge and insights for those going into the field.

This book is much needed and very timely as psychologists in general, and educational psychologists, are in high demand as the world becomes more complex, and the educational system is expected to do so much more than teach the basics. Schools are there to guide young people to well-being and success in life and relationships from hereon.

The chapters by writers from a range of settings address topics relating to registration, professional competence, professional associations which can be so important for collegiality and meeting ongoing professional development requirements, and some history of the profession as well. As I recall it was not till the early 1990s when for example, at the University of Melbourne, we enshrined requirements that Master of Educational Psychology students needed to undertake rigorous research that had to be endorsed by the University's ethics committee. The research undertaken by students under supervision and support has enriched both the trainees and the community. Countless of those research projects found their way into print in refereed journals. Certainly, by the time the Doctor of Educational Psychology program came into being in the early 2000s, it was given that these research projects would be published. Many of those candidates went onto having illustrious careers of their own.

This book also addresses topics such as how to go for an interview; sometimes what seems the most straightforward is the most helpful.

Any professional or would-be professional would benefit by having such a compendium available to them with tips for both an understanding of the profession, as a ready resource, and an ongoing stimulus for reinvigorating as a professional, and sometimes redirection. Today we think about job satisfaction and working with our strengths. A book like this can help us tackle our weaknesses as challenges to deal with and focus on improving our strengths and directing ourselves to that corner of the profession which is most satisfying at any point of time.

As a parent, I know that I grew with the profession as did my interests. When my children were pre-adolescent, I enjoyed working with the early years and focusing on parent skills training and another period was when I became most interested in working with adolescents. Indeed, working with adolescents is what launched me on my research career. Then there are the case studies that remind us how fulfilling a helping profession can be. There is always meaning and purpose to one's work. A famous actor Peter Ustinov once said that he felt that he had never had to do a day's work in his life because he loved his work so much. I really feel like Peter that I have not had to do a day's work and that is why I still work and find it so fulfilling.

There is such a dearth of resources to guide the practice and training of educational psychologists. Therefore, big congratulations to Dr Kelly-Ann Allen for bringing the team together and to the team for making such an important contribution to the field. The delightful artwork and the personal quotes from practitioners bring the volume to life for the reader. This is indeed a significant volume for those embarking or thinking of embarking on a career in educational psychology, or just wishing to refresh their professional knowhow.

Erica Frydenberg, AM, PhD, Hon
Fellow of the Australian Psychological Society

Foreword
from New Zealand

Sonja Macfarlane

Kua tawhiti kē to haerenga mai, kia kore e haere tonu.
He tino nui rawa ou mahi, kia kore e mahi nui tonu.

We have come too far not to go further.
We have done too much not to do more.

(Ta Himi Henare [Sir James Henare]
Ngati Hine tribal elder and leader)

The *whakatauāki* (proverb) given here encapsulates the essence of what I believe this book is promoting—a book that is indeed timely and worthy. Our world is becoming more diverse, more globally connected and interconnected, and we are facing challenges like never before. The COVID-19 pandemic (as one such example) has not only taught us a great deal about ourselves – who we are, and what matters to us the most – but also forced us to revisit what we are doing, what else we may need to do, and how best we could do things in order to preserve the well-being and happiness of those with whom we work, and each other. The demands for, and on, skilled and competent educational psychologists are indeed growing. We value and acknowledge the work that you all do, supporting our *tamariki* (children), *rangatahi* (youth), and their *whānau* (families) through times of challenge and change.

As Fellow of the New Zealand Psychological Society (NZPsS), I have had the extreme honour of working with, and alongside, Educational, Clinical, and Child and Family Psychologists – specifically in the areas of tertiary teaching, tertiary course development and accreditation, registrations, internships, research, supervision, and practice in the field. What I feel proud about is the passion with which our educational psychologists embrace Aotearoa New Zealand's founding document,

Te Tiriti o Waitangi (The Treaty of Waitangi). This bicultural document is an agreement that commits educational psychologists to honouring its articles and principles; codes that serve to uphold the tenets of culturally responsive professional practice. The articles and principles promote the notion that language, culture, and identity count, that we all have untapped potential and unique strengths, and that we are entitled to be supported and scaffolded to taste success – to flourish.

The chapters in this book have created an opportunity for us to hold hands across the Tasman Sea. Australia and Aotearoa; as Australasian siblings, we can teach and learn from each other's histories, cultural narratives, and knowledges, in order to enrich our respective contexts so that we are better placed to support those who also reach out to us for professional help in times of need. What a privilege it is to have this opportunity to work together. To our current educational psychologists, and those of the future; this significant book will be a valued resource which shares real life and practice-based realities.

My sincere acknowledgements to all of the contributors of this book – *he mihi nunui, he mihi mahana hoki, ki a koutou katoa* (immense and warm acknowledgements to you all). And every journey must start with a vision, therefore to you, Dr Kelly-Ann Allen, *he mihi mahana ki a koe mō tō rangatiratanga o te kaupapa nei* (warm acknowledgements to you for your leadership of this project).

Associate Professor Sonja Macfarlane, PhD, FRSNZ,
Te Kura o te Mātauranga, Institute of Education,
College of Humanities & Social Sciences,
Te Kunenga ki Pūrehuroa, Massey University

Preface

Welcome to the world of educational and developmental psychology!

You are reading this book because you are either thinking about a career in educational and developmental psychology, aspiring to be an educational and developmental psychologist or well on your way. This book is designed to help guide you along the path to becoming an educational and developmental psychologist and tap into all the resources and opportunities this rewarding career affords.

This guidebook aims to offer you the most up-to-date advice on a range of topics – starting with preparing for your interviews, to obtaining a job, and maintaining professional development once you are qualified.

You will find that the educational and developmental psychology community is one of the largest psychology communities in Australia and one that is collaborative and connected.

We'd like to welcome you to our community.

A special title

There may come a time in every aspiring educational and developmental psychologist's journey when they realise that obtaining postgraduate training in Educational and Developmental Psychology does not automatically equate to becoming an educational and developmental psychologist. For those of you who are still trying to wrap your head around this, after completing postgraduate study in educational and developmental psychology, graduates are required to complete an additional two-year registrar program to legally use the title of educational and developmental psychologist. This might feel unfair or even illogical. Some will question the point of doing a master's degree in the first place. And others, so tired of the thought of additional study, will feel like there is nothing worse than engaging in the additional two-year registrar program (or an equivalent alternative). They may leave their dreams of becoming an educational and developmental psychologist behind and go forth after completing a Master of Psychology program into the profession of psychology as what is fondly known as a Generalist Psychologist.

In Australia, this means that they cannot refer to themselves as an educational and developmental psychologist (or even educational psychologists for those who like brevity) because the title is protected in Australia under National Law (2009). This means that unless you are registered and endorsed as an educational and developmental psychologist, you cannot use the title.

Of course, there are ways people overcome this:

- Charlie has a background in educational and developmental psychology.
- Ashna has an interest in educational and developmental psychology.
- Sai completed a Master of Educational and Developmental Psychology degree.

These examples can be true statements and do not violate the protected educational and developmental psychologist title. However, there is a fine line to consider, whereby psychologists must avoid being unlawful or reckless in misleading the general public to believe that they are registered and endorsed in an area that they are not.

The simple fact is that becoming an educational and developmental psychologist takes time. The registrar program is an additional hurdle, but as you will see through the course of this book, it is a hurdle that can be rewarding and fulfilling. The additional training helps graduates of postgraduate training in Educational and Developmental Psychology feel more equipped to join the workforce. Many would argue that the supervision provided to new graduates as part of the registrar program is essential regardless of whether graduates decide to seek endorsement in educational and developmental psychology, and so why not complete the registrar program and get endorsed as an Educational and Developmental Psychologist along the way. As an educational and developmental psychologist, you are a part of a growing community – many of whom have contributed to this book.

A much-needed field

As of 2022, there were only 836 endorsed educational and developmental psychologists registered in Australia, and 35,275 registered generalist psychologists, meaning educational and developmental psychologists make up less than 5% of the professional psychological workforce. There is an unprecedented demand for educational and developmental psychologists due to the increased rates of mental health problems following the emergence of COVID-19, a shortfall of preventive to acute psychological treatment, and a lack of availability or long waitlists for psychologists in general. The current situation has precipitated State and Federal governments to increase psychological support. As an example, an increasing number of mental health practitioners have been placed in schools in Victoria. Although this does not fill the vast demand for psychological support, and schools still lack sufficient numbers of psychologists to support students and staff, it is a temporary measure to partially address the professional gap in expertise. We need more educational and developmental psychologists in Australia.

Educational and developmental psychologists are an essential and in-demand profession. Once you have obtained your qualification, it becomes much easier to find work.

A winding, yet interesting path

This book seeks to walk you through the process of becoming an educational and developmental psychologist.

The pathway to becoming an educational and developmental psychologist is a little like choosing your own adventure novel. While a student can leave at any part of the progression – after undergraduate (or even during!), after an honours or four-year degree in psychology, or after a postgraduate degree (such as a master's degree), there are also alternative pathways to becoming an educational psychologist that you will see in this book. Not all paths will lead to becoming an educational and developmental psychologist, but if you are reading this book hoping to enter the educational and developmental field, then you are in good hands. Here's a little bit about what's in store for you:

Chapter 1 will dive into the history of educational and developmental psychology in Australia. It will discuss how educational and developmental psychology is defined and briefly discuss the differences between educational and developmental psychology as an area of professional practice versus educational and developmental psychology as an academic discipline. If you ever wondered why educational and developmental psychology was housed under "education" and not "psychology" within most institutions, this chapter is for you!

Chapter 2 will examine the training requirements of educational and developmental psychologists, specifically the tertiary qualifications that are required. The chapter will also address how prospective students can prepare sample application letters and what they might expect from interviews.

Chapter 3 will address the registration requirements for educational and developmental psychologists in Australia. International requirements and transferring registration for educational psychologists in Australia will also be discussed.

Chapter 4 will outline the eight core competencies in the education and developmental psychology profession. The chapter will specifically focus on educational and developmental psychology competencies as they relate to the eight core areas.

Chapter 5 explores Australian educational psychologists' personal qualities, values, and behaviours, and considers the alignment with best practices.

Chapter 6 discusses what it takes to prepare oneself for a career in educational and developmental psychology. It will provide information on the types of skills and knowledge that are required in educational and developmental psychology.

Chapter 7 includes information about professional associations and member groups. This chapter explores relevant member groups and how they may be harnessed for benefits such as service, conferences, and scholarships.

Chapter 8 focuses on endorsement and registrar program supervision requirements. It provides information about the endorsement process and what to expect from supervision and the registrar program. This chapter really spells out the benefits of being an educational and developmental psychologist

Chapter 9 showcases six perspectives from educational and developmental psychologists working in four contexts: school, private practice, hospital, and an organisation. It will include stories from educational and developmental psychologists in different contexts.

Chapter 10 will offer some tips and techniques for finding employment opportunities and where to look for job listings. It also focuses on tips for your curriculum vitae to make yourself stand out from other applicants.

Chapter 11 includes information that will help prepare future educational and developmental psychologists for a productive professional life. Moreover, the challenges facing professionals today will be underlined, and resources to help prepare for a successful transition into the field will be provided. The chapter explores the transferability of skills to other industries, workplaces, and contexts overseas.

Chapter 12 addresses the challenges and future directions of educational and developmental psychology. Emerging and existing trends in the field are discussed including evidence-based practice and practice-based evidence, Indigenous psychology, and a focus on transdisciplinary collaborations, and prevention and well-being. This chapter also explores and imagines future careers for educational and developmental psychologists in HealthTech and EduTech industries, climate change responses, geropsychology, and even on social media.

There is much to learn about the journey to become an educational and developmental psychologist and this book maps out most of the things you will need to know.

About the authorship team

This book is written by a group of educational and developmental psychologists whose careers span many years in the field. The team members have expertise in a range of areas including professional practice, supervision, endorsement, registration, and professional development. We bring collective experience working in a range of settings including schools, academia, private practice, HealthTech, hospitals, disability, aged care, and early childhood.

I'm (Kelly-Ann Allen) Associate Professor in the School of Educational Psychology and Counselling Psychology in the Faculty of Education at Monash University. I am interested in building communities around my professional interests in educational and developmental psychology – a great match for research interests on our need to belong. Let me introduce you to my co-authors.

Dr Chelsea Hyde is Senior Lecturer and the course leader of the Master of Educational Psychology program at the Melbourne Graduate School of Education, University of Melbourne. After 15 years of work as a school psychologist, she recognises the critical role of educational and developmental psychologists in supporting the mental health outcomes of our young people. As a result, she's committed to training the future workforce of educational psychologists.

Dr Emily Berger is Senior Lecturer in the School of Educational Psychology and Counselling at Monash University. She has worked in the Master of Educational and Developmental Psychology program since 2017 and is passionate about fostering the next generation of educational and developmental psychologists in Australia. Emily has a background working as a psychologist in schools and private practice and is an endorsed and supervising Educational and Developmental Psychologist.

Joe Coyne is Course Coordinator of Postgraduate Professional Training Programs at the School of Psychology and Counselling, Faculty of Health, QUT. He is endorsed as both Educational and Developmental Psychologist and Clinical Psychologist. He began his career with professional training as Clinical Psychologist in 1995. However, his work with people across the lifespan saw a natural transition to becoming endorsed as an Educational and Developmental Psychologist in 2011.

Dr Simone Gindidis is an Educational and Developmental Psychologist passionate about the integration of technology with psychological assessments and therapy. She is Director of SavvyPsych, a private clinic offering developmental assessments, counselling services, clinical supervision, and HealthTech consultancy. She is also the co-founder of GameIQ, a company developing clinician-led digital innovations. Simone was the first Clinical Lead at a leading Australian digital therapeutics company producing digital tools to support executive function development in early childhood. She is an energetic advocate for the role of educational and developmental psychology in the evidence-based development of ethical, quality, developmentally sensitive, fun, digital, and serious game products.

Camelia Wilkinson is an endorsed psychologist at CW Psychological Services in Victoria Australia, who for over 20 years has worked in the field of educational and developmental psychology. She has worked in the disability setting (DHS), educational settings (DET), tertiary setting (the Master of Educational Psychology at the Melbourne Graduate School of Education, University of Melbourne, and the Master of Educational and Developmental Psychology at ACU), and private sector. Camelia is a keen advocate of Educational and Developmental Psychology and is actively participating in work that helps promote the unique skills and expertise of this profession through her executive role as Chair of the College of Educational and Developmental Psychologists and her role as a Fellow of the Australian Psychological Society.

Dr Zoe A. Morris is an Educational and Developmental Psychologist, Board-Approved Supervisor with the Psychology Board of Australia, and Lecturer in the School of Educational Psychology and Counselling in the Faculty of Education, Monash University and Course Leader of the Master of Educational and Developmental Psychology. After working in government primary and secondary schools as a psychologist, Zoe has taught in psychology programs at Monash since 2014 and was the deputy course leader for the Master of Educational and Developmental

Psychology from 2017 to 2021. Zoe is proud to be one of fewer than 1,000 Educational and Developmental Psychologists in Australia and is looking forward to growth of this endorsement area in the future.

Gerald Wurf is a registered psychologist and Senior Lecturer in the School of Educational Psychology and Counselling at Monash University. He is the immediate past-Chair of the Australian Psychological Society's College of Educational and Developmental Psychologists. As a psychologist, he has extensive experience working in disability services, schools, and mental health.

You will also notice that the book is filled with beautiful illustrations – many of these artworks have been created by Kathryn Kallady, also an educational and developmental psychologist who manages to combine art and illustration to help assist in science communication and psychoeducation. Kathryn has worked in several settings including public and private schools and public hospital settings. She is currently in private practice providing psychotherapy and neurodevelopmental assessment. Kathryn is engaged in research and is a sessional lecturer at Monash University.

You can read more about our author biographies in the back of this book.

The authors and illustrator of this book hope that you enjoy reading about the various pathways and proficiencies needed to become an educational and developmental psychologist in Australia. You will also find reflections from experiences in Aotearoa New Zealand courtesy of our colleagues Jean Annan, Rachel Drayton, Michele Blick, and Robyn Stead.

Edited photograph of the authorship team. The authorship team is a group of educational and developmental psychologists at varied stages of their career with diverse backgrounds and experience. We are also fortunate to have Kathryn Kallady's illustrations. From left to right: Camelia Wilkinson, Kathryn Kallady, Kelly-Ann Allen, Joe Coyne, Emily Berger, Simone Gindidis, Chelsea Hyde, Zoe A. Morris, and Gerald Wurf.

Kelly-Ann Allen on behalf of the team!

Understanding the role of educational and developmental psychologists in Australia

"It isn't always an easy job to support those who are struggling, but it is definitely a rewarding career. I love seeing the difference I am making to the lives of children and young people."
—Cindy Hsiao

Introduction

Educational and developmental psychology is variously referred to as *educational and developmental psychology*, *educational psychology*, or abbreviated to *ed and dev* (or *ed & dev*). It is often confused with school psychology, child psychology, and developmental psychology. Sometimes these terms are used interchangeably, and training institutions can mix them up a little! Take Monash University's Master of Educational and Developmental Psychology, located in the School of *Educational Psychology* and Counselling! Or Melbourne University's Master of Educational Psychology, where *developmental* psychology is not mentioned in the degree title, but is indeed taught. This chapter intends to set the scene for how Australian educational and developmental psychology is defined and guided by professional bodies and associations. It will outline the origins of the discipline and field of professional practice, explore how training in educational and developmental psychology has grown in Australia, and discuss the core considerations for deciding to be an educational and developmental psychologist in the first place.

DOI: 10.4324/9781003330974-1

1

Defining educational and developmental psychology

Psychology comes from the Greek word "psyche," which means mind, and "logos," which roughly translates as study. As such, it means the study of the mind and is defined as the science of the study of the mind and behaviour. Educational and developmental psychology, as a branch of psychology, can be seen as much more than simply studying mind and behaviour. Defining educational and developmental psychology becomes complex because of the unique way it sits as both an area of practice and academic discipline. The seemingly innocuous words "developmental" and "educational" have also been known to spark great debates from within and outside the field.

In Australia, there are some misconceptions about educational and developmental psychologists. People often presume that educational and developmental psychologists only work in schools and with children. In fact, many educational and developmental psychologists are employed outside of schools and work with people of all ages, including teens, adults, and older age groups.

Despite the field's breadth and importance, psychology students often report that they discovered educational and developmental psychology by chance. Information about the field can be hard to find, which poses a challenge for psychology students choosing a distinct field of applied practice to study or the general public seeking appropriate psychological services (Gilmore et al., 2013).

Although general awareness of educational and developmental psychology as an area of practice is arguably low, many have worked to raise awareness of the field and promote the identity of educational and developmental psychology as an integral area in the broader practice of psychology.

According to the Australian Psychological Society (APS, 2022a), educational and developmental psychology is a field that concerns itself with well-being across the lifespan. Of note, in the title is the word *development*. This means that educational and developmental psychologists have skills in understanding how people learn and develop throughout their lives (APS, 2022a). Therefore, educational and developmental psychology focuses on the development and learning of people from infancy to old age (Gilmore et al., 2013). The Australian Health Practitioner Regulation Agency (AHPRA, 2020) adopts a similar understanding: educational and developmental psychologists utilise knowledge of psychology, learning, behaviour, and social and emotional development to assist a variety of age groups (e.g. from children, young persons, adults, and older adults).

Educational and developmental psychologists have a range of skills and knowledge in areas such as assessment, intervention, and diagnosis for behavioural difficulties, disability-related challenges, neurodevelopmental disorders, mental health disorders, and learning difficulties, as well as counselling and consulting for a wide range of issues. These issues include relationships, conflict, parenting, stress, and grief, to name a few. In addition, educational and developmental psychologists have an essential role in proactive and preventive approaches that promote psychological well-being and mental health (more about that in Chapter 12).

Figure 1.1 Becoming an educational and developmental psychologist provides a diverse and unique skill set which provides several employment choices

The diverse roles of Australian educational and developmental psychologists are evident in the settings in which they work. Standard settings include private practice, hospitals, schools, disability services, and community organisations. Educational and developmental psychologists can operate under many titles in their respective workplaces. For example, they may be guidance officers, school counsellors, school psychologists, senior psychologists, disability services officers, or geropsychologists (Gilmore et al., 2013). You can read more about the varied contexts in which educational and developmental psychologists work in Chapters 9 and 11.

Educational and developmental psychology as a field

It is unclear when precisely educational and developmental psychology emerged as its own field separate from general psychology or education. However, the origins of educational and developmental psychology have been traced back as far as the classical Greek period, with philosophers such as Plato, Socrates, and Aristotle keenly interested in the role of education and its place in society.

According to Hill (2013), it was not until the post-Darwinian end of the 19th century that psychology emerged as an academic discipline in British universities. It was here that educational and developmental psychology first emerged as a field of psychology concerned with children's education and learning processes.

The development of educational and developmental psychology as an independent discipline was partly due to the introduction of compulsory education by the 1870 Education Act in the UK (Hill, 2013). For the first time, the education system witnessed the growth of a diverse student population with varying needs. Psychology had a crucial role to play in responding to these needs.

Educational and developmental psychology may be one of the least understood or even misunderstood areas of psychology. In most other countries, educational or school psychology is separate from developmental psychology, both in training programs and in professional titles (Gilmore et al., 2013).

In Australia today, educational and developmental psychology is both an academic discipline and a professional area of expertise. When we explain our title to our U.S. colleagues, they are surprised that there is a specific qualification for educational and developmental psychologists. In the United States, educational and developmental psychology is not a distinctive area of applied psychological practice. Most educational and developmental psychologists in the United States will be researchers, while school psychology is the recognised practice specialism.

Educational and developmental psychology as an academic discipline can be split into two areas:

1 Educational and developmental psychology as a teaching and research discipline (e.g. in teacher training and applied areas of practice)
2 Educational and developmental psychology as an applied practice area that is distinct from other areas of psychological practice.

You will see academics fall into one or sometimes both areas.

Educational and developmental psychology as a research discipline focuses on learning, teaching, and students. More specifically, it examines factors such as psychological issues that may arise when teaching, the unique needs of specific students, and student motivation and achievement.

Educational and developmental psychologists who work in applied practice areas often incorporate a wide range of knowledge from such areas as behavioural psychology, cognitive psychology, psychometrics, developmental psychology, and the psychology of individual differences into their practice. The work of educational and developmental psychologists, especially within the Australian context, also emphasises the importance of well-being across the lifespan (APS, 2022a). For instance, within this area of psychology, there is a focus on development across the lifespan and how adjustment at different life stages can either promote or impair well-being (Gilmore et al., 2013). Educational and developmental psychologists have skills in assessing, understanding, and developing approaches for people whose developmental trajectory has been impacted by biological, social, psychological, or environmental challenges.

From an applied practice perspective, educational and developmental psychologists apply their skills and expertise to assist their clients to better understand their presenting issues and meet their goals. Some examples of their work include (but are not limited to) assessing people with cognitive, emotional, social, or behavioural difficulties, implementing intervention programs, counselling, and consulting with teachers, parents, and other stakeholders such as other healthcare practitioners.

It is important to emphasise that educational and developmental psychologists also receive training in working with people without identified problems or challenges. This work might involve working preventively with individuals, groups, organisations, or systems. This work can be concerned with proactive approaches that might involve promoting mental health, social and emotional competencies, coping skills, stress management, or a sense of belonging. It might involve policy development or advocacy, health promotion, or psychoeducation to raise awareness that there are specific things individuals and groups can do to prevent mental health or learning problems from arising.

It might feel overwhelming when first learning about the potential breath of educational and developmental psychology. Dr Nicholas Gamble, Senior Lecturer and Psychologist and Director of the Psychology and Counselling Programs at Monash University, suggests that when starting out,

> Take the time before you start working as a psychologist to get to know the populations you want to work with. If you don't see and experience the typical behaviour, cognition, and interactions of the group, then identifying atypical presentations will be far more complex.

More advice on starting work can be found in Chapters 10 and 11.

The day-to-day tasks of a practising educational and developmental psychologist can be very diverse. Chapter 11 provides more details about the work of educational and developmental psychologists.

The focus of this book is the training of educational and developmental psychologists as practitioners. However, the science-practitioner nature of our profession means that the work of an educational and developmental practitioner is closely tied to academic practice, research, evaluation, and understanding.

In the UK, the public understanding of educational psychology is well aligned with school psychology and the work of Australian educational and developmental psychologists (even though "developmental" is not included in the UK title). Some could say the public understanding of what an educational psychologist does is much broader in the UK. This may be because the role is more clearly defined and identified (i.e. educational psychologists in the UK are mostly based in schools).

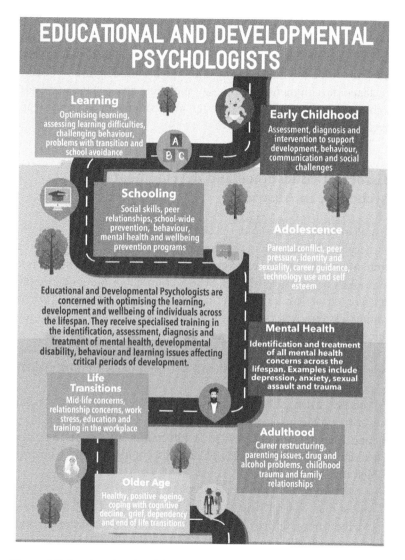

Figure 1.2 An educational and developmental psychologist has received training in working with a broad range of expertise, including assessment, diagnosis, disability, behaviour, well-being, and learning

Source: Image created by Simone Gindidis and supplied with permission from the College of Educational and Developmental Psychologists National Committee.

Also, most school staff in the UK clearly understand the role of educational psychologists, whereas in Australia, the active process of defining the role to potential clients, the community, or within varying work contexts can be essential. Having a good working definition of educational and developmental psychology and being able to give an elevator pitch to others could be your first step in becoming an educational and developmental psychologist!

History of educational and developmental psychology in Australia

Australian educational and developmental psychology has evolved over the decades. Initially, State departments of education employed and often offered training opportunities for teachers to become school counsellors or guidance officers. School counsellors and guidance officers worked almost exclusively in public schools. However, teacher training was removed over time as a specific requirement for entry into educational and developmental psychology programs.

A puzzle has been why educational and developmental psychology commonly sits under education and not psychology in most training courses in Australia.

Professor Michael Bernard, formally a Professorial Fellow at The University of Melbourne, Emeritus Professor, California State University and Founder of You Can Do It Education, reflects on the emergence of educational and developmental psychology at The University of Melbourne.

Some may wonder why it moved, but in fact at The University of Melbourne (UniMelb), educational and developmental psychology did not actually move from anywhere to the Faculty of Education. The program did not exist in any faculty at UniMelb before it was established in 1979 in the Faculty of Education.

At that time, psychology degrees were only offered in Departments of Psychology. At Melbourne, a degree in Clinical Psychology was offered in the Psychology Department.

Frank Naylor, Senior Lecturer, Faculty of Education, approached the departmental head of psychology, Alastair Heron, and enquired whether the Department of Psychology had any interest in offering a master's degree in Educational Psychology. The response was that the Department of Psychology was not interested, and the degree could not be offered in the Faculty of Education. The two-year full-time, four-year part-time course commenced in 1980 with an intake of six to eight students. The founding instructors were Frank Naylor, Gerald Ellsworth, and Michael Bernard. Frank taught individual differences, Gerry research methods and statistics, and I taught psychological assessment, intervention, and consultation.

While the University of Melbourne claimed the first Master of Educational Psychology in Australia, Monash University was not far behind. Eileen Scott Stokes, recently the long-standing psychology programs manager, is considered the backbone of educational and developmental psychology at Monash University, graduating herself from Monash in 1998. Most students who have graduated from Monash University know of Eileen and remember her fondly, with students even referring to her as *Yoda-like* in her level of knowledge and wisdom.

Eileen remembers the original educational and developmental psychology course and how it came about.

The original course commenced as the Master of Psychology in 1990 – with most coursework starting in 1991 and first placements occurring in 1992. Some students commenced in the Faculty's Master of Educational Studies in 1989, undertaking psychology specific units and then transferring to the Master of Psychology in 1992 to undertake placement. This aligns with my memory that the Master of Psychology may have started as a specialism of the Master of Education (MEd) Studies. This was all when the Faculty was known as the School of Graduate Studies. The psychology units were first offered as part of the MEd Studies from 1988 to 1989. The first enrolment in the Master of Psychology (MPsych) seems to be from 1990 when it was a mix of MEd Studies and MPsych. After 1992, two streams were offered in the Master of Psychology course – Counselling and Child and Educational. In 2000, the course was separated into two courses (in October 2000 – for commencement in 2001):

Master of Psychology (Counselling)
Master of Psychology (Educational and Developmental)

In 2007, the combined programs were introduced:

Master of Psychology (Counselling)/PhD
Master of Psychology (Educational and Developmental)/PhD

In 2016, the Master of Psychology (Educational and Developmental) and Master of Psychology (Educational and Developmental)/PhD changed to the Master of Educational and Developmental Psychology and Master of Educational and Developmental Psychology/PhD.

From 2022, Monash University offered the Master of Educational and Developmental Psychology Advanced for psychologists wishing to seek eligibility for the registrar program for endorsement through an alternative pathway. This course was designed for generalist registered psychologists who, after a year of study and placement, would be able to commence the two-year registrar program to become educational and developmental psychologists.

Historically, the State of Victoria has almost had a monopoly on educational and developmental psychology courses. The third course in Victoria currently offered is at the Australian Catholic University (ACU). At ACU, the Master of Psychology (Educational and Developmental) emerged at the Melbourne campus in 2008 after the academic board approved a change in course title for the Master of Psychology (Child and Family).

The Queensland University of Technology (QUT) also offers a Master of Educational and Developmental Psychology program, and like its counterparts at the University of Melbourne, Monash University, and ACU, the course is very well established. Professor Linda Gilmore initiated the Master of Psychology (Educational and Developmental) in 2005. Over the years, she has been instrumental in the course development. She shares:

Overall, student evaluations have been very positive, and entry to the course has become increasingly competitive. The Master of Psychology (Educational and Developmental) program at QUT was initially offered jointly by the Faculty of Education (School of Learning and Development) and the Faculty of Health (School of

Psychology and Counselling). However, since 2020 this program has been now wholly held by the Faculty of Health.

Tim Hannan, Associate Professor at Charles Sturt University, remembers the accredited Master of Psychology (Educational and Developmental) offered at the University of Western Sydney (UWS) from 2002 to approximately 2010, which graduated around 120 students.

It was closed as part of the broad closure of non-clinical programs around 2010, where UWS closed its forensic and sport psychology program around the same time as well.

The Master of Psychology (Educational & Developmental) has been the only accredited two-year course in educational and developmental psychology in NSW. There have been school psychology and Master of Counselling programs, but none offer a pathway to endorsement as an educational and developmental psychologist.

The history of educational and developmental psychology paints an interesting perspective of how the field has developed in Australia. Previous educational and developmental psychology courses have also been run by RMIT and University of Western Australia. At RMIT, educational and developmental psychology training commenced in approximately 1975 with the Graduate Diploma in Applied Child Psychology (fourth year equivalent) was taught by Graham Clunies-Ross, Alan Hudson, Greg Murphy, and Jan Matthews. At the time, this course was pivotal in training Guidance Officers for the Victorian Department of Education.

Over the years, there was a move towards master's level training which provided broader preparation for graduates, with the Master of Psychology (Educational and Developmental) commencing in 1991 under the Phillip Institute of Technology (which merged with the Royal Melbourne Institute of Technology in 1992, later becoming RMIT University). Alan Hudson and Mervyn Jackson from RMIT University recall that the program was very successful:

The program developed and became extremely popular with hundreds of applications each year for only about 10 places. Teaching staff included people such as Alan Hudson, Greg Murphy, Ray

Wilks and Kerry Hempenstall, all of whom had considerable experience as educational psychologists, and Neville King and Roger Miller who had experience in the clinical child psychology area. This range of experienced practitioners made the course very practical in its delivery. Another practical aspect of the course was the involvement of students in the on-campus Psychology Clinic run by the Psychology Department. Over time under the coordination of Jan Matthews, the course produced many graduates who took their places in government and non-government organisations. Many also found their way into private practice. A further development in the psychology area was the beginning of a clinical psychology stream in the professional Master's program. In addition to this, in line with developments elsewhere, the Department started up a 3-year professional Doctor of Psychology program with both educational and developmental and clinical streams. Finally, graduates from the two years of the Masters of Educational and Developmental Psychology program could return and complete one more year and add a Clinical Psychology qualification.

By 2006, it became possible for clinical psychologists to get Medicare rebates for fees charged in private practice. This was a major factor in making professional programs in clinical psychology much more popular than those in educational and developmental psychology. As the number of applicants for the clinical program soared, the number for educational and developmental programs reduced dramatically. Finally, because of the dwindling number of applicants, the University decided to stop the intake into the Educational and Developmental Masters program.

To recap, there are currently four universities in Australia where you can study Master of Educational and Developmental Psychology; Australian Catholic University, Monash University, Queensland University of Technology, and the University of Melbourne. Future educational and developmental psychology courses are on the cards and we expect updates shortly (so watch this space). Course availability is instrumental in maintaining the ongoing supply of educational and developmental psychologists, impacting the current distribution of trained practitioners throughout Australia. In Victoria, where three courses are currently available, the growth of educational and developmental psychologists has been faster than any other endorsement area at the national level (see Chapter 8 for a deeper dive into this trend).

Deciding to be an educational and developmental psychologist

Despite the many benefits of educational and developmental psychology (see Chapter 8 for an overview), the decision to become an educational and developmental psychologist can be challenging. When deciding to become an educational and developmental psychologist, comparisons will be made to the other endorsement areas in psychology. The authors of this book encourage readers to be aware of these other practice areas and how they differ. There are nine, endorsed practice areas in Australia of which educational and developmental psychology is one. Other endorsed practice areas are clinical neuropsychology, clinical psychology, community psychology, counselling psychology, forensic psychology, health psychology, organisational psychology, and sport and exercise psychology. The book series, from which this book emerges, is a source of further advice on the distinctive practice areas of psychology in Australia. This series may help inform decisions concerned with course or career pathways.

Eileen Scott Stokes says,

> [p]rospective students are sometimes unsure which course they should apply for and study. Determining whether to apply to an educational and developmental course as opposed to one of the other areas of practice is an important first step. A Masters course leading to registration as a psychologist is a demanding course of study, both in terms of the professional competencies students need to develop and the personal growth involved in studying to become a psychologist. It is important that the prospective student undertakes a course that aligns with their passion and values.
>
> The APS College website is an excellent starting point to understand what an educational and developmental psychologist does – the types of presenting issues and range of client ages they work with and the types of settings in which they work.

Prospective students can further understand the role of an educational and developmental psychologist – in contrast to the roles of clinical, clinical neuropsychology or counselling psychologists – by exploring in depth the content of the courses they are considering. Course summaries and specific unit content and unit objectives set out the knowledge, skills and competencies students will achieve on completing the units and the course. Lists of possible placement settings provided as part of the course descriptions also indicate the type and range of settings and workplaces graduates will find employment.

A fuller understanding of an educational and developmental psychologist's work will assist prospective students in deciding to study an educational and developmental Masters course and help them articulate what they have done in readiness to become such a professional. This more precise understanding will also help them understand why they wish to become an educational and developmental psychologist, which will assist them in the interview to enter a Masters course.

See Chapter 2 for more information about this aspect of interviews. Furthermore, most prospective educational and developmental psychologists will have a passion and interest in working with people. This might be an interest in working with people of all ages, but some will be mainly attracted to working with younger age groups. According to educational and developmental psychologist Darren Stops (2022), a career in educational and developmental psychology can be enriching if it aligns with an individual's values and passions. Before a person decides to pursue the profession, they should know that it must align with their inherent abilities, values, and beliefs. You have to enjoy working with people, be empathetic, and respect other people's points of view. It would help if you also were self-aware, free of judgement, and able to separate your own opinions from your work (Stops, 2022). Finally, anyone who intends to pursue educational and developmental psychology must be prepared to cope with some of the complexities that will naturally come with the profession. These include, but are not limited to, managing high client demands, complex presentations, and a lack of emphasis on the importance of prevention in some contexts.

A New Zealand Perspective

Jean Annan

Although this chapter has been written with the role of the Australian educational and development psychologist in mind, much of the information in this section is relevant to this role in New Zealand. Information about work as an educational psychologist and how to become a registered practitioner is not always available for prospective psychologists, particularly at the outset of their career journeys. Often the first time students learn about the existence of educational psychology is after their study is well underway and unforeseen events pique their interest. As the writer points out, discovering the profession, its particular work and training pathways is often a matter of chance.

The scarcity of information about the role of the psychologist leaves room for misconceptions about the role. One common misconception is that educational and developmental psychology is restricted to working in schools, early learning centres, and school communities. Many psychologists do work in these settings but the practice itself extends beyond schooling. Learning and well-being are life-long concerns and it is not inconceivable for educational and developmental psychologists to work with adults (e.g. literacy challenges and particular disabilities). Furthermore, educational and developmental psychology work in New Zealand, as for other groups of psychologists, is located across a range of sites. For example, psychologists may work in government agencies, publicly funded mental health agencies, private practices, and non-profit support organisations. The distinction between psychologists working within different fields in New Zealand is possibly a little narrower than that in Australia. In New Zealand, all registered psychologists practise within a general scope but can apply for the addition of specific scopes (e.g. educational, counselling) on the basis of their initial training and subsequent professional learning.

As in Australia, New Zealand educational and developmental psychology practice assumes a dynamic, ecological perspective, reflecting the country's unique cultural context. A particular point of difference for psychologists working in New Zealand is the value of and the requirement to work in accordance with the principles of Te Tiriti o Waitangi. New Zealand is a bi-cultural nation, and psychologists recognise and support concepts such as rangatiratanga (chieftainship and authority), whanaungatanga (family and belonging), and mana ōrite (equal power sharing). Critical aspects of educational and developmental psychology in New Zealand are promoting equity and working within a culture of collaboration.

Concluding comments

Educational and developmental psychology has a rich history as a discipline and a distinct area of professional practice. In Australia, educational and developmental psychology has developed uniquely compared to other countries and continues to establish its identity.

Chapters 6 and 11 detail critical considerations for choosing the pathway to become an educational and developmental psychologist, but often the decision to become an educational and developmental psychologist will occur at university! Chapter 2 outlines the study requirements and pathways to becoming an educational and developmental psychologist.

Tertiary study and professional practice requirements

"I feel I have had so many more valuable experiences and learned so much more since I became more comfortable to take on different challenges."

—Cameron Lee

Introduction

Becoming a psychologist in Australia is a very long and challenging journey. From starting an undergraduate tertiary degree, then moving to an Honours or fourth-year psychology program, and then undertaking a Master of Psychology degree, people spend several years training to qualify as a psychologist. For people who decide to complete a Master of Educational and Developmental Psychology degree, the pathway to becoming an educational and developmental psychologist is longer, with some deciding to undertake further training of up to two additional years to become an educational and developmental psychologist (see Chapter 3 on the different pathways to becoming a psychologist).

This chapter will explore the stages people undertake when applying for a postgraduate degree in educational and developmental psychology, including information about how to apply and what to expect from interviews. The chapter will discuss placements and research project requirements when students complete Master of Educational and Developmental Psychology.

DOI: 10.4324/9781003330974-2

Australian Psychology Accreditation Council (APAC) accreditation

APAC is an independent group responsible for developing, reviewing, and mandating the accreditation standards of tertiary psychology courses in Australia. APAC is responsible for accrediting over 700 psychology programs (including Educational and Developmental Psychology Master's programs) across higher education institutions in Australia, Malaysia, and Singapore on behalf of the Australian Health Practitioner Regulation Agency (AHPRA) and the Psychology Board of Australia (PsyBA). APAC's responsibility is to develop standards for the education and training of psychologists in Australia, Malaysia, and Singapore, assess and monitor tertiary programs and providers to ensure they meet the APAC accreditation standards, and advise the PsyBA, government departments, and other bodies on matters related to the education and training of psychologists (APAC, 2022). The structure of APAC accredited training programs spans four "levels" of training as shown in Table 2.1.

Table 2.1 The Structure of APAC accredited Training Programs

APAC Accreditation Level	AQF Qualification	Example degree titles
Level 1 Foundational competencies	Bachelor's degree	Undergraduate degrees such as Bachelor of Psychology, Bachelor of Arts or Science (with a major in psychology), or Bachelor of Science/Education (with a major in psychology).
Level 2 Pre-professional competencies	Bachelor Honours degree or Graduate Certificate	A fourth year can be undertaken at the undergraduate level via an Honours degree (e.g. Bachelor of Arts [Psychology] Honours) or postgraduate level (e.g. Graduate Certificate in Professional Psychology).
Level 3 Professional competencies	Master's degree or Graduate Diploma	A postgraduate program such as Master of Professional Psychology (5 + 1 pathway).

APAC Accreditation Level	AQF Qualification	Example degree titles
Level 4 Professional competencies for endorsed areas of practice	Master's degree	Stand-alone postgraduate programs of study such as the Master of Educational and Developmental Psychology Advanced.

Note: AQF = Australian Qualifications Framework is a national body that specifies the standards for educational qualifications in Australia.

While the pathway is highly regulated, you can choose the specific degrees that enable you to navigate the path and whether you have a break between various stages to gain more work and life experience. Many students study at different institutions throughout their training, while some remain at one institution for the entirety of their training. Increasingly, training providers are offering combined courses that provide multiple APAC levels of training within one program. For example, the Master of Educational and Developmental Psychology combines training at Levels 3 and 4 – and you might have noted it was missing from the above table for that reason. Some undergraduate degrees combine the bachelor's degree (Level 1) and honours degree (Level 2), pending meeting any minimum academic requirements of moving to Level 2. It is anticipated that we may see more combined courses in the future as they provide more certainty to students and reduce the number of transitions needing to be made throughout training. You can search currently accredited programs at each level via a handy search tool on the APAC website (https://apac.au/).

When planning your study timeline, be mindful that APAC rules there can be no more than ten years between undertaking Levels 2 and 3 (i.e. there can be no more than ten years between the fourth year of training and commencing a master's program). Students who leave it longer will need to undertake additional refresher units typically to maintain knowledge in areas such as ethics and assessment.

Training requirements and pathways

While Chapter 3 will discuss the many stages and pathways to registration as an educational and developmental psychologist, this chapter details the training that enables eligibility for registration. To become a general psychologist in Australia, you will need to complete APAC accredited training at Levels 1–3 at a minimum, and this can take approximately six years (or part-time equivalent) – note this can take longer if you undertake double degrees or shorter if you already have a bachelor's degree outside of psychology). To become an educational and developmental psychologist, you must complete APAC accredited training at Level 4 and afterwards a registrar program to gain an Area of Practice Endorsement (AoPE) in educational and developmental psychology (see Chapter 8 for more information). This means it can take at least eight years (full-time) to become an educational and developmental psychologist. A list of APAC-accredited Educational and Developmental Psychology Master's programs in Australia is included in this chapter.

To provide an example of a common pathway for students, many start by completing an undergraduate degree, followed by a fourth-year degree in psychology, such as an honours year or postgraduate diploma. After this, students will usually complete a two-year (full-time) or four-year (part-time) Master of Psychology which may or may not be Master of Educational and Developmental Psychology. However, students who complete Master of Psychology not in the discipline of educational psychology will be required to complete an additional one-year (full-time) or two-year (part-time) degree. These are called Level 4 Stand-alone programs for endorsement (see Chapter 8 for more information), and currently, the only program of this type is the *Master of Educational and Developmental Psychology Advanced* at Monash University (see details later in this chapter). After completing a Master or Advanced Master of Educational and Developmental Psychology, graduates will be eligible to register with AHPRA as a generalist psychologist, complete two additional years of supervised practice with an educational and developmental psychologist, and then register with AHPRA as an educational and developmental psychologist. The APS (2022d) also lists the stages and steps to general registration and completion of an area of practice endorsement (AoPE) in psychology (https://psychology.org.au/

psychology/careers-and-studying-psychology/studying-psychology/study-pathways).

In addition, programs in Victoria allow students to complete a combined Master of Educational and Developmental Psychology and PhD.

Educational and developmental psychology master's programs in Australia

People seeking to study and qualify in the specific area of educational and developmental psychology will need to complete a Master of Psychology program in this area of practice. This means identifying a university that offers an accredited Master of Educational and Developmental Psychology course. The following is a list of Master of Educational and Developmental Psychology courses which are APAC accredited and offered in Australia. These courses are offered only in two states, Victoria and Queensland. Monash University in Victoria is the first and currently the only university accredited to provide a Master of Educational and Developmental Psychology Advanced degree for generalist registered psychologists seeking further training to become an educational and developmental psychologist.

Victoria

- Master of Educational and Developmental Psychology at Monash University, the Monash University Master of Educational and Developmental Psychology Advanced degree for registered psychologists, and the Master of Educational and Developmental Psychology/PhD combined degree at Monash University.
- Master of Psychology (Educational and Developmental) at Australian Catholic University and the Master of Psychology (Educational and Developmental)/PhD at Australian Catholic University.
- Master of Educational Psychology at the University of Melbourne and the Master of Educational Psychology/PhD at the University of Melbourne.

Queensland

- Master of Psychology (Educational and Developmental) at Queensland University of Technology

---

Keep an eye on the APAC website as new courses are planned. Often Master of Psychology programs are only accredited by APAC to be delivered face to face, meaning that prospective students from other states must reside in Victoria or Queensland while undertaking their studies (though some dedicated students have undertaken degrees interstate by flying in and flying out every week for family/employment reasons). However, the Master of Educational and Developmental Psychology Advanced course at Monash University is delivered in *mixed-mode* allowing students to continue living in their home state while completing the course and only needing to be on campus for two short intensives. This is a significant development to ensure that educational psychologists can continue to offer their services across Australia.

Preparing your application for postgraduate study

While selection for Level 2 training (i.e. "fourth-year") focuses solely on academic achievement, under APAC rules, universities must undertake a broader selection process for entrance to training at Levels 3 and 4 (i.e. Master of Educational and Developmental Psychology). This involves an application form, referee reports, and an interview. Figure 2.1 outlines some of the critical aspects upon which selection is based, each institution may evaluate and prioritise aspects of the applicant uniquely according to their program preferences, so it is a good idea to apply widely.

Suppose that you are undertaking the early years of psychology training now. In that case, it can be helpful to reflect on the above components and consider your current areas of strengths and how you might take action to improve areas requiring further development, perhaps through volunteering to gain relevant practical experience.

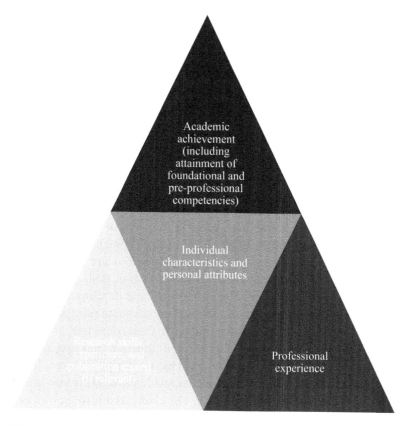

Figure 2.1 Key selection criteria for postgraduate studies generally include Academic achievement (including attainment of foundational and pre-professional competencies), Individual characteristics and personal attributes, Professional experience, Research skills, experience, and publication record (if relevant)

In addition to completing an application to each respective university, prospective students are often required to prepare and submit additional online supplementary forms when applying for a place in a Master of Educational and Developmental Psychology course in Australia. These online application forms ask applicants to provide demographic information, contact details, provide information about prior degrees completed, list prior and current employment (including paid and voluntary work), list any professional memberships the applicant may hold, provide details of research, including Honours or postgraduate research completed, and list published journal articles, conference presentations, or other academic pieces of work completed. Applications may also ask prospective students to answer open-ended questions to assess the motivations of the applicant to work as a psychologist, to understand their skills and interests in the field of psychology (and more specifically, educational and developmental psychology), and to assess what the applicant has done to date to prepare to become an educational and developmental psychologist. It is vital that applicants consider their responses to these questions in line with the requirements of the course they are applying to and the educational and developmental psychology field more broadly. Responses to these questions are a chance for applicants to demonstrate their academic writing skills, knowledge of the discipline, and interest in educational and developmental psychology. Applicants should give themselves adequate time before the application due date to consider and write their responses, ask questions if aspects of the application form are unclear, and prepare any supplementary materials such as academic transcripts, referee documents, and, for international students, evidence of their visa status and English Language competency. Once accepted into a program, to obtain provisional registration with the PsyBA, students need to provide proof of enrolment in their course and meet English Language requirements.

On the topic of preparing your application to enter a Master of Educational and Developmental program, Cameron Lee, a current Master of Educational and Developmental Psychology student (and successful applicant), wrote:

> Professional and personal (life) experience adds value to your application. I wish I knew the value of these experiences when writing my application as I would have felt a lot more confident about my chances. Many of those experiences have held me in good stead throughout the Masters, particularly in my placements.

Referee reports

When applying to enrol in any psychology master's course, including Master of Educational and Developmental Psychology, students must obtain referee reports from academic and professional referees. The academic referee for many applicants will be the student's supervisor for their thesis in their Honours or fourth-year psychology program. Applicants may also select a lecturer or academic mentor who knows their skills, attributes, and potential (see Chapter 5 on important skills and attributes of psychologists). The professional referee could be an employee through paid or volunteer work of the applicant. Completion of the referee reports is managed centrally through the Heads of Departments and Schools of Psychology Australia (HODSPA) Reference Request System, which means that each referee is only required to complete one online referee form, and the report will be available to all Australian institutions that the applicant has applied to. There may be different referee forms required for students applying to programs outside of Australia. The types of questions available to referees completing forms through HODSPA include the applicant's ability to work independently and with others, the applicant's motivation and maturity, and the capacity of the applicant to study and work in the field of psychology. Given the types of questions that referees will be called to answer, make sure your referee knows you. If they have not worked with you previously, referees can indicate this on the form, which asks, "[H]ow well do you know the applicant?" After completing the online application form and referee reports, applicants may be contacted by the university they applied to in order to progress to the next stage, which involves participating in an interview. If you are not contacted for an interview or are unsuccessful following your interview, please read the section on managing a rejection in this chapter.

You may be asked when applying to provide a letter or personal statement which should outline your interest in the area of educational and developmental psychology, your experience relevant to the field, your motivation and enthusiasm for studying at the university you are applying to, and any other information which you believe will show that you are prepared and suitable for educational psychology. It is essential to also show that you can write clearly and concisely. Remember that your application will be one of many. We have provided an example sample letter from a former student when applying for a Master of Educational and Developmental Psychology degree, as well as a personal statement from another student who applied for a program and was successful.

Sample Letter 1

Miss Grace Mackie
[insert street number and street name of applicant]
[insert suburb, state, and postcode of applicant]
[insert date of letter]

[insert name of psychology program director/course leader]
[insert name of university]
[insert building number, street number, and street name of university]
[insert suburb, state, and postcode of university]

Dear [insert name of psychology program director/course leader],

I have long been attracted to the educational and developmental psychology branch, as it provides an opportunity to concurrently intervene at different levels (e.g., school, familial, individual) and at different points across the lifespan. It is my understanding that this broad yet specialised scope of practice allows psychologists to work with children and the people who care for and educate them, in order to help turn challenges into resilience, and improve developmental outcomes of children and youth.

The Master of Psychology (Educational and Developmental) is the next step in my academic career, which will provide me with a solid foundation for fulfilling my goal of becoming a school psychologist. I could target areas such as bullying, anxiety, and behaviour management in one setting and across multiple groups, allowing children the best chance to reach their potential. The Master of Psychology (Educational and Developmental) appears to offer research, educational, and practical opportunities that will allow me to carry out the role of a school psychologist successfully.

After my experience volunteering at a primary school, I have come to realise the wide range of knowledge and skills required to be an educational and developmental psychologist. For example, choosing appropriate psychological assessments for presenting issues, information gathering from various sources, writing detailed psychological reports, and understanding, applying, and implementing appropriate

---

interventions. I believe the focus of your degree on therapeutic, clinical, and research skills will provide me with the best opportunity to become an excellent educational and developmental psychologist in the future.

I look forward to the opportunity to discuss my application with you at an interview.

Yours sincerely,
[insert signature]
Miss Grace Mackie

Sample Letter 2

Personal Statement – Rhys Mawson

Across almost eight years as both a teacher and a youth worker, I have had a drive to effectively respond to the diverse and highly individual needs of young people. I strongly believe completing the Master of Educational Psychology course will help me to do this.

I want to be considered for this course because I know the benefits of a young person's continued and meaningful engagement with the school environment. I began my career as a Maths and English teacher in the northern suburbs of Geelong. In this environment, I learnt that schools can and do provide much more than a space for teaching and learning, and that the best outcomes come about when those environments strive for a holistic understanding of young people and can respond to their needs across a range of life domains. However, I know firsthand that doing this effectively in schools is challenging. Having also worked in the youth development space for almost three years, I have seen how feeling unsupported and unheard by schools affects young people, as well as the many challenges that come about after or alongside their disengagement from school. In a position as an educational psychologist, I will have a greater ability to respond to individual young people's needs and hence keep them engaged as a result. I know the role teachers play in this and want to help enhance their capacity to respond to students' needs, especially those with developmental disorders like autism – the focus of my thesis – and those who have been affected by trauma.

I bring skills and knowledge that will help me excel not only in this course but also in a career as an educational psychologist. I have had extensive experience engaging with young people in a variety of environments, honing my ability to show genuineness, empathy, and a sincere interest in their lives. As an educational leader, managing the maths domain across a multi-campus school in my second year of teaching, I know what it takes to ensure that school staff feel supported and confident to meet the needs of students. In my youth work role, I developed collaborative relationships with a range of professionals, implementing targeted programs and activities that supported young people both in school and in the community. Having worked successfully with such a wide variety of people, I believe I am an effective and engaging communicator.

I expect to be challenged when adapting these skills, strengths, and experiences to this course. However, in knowing I will be surrounded by passionate and knowledgeable peers, I feel confident I can meet that challenge.

Preparing for interviews

After you are contacted by the university and offered a time and date for your interview, you will need to start preparing for your interview. Interviews are often with a panel of academics who work as lecturers or teaching associates in the program you have applied for. Applicants should re-familiarise themselves with the course structure and lecturers who teach in the program before their interview. They might also want to familiarise themselves with the types of research, placement opportunities, and specific units offered in the course. Applicants should also review their original online application, noting aspects of their professional experience, achievements, and personal circumstances they would like to share with the panel. Since the COVID-19 pandemic, many interviews have changed from face-to-face delivery to online delivery via video conferencing platforms. This has benefited many applicants because they can complete the interview from home and in a more familiar and comfortable place. It has allowed prospective students to be interviewed remotely, providing better access to students in rural and overseas settings. Although, if you are interviewed online, ensure you have sufficient internet connectivity; otherwise, you might consider requesting a telephone interview.

Online interviews require applicants to also consider how they present themselves professionally and how they can engage the interview panel. For example, consider your virtual background during the interview, ensure that you are dressed in a neat, casual manner, and that you engage with the interviewers rather than relying on reading written notes. Examples of skills and attributes that selection panels will be interested in include:

- Does the applicant understand the course structure, placements, and units?
- Does the applicant show enthusiasm for the course, faculty, and university?
- Does the applicant know what an educational and developmental psychologist does? (applicants can visit the APS College of Educational and Developmental Psychologists website *https://groups.psychology.org.au/cedp/* to obtain a better understanding, as well as visit the website *https://groups.psychology.org.au/cedp/about_us/* which details the skills of educational and developmental psychologists).
- What professional experience does the applicant have? Can the applicant articulate how their professional experience relates to the field of educational and developmental psychology?
- Has the student published a journal article, prepared research reports, or presented at a conference?
- Has the applicant thought about how they will balance work-life-university commitments?
- Does the applicant have the maturity, stability, independence, and teamwork skills to be successful in the program?
- Is this the right time for this applicant to complete a Master of Psychology course? Is the applicant ready to work with clients and will they be able to manage the workload?
- Will the applicant collaborate well with their lecturers, peers, and uphold the standing of the profession?

During the interview, applicants should be aware that interviews are typically completed by academic staff over consecutive days and weeks because of the large number of applicants. For this reason, applicants must provide clear and succinct responses to questions from the panel. Consider what will make you stand out to the panel for the right reasons (and avoid standing out for the wrong reasons). An essential skill of psychologists and therapists is their capacity to engage in self-reflection for personal and professional growth (Mcgillivray et al., 2015). Show your interview panel through your demeanour and responses to their questions that you understand and can use self-reflective practice. Self-reflection is also crucial if you are not invited after applying to participate in an interview, or after your interview, you are not given a place in a Master of Psychology program (see the section in this chapter on managing a rejection).

Practise Interview Questions

1   What prior experience (voluntary or paid) has prepared you for studying educational and developmental psychology?
2   What is your understanding of educational and developmental psychology and how this specialisation differs from other areas of psychology?
3   What personal or professional attributes do you have that you think will help you most when studying or working as a psychologist?
4   Completing a Master of Psychology course can be very demanding on your time, professional, and personal life. What have you done to prepare for this commitment?
5   What are you most looking forward to about the course if you are successful in obtaining a position?
6   Where do you see yourself professionally in five years and how will this course help you to achieve your goals?

Helen Johansen, a current Master of Educational and Developmental Psychology student, reflected on her interview experience:

> I found I was so nervous about answering the questions "correctly" that I lost a bit of my own authenticity in my answers. In hindsight, I wish I had been less concerned about getting the answers "right,"

and concentrated more on capturing my own individual passions, beliefs, and journey in my answers.

The final stage of preparing for your interview is to think about potential questions that you want to ask the interview panel. Example questions can include:

- How many offers are made to the program?
- What are the course fees for the program?
- If I receive an offer, can I defer my place?
- Can I enrol in the program full-time or part-time? Can I change between full- and part-time enrolment during the course?
- What is the expected study time for the course?
- How many contact hours are required for full-time and part-time enrolled students?
- How much independent study time is required for full- and part-time enrolled students?
- What types of placement opportunities are offered during the course? How many placement hours are required?
- What types of minor research thesis topics are available to students? How are research topics allocated and how do students find a supervisor?

Accepting your offer

Offers may be made very quickly after the interviews have concluded. Applicants are typically sorted from highest to lowest ranked by the panel and the highest ranked applicants are offered a first-round offer into the program. Depending on the number of first-round offers that are accepted by applicants, course leaders may be able to offer second- or third-round offers. This is typically a period of great anxiety and uncertainty for applicants.

Master of Educational and Developmental Psychology student, Jessica Rodaughan, stated when reflecting on her experience of accepting her offer:

I wish I knew that while I was accepting an offer to become a student, it was also an offer to become a professional. I first saw Masters as another degree in the process towards becoming a psychologist, but I later learnt that I was actually taking my first steps as a Psychologist. Becoming provisionally registered, beginning placement and learning skills which are exclusively understood and practised by psychologists, all helped me realise I was not just a student but a practitioner.

Many Master of Psychology programs provide students with information sessions and orientation events prior to the start of the programs. Students will also receive information about how to enrol in the program, enrol in the first units of the degree, and information about the next stages. When enrolling in the program, students may have the opportunity to apply for a scholarship or financial support to help them complete their master's degree. There are various scholarships open to students who can demonstrate the exceptional academic achievement they have obtained throughout their university life, and for marginalised groups or groups not well represented in university settings (e.g. Aboriginal or Torres Strait Islander people, women, and people from disadvantaged backgrounds). Financial support and advice can often be accessed by university students through university student services if the student is facing financial challenges, or through FEE-HELP which helps many students to access university courses. FEE-HELP is a loan system by the Australian Government designed to help university students to pay all or part of their tuition fees (Australian Government, n.d.). FEE-HELP is a loan provided to eligible domestic fee-paying students and can be provided to students who enrol in a master's programs that is not subsidised by the Government. HECS-HELP is a different scheme designed to help students cover the costs of a master's program. HECS-HELP is a loan for eligible students with a Commonwealth-supported place. As per earlier comments in this chapter on preparing for interviews, students should ask during their interview about costs and fee help available to students who are successful in obtaining a position in the course.

Figure 2.2 Receiving an offer can be an exciting day, but it is important to keep in mind that knock-backs do occur and educational and developmental psychology courses can be competitive

Managing a rejection

Due to the number of applicants and interviews completed for Master of Educational and Developmental Psychology programs, individual feedback is typically not provided to applicants who are not offered a place. There are a few important things to remember if you are not offered a place in a Master of Psychology program:

- There are typically hundreds of applications and very few positions available.
- You are not alone! Some successful candidates had applied a few times before they were accepted into a program.

- Celebrate if you had the opportunity to attend an interview. This is an achievement to make it to this stage. Think about your interview responses, the questions the panel asked, and what you can do to improve your skills and knowledge before applying again. Make sure if you apply and are interviewed again, you remind the panel of your earlier application and what you have done between then and now to improve your skills and knowledge.
- If you have not had the opportunity to participate in an interview, consider your online application and how you can improve your responses so that you have a better chance to be interviewed when you apply again (see the section in this chapter on Preparing your Application for Masters).
- Consider your other options. Perhaps this is an opportunity to publish your Honours thesis or volunteer to work for a research group, charity organisation, or mental health service.
- Finally, apply in future years. It is very common for applicants to apply once, twice, or three or more times. There are many different pathways to becoming a psychologist (or an educational and developmental psychologist) so keep trying, improving your skills, and exploring the different options available to you (see Chapter 3 on the different pathways to becoming a psychologist).

Placements and supervision

At Monash University, Eileen Scott Stokes in her role as a program manager in educational psychology and counselling has been organising and supporting educational and developmental psychology students through their placements for over 30 years. She reflects on the stages, considerations, and lessons she has learned over the years when students undertake placements.

A major component of an educational and developmental psychology course is the requirement to successfully complete a minimum of 1,000 hours of supervised practice. These hours must include a minimum of 400 direct client contact (DCC) hours and a minimum number of supervision hours. Some courses commence these supervised hours in year one, with the majority (if not all) of the hours completed in year two.

This is a major transition point in the study pathway to becoming an educational and developmental psychologist and can lead to additional stress. Placements involve working as a provisional psychologist under supervision in various workplaces in the field. Obtaining the minimum hours required by APAC, involves working three days per week for a full calendar year. For many students, this might be their first professional role in the workplace, involving an adjustment to the working world as well as to working as a provisional psychologist. While undertaking their placements there are often additional costs to the student around travel and obtaining clothing more appropriate to a professional role.

Students on placement are seen as future colleagues and expected to immerse themselves in all aspects of the day-to-day activities of the Agency where they are placed. As the placement progresses students take on a caseload of clients and are expected to work more independently.

Placements involve a steep learning curve for students. In addition to developing the competencies required to become registered psychologist students are also expected to develop skills involving self-reflection. Working as a provisional psychologist under supervision involves personal and professional growth as students reflect on their practice.

Placements also include a substantial amount of administrative tasks. Students are expected to professionally manage placement documentation required by APAC for the course as well as maintain accurate records and client files.

Adding to comments from Eileen, Tasma Dunn, a current Master of Educational and Developmental Psychology student, found that it is important to have an open mind when starting a placement: "To be open to placement experiences – what you think you don't like or don't want to do may turn out to be something you enjoy."

Research project and supervision

A component of Educational and Developmental Psychology Master's programs is for students to complete a research project. This may involve students completing an extended literature review related to their research topic, and a piece of independent research that students complete and prepare as a research report, including an abstract, introduction, method, results, and discussion section. APAC sets out requirements for types of methodologies that qualify for a research project for a Master of Psychology program. These methodologies include:

- An evaluation of a program or service
- An experimental single-case design study
- A pilot research project and grant application
- A systematic review or meta-analysis
- A study using primary or secondary qualitative or quantitative data
- A traditional research project
- A capstone experience

(APAC, 2019)

This is one example of how Psychology Master's programs can differ in how they meet APAC requirements, in addition to variation in course structure and unit offerings available. Some universities also offer programs where students can articulate from completing a minor thesis in psychology to a PhD degree in psychology. Students who decide to undertake this articulation pathway will still graduate with a master's degree in Educational Psychology and a PhD degree after a few more years of study! For students not enrolled at one of these universities that offers this articulation pathway, there are opportunities for students to complete a PhD thesis after completing their research project during their master's program.

It is relatively common that the master's research project will take the form of a minor thesis which is undertaken with academic supervision. Thus, the first stage of starting any thesis is to search the website of your University's School or Faculty to review the types of research topics and supervisors available to supervise your thesis. While it is not a requirement that a student's research supervisor is an endorsed and registered educational and developmental psychologist, students should be aware that academics not endorsed in this area may not be aware of accreditation requirements for the thesis as set out by APAC.

Choosing a research supervisor

When choosing a suitable research supervisor, students should consider what methodology they prefer, possible project ideas, and the research interests of prospective supervisors. Students should remember that starting a supervisory relationship is the beginning of a long collaborative relationship. Maintaining a good working relationship through having clear expectations and good habits around communication is essential. There are several considerations students should think about when choosing a research supervisor:

- Does their research interest align with my research interests? Will I still be motivated to explore this area of research in a year when completing my thesis?
- Does the supervisor use research methods I am interested in and have relevant skills? What additional training will I need to undertake to learn the research method required for my thesis?
- Does the supervisor apply a theory or theories in their research that I am interested in?
- Does the supervisor have a similar style of working to me? For example, do they prefer students to work independently or in teams with other students, do they prefer to work online or have face-to-face meetings, or do they enjoy keeping to deadlines, or are they more relaxed with time frames?

Helen Johansen, a current Master of Educational and Developmental Psychology student, advice for selecting a research topic and supervisor for the Master of Educational and Developmental Psychology thesis is:

> I believe it is really important to choose a research area about which you are passionate and interested, as this really helps to motivate you to work on your thesis in the midst of all the other work there is to do in the course. It is also so important to choose a supervisor who works in a similar way to which you work, so that you are pulling together.

Publishing your thesis

Students may have the opportunity to publish their master's thesis as a co-author with their supervisor or supervisory team. Publishing your thesis is a great way to add knowledge to the profession and will add to your research skills and credibility when applying for work (see Chapter 4, which addresses research as one of the eight core competencies in the profession). Before writing their thesis, students should converse with their supervisor about the possibility of publishing their thesis as a journal article or book chapter, or disseminating their research findings through other forums (e.g. at a conference or industry briefing). Students and supervisors may choose to develop an authorship agreement that outlines what students (and supervisors) can expect from the process of publishing a student thesis. For example, the agreement may outline who is responsible for preparing the thesis for publication, the anticipated timeline for the manuscript's production, and who will manage submission and revisions of the article with the journal or publisher.

A graduate of the Monash University Master of Educational and Developmental Psychology program and now registered psychologist, Jenna Miller, reported about publishing her master's thesis:

> The main thing I learnt about the publication process was how incredibly important it was to have an invested and supportive supervisor. Without my supervisor to keep me on track, I don't think I would have got to the point of publication. But overall, it was really worth it and I am proud that we made it- I hope that our findings contribute to the literature and practice on the ground in some, if not tiny, meaningful manner!

Maintaining good peer relationships (and not isolating yourself!)

A final note for this chapter about preparing and undertaking a Master of Educational and Developmental Psychology course is the importance of maintaining good peer relationships, good working relationships with your lecturers and supervisors, and enjoying the experience of being part of our very small community of educational and developmental psychologists.

Many students benefit from these collaborative relationships both during and after they complete their Master of Educational and Developmental Psychology, whether it is through an opportunity to work as a research assistant with your thesis supervisor, the offer of a job by your placement supervisor, or the continued supervision that you engage in with your peers long after you complete your master's program. Our network is small, but many opportunities come from being open to experience, learning, and generosity towards fellow educational and developmental graduates.

A New Zealand Perspective

Rachel Drayton

To become an Educational Psychologist in New Zealand, you must undertake a minimum of seven years study. A Bachelor Honours degree or a Graduate Certificate must be completed in Psychology (full or combined degree).

Following undergraduate study, a Master of Educational Psychology degree must be completed. This consists of full-time study and part-time options, within four years. Upon successful completion or a master's degree the final stage, the professional practice component, can be applied for.

There are three tertiary providers that offer a pathway to psychology registration; Massey University's Postgraduate Diploma in Educational and Developmental Psychology, or Victoria University of Wellington's Postgraduate Diploma in Educational Psychology Practice and Postgraduate Diploma in Child and Family Psychology at Canterbury University.

There are two options available; and the majority apply for an Educational Psychology Internship Scholarship with the Ministry of Education. If accepted you will be undertaking full time study, also be placed at one of the Ministry of Education offices across the country and provided with supervision. In addition to academic course work, students will need to complete 1,500 hours of supervised practice in order to apply for full registration with the New Zealand Psychologist Board.

Qualified teachers such as Resource Teachers of Learning and Behaviour (RTLB) or employees or other services such as Explore Behaviour Supports may be supported by their employers to complete the pathway to registration. They will therefore not be eligible for a scholarship but required to register with a University programme and also complete the 1,500 supervised practice component in their work setting.

There are limited places available each year and it is highly competitive. Applicants are required to demonstrate experience in the field and meet a minimum academic standard to progress. During the application and interview phases, applicants are required to do the following:

- demonstrate relevant work experience
- discuss what theories and approaches relating to psychology in education are important in their work
- discuss how these approaches/theories be applied during your internship year?
- demonstrate knowledge and experience of tikanga Māori, Pacific cultures, and/or other cultures and how this knowledge has been applied in your work.

Students enrolled at Victoria or Massey University can reside anywhere in the country and can attend in person block courses as required.

> I had been working with children and families for 15 years when I started a Master of Educational Psychology. I was employed full time as a manager of a youth services team and was enrolled as a part time student at Victoria University, Wellington. I started working for the Ministry of Education during this time who supported my career progression and my internship placement as an employee. I don't think I would have been provided this opportunity without my many years of prior experience in the field.

The Ministry of Education has produced a video series about being an Education Psychologist:
www.youtube.com/playlist?list=PLy7eFR9M9r0Wjv2szZfbaV
vXLwWJYXUQx

Concluding comments

Preparing your application and participating in a Master of Educational and Developmental Psychology program can be an anxious, exciting, and busy period. Applicants must ensure their application is completed and submitted by the due date and addresses the criteria and areas of practice relevant to educational and developmental psychology. We wish you all the best when preparing your application and hope to see many of you at our interviews and within our programs in the future. The next chapter will take you through the next stage after applying for and starting an Educational and Developmental Master's program – registration requirements for psychologists in Australia.

3 | Registration requirements

> *"My training as an Ed and Dev set me up for working in schools in a way that I cannot imagine any other stream does. I believe we are uniquely prepared for the variety of work that can arise in these settings."*
>
> —Sally Kenney

Introduction

Registration as a psychologist is the first official hurdle to becoming an educational and developmental psychologist. This chapter provides an overview of what it takes to become registered as a psychologist in Australia, including a brief overview of registration, the pathways to registration as they currently exist, the different types of registration, and the ongoing requirements to maintain registration. Underpinning this chapter is the *Health Practitioner National Law*, which all Australian states and territories have enacted. The National Law provides the regulatory framework for the registration of psychologists, and other health professionals, and details specific undertakings that all registered psychologists must meet and uphold. There is no exception to the need to maintain registration and practice under the National Law for psychologists who hold an Area of Practice Endorsement (AoPE) in educational and developmental psychology. This chapter will explore what you need to know.

Being a part of a registered health profession is a privilege that confers a range of subsequent benefits to the holder and protects the public from unqualified practitioners. Access to professional roles, Medicare

42   DOI: 10.4324/9781003330974-3

funding, and the ability to provide authoritative input into high-level decision-making in multiple service areas is made available through registration. Upholding the standards required by registration is critical to the abiding faith that the public and other professionals hold in psychologists. When you attain registration, you can *borrow* from the integrity and diligence of all currently registered psychologists who uphold the standards and requirements of registration to enhance your own professional reputation. Maintaining these standards in your own practice is essential and will provide a legacy to the psychologists who will come after you.

Psychology as a registered profession in Australia

Although separate state registration systems for practising psychologists have operated in Australia for many decades, national registration has a relatively recent history, only being established with the enactment of the Health Practitioner Regulation National Law in 2009. This Act establishes the conditions and provisions for regulating health professionals who are required by the law to be registered with the Australian Health Practitioner Regulation Authority (AHPRA). Under the Act, regulated health professions currently include:

- Aboriginal and Torres Strait Islander health practitioners
- Chinese medicine practitioners
- Chiropractors
- Dentistry
- Medical practitioners (Doctors)
- Medical radiation practitioners
- Registered nurses and midwives, endorsed enrolled nursing
- Occupational therapists
- Optometrists
- Osteopaths
- Paramedics
- Pharmacists
- Physiotherapists
- Podiatrists
- Psychologists

The profession of psychology is overseen by the Psychology Board of Australia (PsyBA – colloquially known to psychologists as *the Board*), which is constituted under the National Law. PsyBA has formed four Regional Boards to support and regulate the practice of psychology. The Regional Boards are: The Australian Capital Territory/Tasmanian/Victorian Board; the New South Wales Board; The Queensland Board; and The Northern Territory/South Australia,/Western Australian Board. Applications are made to the Board for registration, queries regarding practice, and complaints from the general public concerning the conduct of psychologists.

The title "psychologist" is regulated under Australian law as a registered profession. The title can only be used by practitioners who have completed a board-approved education and postgraduate training program, ensuring the public that the practitioner has threshold competencies to practise safely. Furthermore, only psychologists who hold an area of practice endorsement (e.g. educational and developmental psychologist) can use the titles associated with their relevant practice endorsement. As mentioned in Chapter 1, and discussed later, psychologists are required to only provide services in areas where they can demonstrate their current competence.

The primary aim of AHPRA, and therefore the PsyBA, is to ensure public safety through regulating the profession. Arguably, the Board exists for the protection of the public more than for the profession. Its first duty is to ensure that practitioners adhere to all requirements defined under the Act.

The categories of registration

Categories of registration for psychologists in Australia are provisional registration, general registration, and non-practising. It can be confusing, but it is essential to be aware that psychologists in Australia do not have specialist registrations (i.e. the way a Medical Practitioner may have a specialty in Psychiatry or Paediatrics). Instead, psychology AoPEs provide recognition of advanced training and practice without granting specialist registration under the Health Practitioner Regulation National Law (2009). This is an important distinction under law. Specialist registrations are reserved for areas deemed to carry significant risks to the public. Because of this, specialists tend to have more narrowly defined scopes of practice.

Pathways to registration

There are several pathways to registration as a psychologist in Australia. All professional pathways require completing Level 1 (Bachelor's degree) and Level 2 (Honours or equivalent four-year degree) in psychology. Level 1 and Level 2 courses must be accredited by the Australian Psychology Accreditation Council (APAC). Before 30 June 2022, there were three pathways for psychology graduates to attain general registration in Australia. The first and oldest of these pathways was the 4 + 2 pathway, referring to the requirement to have a four-year undergraduate training at honours or equivalent level and then to practise under supervision as a provisionally registered psychologist (or intern) for a further two years. This pathway has been retired, leaving two existing pathways for general registration.

The 5 + 1 pathway for registration requires the completion of a one-year full-time (or part-time equivalent) postgraduate master's degree accredited by APAC at Level 3 (e.g. Master of Professional Psychology). This is followed by one-year full-time (or part-time equivalent) supervised practice as a provisionally registered psychologist (i.e. intern psychologist). In short, the 5 + 1 pathway to general registration involves five years of accredited study and one year of supervised practice.

The pathway most relevant to educational and developmental psychologists is the higher degree, postgraduate pathway, as detailed in Chapter 2. This pathway requires completion of a 4-year sequence of study as detailed earlier, followed by completion of an APAC-approved packaged Level 3/4 master's degree, equivalent to 2 years of full-time study (or a packaged PhD program). Graduates from packaged Level 3/4 programs are eligible for general registration as a psychologist. For subsequent endorsement as an educational and developmental psychologist, graduates from packaged, Level 3/4 master's or PhD programs are required to complete the PsyBA registrar program (see Chapter 2 for more information on APAC accreditation of courses and the application process, and Chapter 8 for further information on endorsement as an educational and developmental psychologist).

Provisional registration

In all pathways to registration, there is a minimum period of 2 years of provisional registration as a psychologist. During the period of provisional registration, students and interns can only deliver psychological services under the direct supervision of an appropriately experienced and qualified psychologist who must be *Board-Approved Supervisor*.

Options for generally registered psychologists with appropriate experience to return to postgraduate study to complete standalone Level 4 training as an educational and developmental psychologist have recently become available (e.g. Master of Educational and Developmental Psychology Advanced Entry). Generally registered psychologists undertaking Level 4 stand-alone programs that lead to an area of practice endorsement are required by APAC to receive supervision by a board-approved supervisor who also holds a relevant AoPE (see Chapter 8 for details of registrar requirements, and see the following for what it means to be a board-approved supervisor).

General registration

"Congratulations!" You will hear this from your supervisors and teachers once you attain general (or colloquially *full*) registration. It certainly will feel like an achievement coming at the end of a long period of training, support, and evaluation to ensure that you have the required competency to hold general registration as a psychologist in Australia. This extended period of training is required to ensure that, as a psychologist, you can work confidently and competently and adhere to the required professional standards.

General registration is the category of registration that all practising psychologists must attain and hold to practise independently. As such, the requirements of programs outlined in Chapter 2 are essential to developing the required competencies. Independent practice can be daunting at first, but ideally, the period of provisional registration has provided adequate training and support to take this step with some confidence. Of course, supervision and requirements for peer consultation do not stop once general registration is attained. Remaining a generally registered psychologist requires maintaining one's knowledge

Figure 3.1 It will feel like a huge accomplishment to reach general registration, and it will allow you to practise as a psychologist in Australia

through ongoing professional education and development. One excellent means for this is to continue to have regular, ongoing supervision from a senior psychologist who can continue to develop your skills and knowledge. This ongoing supervision is one of the benefits of undertaking the PsyBA registrar program to become endorsed as an educational and developmental psychologist (see Chapter 8).

Non-practising registration

There are times in a psychologist's career when they may wish to continue to be recognised as a psychologist and (importantly) maintain the continuity of their registration status, but they do not intend to work as a psychologist for an extended period. Common reasons for seeking extended leave from the profession include carer's leave, parental leave, adoption leave, grandparenting leave, sick leave, and time off to pursue lifestyle or other interests. During periods of extended leave, approved non-practising registration enables psychologists to remain registered for a period of up to five years before returning to practise.

Additionally, this category of registration may suit the needs of psychologists who:

1   Are retiring, but who want to continue to use the protected title of *psychologist* and remain on the register.
2   Are practising overseas, but wish to retain registration in Australia either for continuity or because they intend to return to practise in Australia.
3   Are ceasing work in a role that provides psychological service and are moving into roles requiring non-psychological work (e.g. management, policy development, or advocacy), but who can foresee returning to practise as a psychologist in the future.

Non-practising registration requires the psychologist to make an application to the Board. Significantly lower fees are charged for non-practising registration and psychologists are not required to meet annual continuing professional development (CPD) or recency of practice requirements. Endorsements and supervisor approvals are inactivated while holding non-practising registration. After five years, non-practising psychologists are not immediately eligible to return to general registration. In such cases, a psychologist may be required to undertake remedial actions, such as a period of supervised practice or passing the National Psychology Examination.

Overseas registration considerations

In a global world, the ability to work internationally is highly valued. Many psychologists consider working or living for brief or extended periods in jurisdictions outside of the country where they obtained their psychology qualifications. In reading this book, it will be clear to you that the path to becoming registered, and subsequently recognised as an endorsed educational and developmental psychologist, is challenging. It is the result of sustained work over an extended period of time. Obviously, it would be beneficial to know that you could take your qualification, skills, and expertise with you should you travel outside Australia to live and work. As noted earlier, leaving Australia and preserving your registration status (for at least five years) is relatively straightforward. Before leaving Australia, you can apply for non-practising registration, and if approved, you can remain on the Psychology Board register as a psychologist. However, recognition of Australian psychology qualifications elsewhere is often less straightforward except for New Zealand registration.

Each country has its own specific requirements for practising as a psychologist and some countries (e.g. Singapore) do not currently have nationally legislated registration requirements for psychologists. In the UK, there is a clear pathway for internationally qualified psychologists to seek equivalence and obtain registration (see www. hcpc-uk.org/registration/getting-on-the-register/international-applications/). Educational psychologists are recognised within the UK (see www.aep.org.uk/).

In the United States, an attractive destination for many Australians, obtaining a licence to practise as a psychologist can be complex. While Australian qualifications at the tertiary level (especially PhD degrees) are likely to be recognised, each U.S. state has a licensing board that sets the specific criteria required to work as a psychologist. Applicants must approach the relevant body in the state they intend to practise. The American Psychological Association has a recognised speciality in School Psychology, but in each state there may be both specific licensing requirements and practice conditions (see www.apa.org/ed/graduate/specialize/school). Further information about working internationally as an educational and developmental psychologist is provided in Chapter 11.

For psychologists who hold international qualifications and registration in jurisdictions outside of Australia or New Zealand, the Psychology Board of Australia provides up-to-date advice for overseas applicants (www.psychologyboard.gov.au/Registration/Overseas-Applicants. aspx). Several points are worth noting for overseas applicants. First, it is going to require a lot of paperwork! Extensive documentation about your university degrees, coursework units, professional experience, and work history will be required to assess the equivalency of your qualification.

Two other pieces of information are also useful. First, The Australian Psychological Society can assess and provide a letter of recognition for overseas qualifications and the equivalence to Australian programs of study. However, as they and Psychology Board clearly state, this is not recognised for registration purposes, but for applying to study an Australian accredited psychology program. Scrutiny of international qualifications for Australian registration is conducted by the Psychology Board. Second, registration in Australia, both as a provisional psychologist and as a generally registered psychologist, requires English language proficiency, and evidence of proficiency must be provided. The Board considers international applicants' school education and the language of instruction used by the school system to help establish English *native speaker* proficiency. Applicants who have undertaken their primary and secondary school education in a recognised country such as Australia, United States, the UK, Canada, New Zealand, Republic of Ireland, or South Africa are likely to be recognised as proficient in English language. This can be confusing for international applicants who have completed a postgraduate degree where English was the language of instruction. Still, because their childhood education was not in a recognised country, they are asked to complete a language proficiency test before their application for registration can proceed.

Registration and becoming a board-approved supervisor

As previously noted, supervision is required for all provisionally registered psychologists, and the psychologist providing supervision must be a board-approved supervisor. Board-approved supervisors must have practised psychology for a minimum period of three years after achieving general registration (see Chapter 8 for more information about supervision and endorsement). There is clear merit in these timeframes. A supervisor needs to have enough experience to draw on to guide a less experienced psychologist through the early stages of their career. Having a specific period of practice under supervision and consolidating your own understanding of the AoPE are also essential to support others in building their identity as educational and developmental psychologists.

In addition to post-registration practice experience, board-approved supervisors must complete an approved supervisor training course and pass the assessment requirements. Details of these approved supervisor training programs can be found on the Board's website under "Supervisor training." Training programs ensure supervisors have the requisite skills to conduct the three critical components of supervision: teaching, administration, and evaluation. As a teacher, the supervisor passes on fundamental knowledge regarding psychological practice. All supervisors must ensure compliance with Board standards and be familiar with legislative and administrative requirements for provisional psychologists. Supervisors are the key gateway for evaluating provisional psychologists' attainment of the core competencies for registration (see Chapters 4 and 8). Once supervisor training has been completed and passed, there is a recognition that ongoing development and maintenance of supervisory skills are required. Therefore, the Board requires all approved supervisors to complete one Masterclass at least every five years after initial approval to maintain their status.

Ongoing registration requirements

Once you have obtained general registration as a psychologist, you are by no means at the end of your journey with the PsyBA. Ongoing compliance with registration standards, guidelines, and ethical practice are the obvious preconditions of maintaining registration. However, there are three other specific requirements for maintaining registration. All psychologists must hold Professional Indemnity Insurance (PII) while practising as a registered psychologist. This is either directly acquired by the psychologist or provided by the employer. Training institutions hold PII for provisionally registered students who are undertaking postgraduate training. Psychologists holding non-practising registration require "run-off cover," insurance for any claims that arise from past practice.

Second requirement is psychological knowledge and the evidence-based changes. Therefore, the Board requires registered psychologists to complete a minimum of 30 hours of continuing professional development (CPD) annually. Of this, 10 hours must be peer consultation where practitioners actively reflect on their practice.

Third, registered psychologists must maintain *recency of practice*. A minimum of 250 hours of practice as a psychologist (including for provisionally registered psychologists) must be completed within five years. Recency of practice requirements can also be met by having completed either an accredited program of study within the past five years or a board-approved internship or supervised practice within the five-year period.

Last, it is not unusual for provisionally registered psychologists completing postgraduate degrees to be offered part-time, paid work outside of their program of study or their university professional experience placements. Part-time employment as a provisionally registered psychologist is permitted; however, students are required to inform the Psychology Board by completing the *Working in addition to placements* (AWOP) application form. Key to such private arrangements is the need to document the supervision arrangements that are in place to cover the duration of the additional work and to ensure that appropriate professional indemnity insurance is held before the work commences.

A New Zealand Perspective

Kelly D. Carrasco

Similar to Australia, psychology is a regulated profession overseen by the New Zealand Psychologists Board (i.e. the Board), whose authority was appointed under the Health Practitioners Competence Assurance Act 2003. Only those individuals who are registered with the Board may legally use the title "Psychologist." Practitioners register under scopes of practice based on their training, meaning individuals who completed educational psychology training programmes register as and use the title of "Educational Psychologist."

When students are completing the professional practice component of training as part of their postgraduate diploma programmes, they must register with the Board as an "Intern Psychologist." They must successfully complete 1,500 hours of supervised training as part of their degree programmes before they can move to full registration as an "Educational Psychologist." All "Educational Psychologists" practising in New Zealand must meet the core competencies under the "Psychologist" scope of practice as well as the additional core competencies of the "Educational Psychologist" scope of practice as described by the Board.

In addition to registration, educational psychologists must hold a practising certificate that is renewed annually. To maintain registration and good standing with the Board, educational psychologists must engage in supervision, either from a more senior psychologist or peer supervision if already a senior psychologist, and the Continuing Competence Programme (CCP). The CCP serves to ensure that practising psychologists are maintaining a required standard of competence as part of their professional obligation. While there are no minimum number of hours of professional development as part of the CCP, psychologists are expected to be self-reflective and commit to as much learning as is required to maintain all their core competencies.

New Zealand-registered educational psychologists will have many of the same overseas registration considerations as their Australian counterparts. Since the documentation you may be asked to produce will vary by country (and even states within countries), it is good practice to maintain all educational and training-related materials, such as course syllabi, readings, or logbooks of practice-related work.

For more information about registering and practising as an educational psychologist in New Zealand, please see the Board's website (https://psychologistsboard.org.nz/).

Concluding comments

This chapter has highlighted the requirements surrounding the various forms of registration that you will encounter on your journey to becoming an educational and developmental psychologist. At a minimum, you will pass through provisional registration to general registration. Beyond that, you will need to pass through the registrar program to become an endorsed educational and developmental psychologist.

After the minimum period of registration, you may become a board-approved supervisor. Two years after your endorsement is achieved, you would be able to support others to pass through the registrar program. There may also be occasions where you enter a period of non-practising registration. Along the way, in this official part of your journey the PsyBA website (www.psychologyboard.gov.au/) is an essential point of reference and guidance in understanding what is expected of you. At the core of registration are the demonstration, maintenance, and application of the core competencies required by the Board. The next chapter will discuss the professional competencies upon which psychological practice rests.

Professional competencies

> *"Nothing compares to the satisfaction gained through the development and application of new knowledge and skills in Educational and Developmental Psychology; practitioners have opportunities to enhance and support growth, development, learning, and wellbeing in children, adolescents, parents, families, and older adults in contextually responsive ways."*
>
> —Louise Laskey

Introduction

The training of psychologists in Australia is highly regulated to protect the public. As a result, clear guidelines stipulate the core competencies required of all registered psychologists in Australia. In addition, there are competencies specific to each endorsed area of psychology. In this chapter, we will explore the competencies specific to the field of educational and developmental psychology.

In December 2019, the Psychology Board of Australia published the *Guidelines on Area of Practice Endorsements* (Psychology Board of Australia, 2022a). The competency areas for educational and developmental psychologists highlight the importance of knowledge in learning and development across the lifespan. The guidelines also recognise the breadth of clients (individual, familial, and organisational) that educational and developmental psychologists typically provide services to, namely children and families, schools and institutions, welfare, and community agencies. This chapter will detail the eight core competencies: (1) knowledge of the discipline; (2) ethical, legal, and professional matters; (3) psychological assessment

DOI: 10.4324/9781003330974-4

Figure 4.1 There are eight core competencies that underpin work for psychologists in Australia

and measurement; (4) intervention strategies; (5) research and evaluation; (6) communication and interpersonal relationship; (7) working in a cross-cultural context; and (8) practice across the lifespan and discuss how they relate to the work of an educational and developmental psychologist.

The eight core competencies

(1) Knowledge of the discipline

Knowledge of learning and development across the lifespan is a critical competency of an educational and developmental psychologist. One must possess an applied understanding of key theories of social, emotional, and cognitive development and exceptionalities. This knowledge informs the appropriate selection and application of assessments and interventions in client work.

Knowledge of associated disciplines and fields is vital as best-practice often requires a multi-disciplinary response. Understanding of paediatrics, psychiatry, neuropsychology, psychopharmacology, gerontology, and behavioural science is often required when providing psychological services to typical client groups.

Awareness of neuro-typical and neuro-diverse development is critical. Not only does this knowledge aid diagnosis but also enables differential or comorbid diagnosis. An example of this may be an educational and developmental psychologist assessing whether a child has a comorbid presentation of autism and social anxiety disorder or a differential diagnosis of attention-deficit/hyperactivity disorder or posttraumatic stress disorder. Furthermore, in working with parents or caregivers of children, educational and developmental psychologists will be exposed to different psychiatric conditions more common in adulthood, such as personality disorders and substance abuse disorders. Thus, educational and developmental psychologists must have a strong understanding of developmental and psychiatric conditions to accurately diagnose childhood presentations and develop appropriate interventions for clients and families.

Educational and Developmental Psychologists have knowledge in a broad range of areas which is critical for skills in diagnosis and differential diagnosis. Therefore, educational and developmental psychologists may work with various presentations and disorders rather than focus on one area. The Australian Psychological Society's College of Educational and Developmental Psychologists (CEDP) provides a list of evidence-based knowledge areas needed for work as an educational and developmental psychologist.

Knowledge areas for Educational and Developmental Psychology

Assessing developmental, learning, and behavioural difficulties throughout the lifespan

Diagnosing disabilities, neurodevelopmental disorders, and mental health disorders
Differential diagnosis
Identifying and using evidence-based interventions
Counselling
Consulting with individuals and groups
Designing training programs
Evaluating programs and interventions
Designing and implementing professional development programs
Case management and liaising with other specialists
Writing reports for multiple audiences (e.g. parents, teachers, and other professionals)
Psychological consultancy and professional learning
Areas of Expertise – Across the Lifespan
Early childhood
Parents or professionals (e.g. GPs, Paediatricians, Child Health Nurses, and Child Care Centre staff) may refer a child to an Educational and Developmental Psychologist for the following reasons:

Concerns about a child's cognitive, behavioural, or emotional development

Assessment of a developmental delay
Assessment of specific conditions (e.g. Intellectual Developmental Disorder and Autism)
Assistance with feeding, sleeping, or behaviour problems
Infant mental health problems (e.g. anxiety and disordered attachment)

Managing a child's difficult temperament
Assistance with attachment issues, or with "goodness of fit"
between parent and child
Parenting issues
Sibling rivalry within the family
Assessment of school readiness
Assistance with treatment planning and early-intervention
programs
School years
Parents, teachers, or other professionals (or children themselves)
may seek assistance for the following reasons:

*Problems with the transition to school, or from one phase
of education to another*

Separation anxiety or school avoidance
Psychoeducational assessment
Assessment, diagnosis, and treatment of learning difficulties and
disorders (e.g. dyslexia)
Poor peer-relationships
Behaviour problems and disorders (e.g. attention-deficit
hyperactivity disorder)
Specialist behaviour management planning
Low self-esteem
Well-being issues
Mental health problems (e.g. mood disorders)
Assessment of giftedness
Family relationship issues
Physical or sexual abuse
Assistance with treatment planning and specialist
support
Whole school consultancy or intervention (e.g. social-emotional
learning programs and critical incident intervention)
Adolescence
Adolescents, their parents, or others concerned with their
welfare may seek help to deal with:

Conflict between the adolescent and parents

Friendship issues
Peer pressure
Behaviour problems
Sexuality issues
Disability issues
Identity issues and the transition to adulthood
Mental health problems
Drug and alcohol problems
Career guidance
Adjustment and transition issues
School to work transition
Whole school community issues
Adulthood
Individuals, their partners, or employers may seek assistance with:
Mental health (including perinatal mental health)

Relationship problems

Divorce/separation
Parenting and child-rearing
Adoption issues
Mid-life concerns
Career restructuring
Work stress
Education and training in the workplace
Later adulthood
Elderly people or their adult children may seek information or assistance with:

Healthy ageing

Coping with decline in functioning
Dependency

Adjustment and transition issues
Issues of loss or grief

Proactive and preventive approaches

Mental health promotion
Well-being interventions and approaches
Relaxation strategies and mindfulness
Positive psychology (positive education)

What does this look like in practice?

Competence in knowledge of the discipline is really the integration and application of theory and research to practice. Psychologists are highly trained, and as a result of years of tertiary education, well versed in psychological theory. Picture a situation where you are assessing a child who has been referred for suspected developmental delay. In conducting a comprehensive assessment of this child, you will need to draw on your knowledge of social, emotional, and cognitive development, learning theory, understanding of milestones, impacts of ecological factors on development, and consideration of psychopathology. How will this knowledge inform your work with this child? Knowledge of the discipline requires that the psychologist has ready access to this information, or if not, can access it through supervision or professional resources.

Let's hear from the field

In my practice as an educational psychologist I require broad knowledge in a range of areas. One area that informs my practice daily is the knowledge of developmental norms and most importantly, what isn't developmentally appropriate. I apply this understanding when recording developmental histories with parents and caregivers, such as knowing appropriate developmental milestones at different ages. In classrooms when completing observations, I have awareness of what behaviour is age appropriate and then identify what is and isn't expected at that age. This can also include academic abilities (for example being able to read "cat" at age 6 versus age 12) and motor abilities (for example being able to write "cat" at age 6 versus age 12). My knowledge of age-appropriate skills are applied to assessment decisions to ensure the most accurate assessment is used quantitatively to compare a student's abilities to same aged peers. All this information is then used for case conceptualisation, such as in a report, to provide schools and families/caregivers with appropriate recommendations to support the student or inform referrals to other services to further assist the student.

—Jessica Smead (School Psychologist and Registrar)

(2) Ethical, legal, and professional matters

Ethical competence and practice is integral to the work of all psychologists as we are legally bound to practise ethically and in accordance with relevant Codes (e.g. currently the APS Code of Ethics and soon to be the PsyBA Code of Conduct). Ethical competence is essential because many educational and developmental psychologists work with children and young people (i.e. minors, and other stakeholders such as parents, teachers, and schools). Work in the context of educational and developmental psychology can often present ethical dilemmas and issues due to the need to balance ethical obligations to different parties, such as parents and schools, and handle conflicts of interest. The most common ethical challenges often pertain to privacy and confidentiality concerns. In a school context, a psychologist is obligated to protect a young person's right to privacy and confidentiality, however, not all information can remain confidential. Disclosures of risk of harm, child safety issues, or legal requests for information (e.g. by the family court) are situations where information may be requested (or needs to be shared). Ethical competence in such situations ensures that ethical obligations are upheld and the client is protected.

If ever in doubt, psychologists should seek support for their ethical decision-making. This may mean consulting the codes and guidelines, seeking consultation from a peer, supervisor, or senior colleague, or, if necessary, seeking legal advice such as through your professional association (e.g. APS) or professional indemnity insurer.

The other aspect of ethical competence is the ability of educational and developmental psychologists to effectively communicate their ethical obligations to others, such as to families or to community agencies or schools. In theory, this might sound straightforward, but in practice, several considerations can impact how or what information you share with others while upholding ethical boundaries. Capacity to provide informed consent, limits to confidentiality, working with mature minors, ethical storage of information, consent in separated families, handling conflicts of interest, and managing dual relationships, particularly in school settings, are common ethical issues to be navigated.

In addition, various legal and professional matters can arise that require careful consideration and an informed response. Requests to access client information may come from law enforcement or other agencies, notes can be subpoenaed, or a psychologist might be required to provide expert testimony in court. In such matters, the psychologist should be aware of their obligations and seek additional support (i.e. legal advice or forensic supervision that may come from your professional association or insurer) when needed to ensure ethical practice is upheld.

What does this look like in practice?

Ethics is a cornerstone of psychology training. All graduate psychologists are well equipped to navigate ethical matters in the field, but it is the nuances that can at times present challenges. Think of the following situations: you are employed as a school psychologist and the principal requests a list of students you are seeing and asks to access your files. How would you respond? Or, you have received a private practice referral to see a 10-year-old child, the parents are separated and you have consent from one parent. How would you respond?

These are typical examples of situations where an educational and developmental psychologist would be required to demonstrate ethical competence. Let us look at an example of how Sarah demonstrates ethical competence within the school setting.

Let's hear from the field

As an educational and developmental psychologist working in a secondary school, I am regularly faced with ethical "dilemmas" that require me to consider competing laws and ethical standards, and manage competing expectations from students, families, school staff and external agencies.

For example, most students that self-refer want to talk in complete confidence and mature minors can provide informed consent for psychological support without parent/carer involvement. However, there are times when confidentiality needs to be breached to reduce risk of harm. In such situations, informing the young person of such obligations helps to preserve the therapeutic relationship. What is in the "best interests" of the student is not always clear, or in line with organisational policy. Occasionally, I conclude it is in the best interests of a child to withhold information pertaining to risk of harm from parent/carers that I deem to be incapable of providing a protective response e.g., because they have consistently exhibited unhelpful responses to past disclosures, or where there is a genuine risk of family violence. In such cases, it is imperative that I clearly communicate my ethical decision-making process to Principals and where appropriate, child protective services so that that they too can make informed decisions to protect the young person, now and in future, in their own roles.

—Sarah Pearson (Educational and Developmental Psychologist, School Psychologist)

(3) Psychological assessment and measurement

Assessment is an essential component of psychological practice. Educational and developmental psychologists require competence in the application of multiple methods to assess learning and developmental problems across the lifespan. This includes the ability to select appropriate assessment tools. To do this, educational and developmental psychologists must have adequate knowledge of assessment theory and research, the capacity to consider limitations of the assessment tools selected, such as their reliability and validity, and the ability to interpret non-typical profiles and outlier scores.

Assessment work of the educational and developmental psychologist most commonly includes (but is not limited to) the following types of assessment.

Common types of assessment:

Psycho-educational (cognitive and academic)	Diagnostic inventories	Functional and adaptive behaviour assessment
Educational attainment	Developmental delay	Behaviour ratings
Career interests and/or work preferences	Executive function and memory	Personality (sometimes referred to as character)
Social and emotional competencies (including coping skills)	Strengths and emotions	Mental health and well-being screening and assessment

Educational and developmental psychologists perform a key assessment role in the identification and diagnosis (and differential diagnosis) of many disorders. Many of these first emerge during childhood, such as *Specific Learning Disorder, Intellectual Developmental Disorder, Autism,* and *Attention-Deficit/Hyperactivity Disorder (ADHD),* but can be identified and diagnosed at other times across the lifespan. Competent assessment of these and other disorders also requires educational and developmental psychologists to have knowledge and assessment skills of other disorders, such as anxiety disorders, depressive disorders, trauma and attachment-related disorders, and emerging personality and psychotic disorders. Some diagnostic tools for specific areas require additional training by the psychologist in order to access a licence or permission to be able to administer the tools (e.g. Autism Diagnostic Interview-Revised (ADI-R), the Autism Diagnostic Observation Schedule, Second Edition [ADOS-2], and Griffiths Mental Development Scales – 3rd Edition [Griffiths III]).

Assessment competence includes not only the selection and administration of psychological, developmental, and educational measures but also the accurate scoring, interpretation, and synthesis of this data. In addition, the ability to provide feedback and effectively describe the information to the relevant stakeholders in a meaningful way is essential. When such measures are used to inform clinical judgement about whether a client meets criteria for diagnosis, standardised administration and accurate scoring are critical.

Educational and developmental psychologists also have an ethical obligation to maintain the integrity of tests used and assessment outcomes by safeguarding confidentiality, ensuring secure storage of the test materials, and upholding the copyright requirements.

Psychological measurement tools are frequently revised.

An educational and developmental psychologist needs to ensure that the assessment tools they select are up-to-date and valid. The use of an outdated test will result in the use of outdated norms; this has implications for diagnosis (e.g. the observed rise in Full Scale IQ scores over time known as the Flynn effect).

Context is also important. Educational and developmental psychologists will ask questions like, *for what purpose is the assessment measure being used? Is the assessment for diagnostic purposes or to inform intervention progress?* Understanding the context in which the assessment tool is being used informs the selection of different tools and tests. Understanding diagnostic criteria is also important to inform the selection of assessment tools. For example, diagnostic criteria may require measurement of a person's symptoms across multiple contexts, requiring the psychologist to collect information from the child's school and home, or diagnostic criteria may require symptoms to be present in the early developmental period, which requires the psychologist to conduct a detailed developmental history.

What does this look like in practice?

In practice, educational and developmental psychologists will select assessment tools that enable them to answer the referral question. There are best-practice and gold-standard tools recommended for diagnosing particular disorders and problems. Educational and developmental psychologists are guided by knowledge in test selection and a client-centred perspective that considers the needs and capabilities of the client during an assessment. Several other factors can and do also impact a psychologist's selection of tests. For example, government or bureaucratic requirements, accessibility or availability of tests, familiarity with tests, confidence with administration, and test duration are common factors. Clinical judgement is exercised in this process, and as a result, it is possible that two different educational and developmental psychologists could provide the same diagnosis utilising two completely different assessment batteries.

Let's hear from the field

In my work as an educational and developmental psychologist I show competence in this area by using a range of assessment tools – behavioural, social/emotional, intellectual and adaptive functioning, for funding purposes as well as for diagnosis of neuro-developmental disorders, and for differential diagnosis. I conduct functional behaviour analysis to understand what a child's behaviour is communicating. I have recently trained to use a nonverbal intelligence test which has been illuminating, showing me how some seemingly low functioning children perform well during a nonverbal assessment, reminding me how much language can impact on someone's presentation and how they function in school. I tailor the assessment tool and method of assessment I use to the individual's needs after exploring their concerns and background. I do continual training to expand the range of assessments I can competently use. I continually adapt my client focused reports to improve readability, considering current ideas about neurodiversity. I use my knowledge of psychometrics to help parents, teachers, and clients to understand the assessment scores and profiles – such as explaining why two different test batteries both measuring the same thing get different results. I have continual supervision (both peer supervision and supervision one-on-one with someone with specific expertise), which is vital to talk through non-typical profiles and tricky cases which have complex presentations and backgrounds, such as trauma histories.

—Dr Cheree Murrihy (Educational and
Developmental Psychologist and Lecturer)

(4) Intervention strategies

Educational and developmental psychologists are competent in delivering interventions for learning and developmental problems and prevention at both the individual and group levels. Knowledge of best-practice intervention in treating a broad range of disorders and presenting issues is crucial. Educational and developmental psychologists are also trained in preventive interventions and approaches that support learning and well-being. Psychology is a highly regulated profession to ensure the protection of the public. The pathway to registration and subsequent route to endorsement ensures that educational and developmental psychologists are competent interventionists, meeting the needs of their clients via evidence-based practice.

The competency of intervention strategies is delineated into psychological intervention provided at the individual and the group level. At the individual level, intervention is designed to target the presenting issue with a view to improve functioning or well-being. Guidelines and reviews such as "Evidence-based psychological interventions in the treatment of mental disorders" (APS, 2018) exist to support clinicians with intervention strategies. In such guides, evidence for a range of psychological interventions is provided to assist decision-making about optimal treatment. When working with the individual, the focus of intervention may include one or more of the following: counselling or psychotherapy, psychoeducation, behavioural support, learning, and educational strategies, emotional regulation, social skills training, development of life skills, functional behaviour analysis, and training of parents, teachers and carers. This list is not exhaustive but reflects the breadth of intervention work educational and developmental psychologists engage in. Diagnostic presentations often require the application of recommended and established psychological interventions such as exposure therapy for anxiety disorders, however, clinicians use a range of intervention strategies to support their individual client work. When devising an intervention plan, educational and developmental psychologists consider the range of presenting issues, their severity, and their impact on functioning, and will regularly review the client's progress to ensure that intervention is targeted and specific. Working in partnership with the client, intervention goals are devised and revised iteratively.

Educational and developmental psychologists can effect change across multiple levels of a system; in this capacity, they can impact the culture or climate of a setting. At the group level, educational and developmental psychologists may provide intervention to families or client groups in a range of settings (e.g. schools, hospitals, community organisations, or private practice) focusing on prevention, intervention, or professional development. In a school setting, psychologists use their intervention knowledge to provide consultation and inform program development and implementation. This intervention may be a whole-school approach to address school-wide priorities such as reducing bullying or increasing or maintaining attendance, well-being, inclusion, or school belonging as some examples. Smaller targeted groups at a cohort level may also occur (e.g. study skills groups).

What does this look like in practice?

So how does the educational and developmental psychologist choose an intervention? What informs this decision? As we discussed earlier in the *Psychological Measurement* competency, several factors impact the type of assessment selected, the same applies to selecting interventions. Such factors include training experiences of the psychologist and efficacy of delivering a certain intervention, access to intervention resources and programs, nature of delivery (individual vs. group), and available research evidence. Above all, the needs of the individual or group are a core consideration. This may be driven by a referral question, a social trend or concern, or an understanding of evidence-based best practice.

Evidence-based intervention for reading problems has received a lot of media attention. It is a point of contention among educational professionals who may subscribe to different pedagogical philosophies due to an evolving evidence base (e.g. the so-called, *reading wars*) (Buckingham, 2020; Solity, 2020; Wheldall et al., 2020). Educational and developmental psychologists must navigate the rhetoric to recommend an evidence-based intervention and, where necessary, present evidence to support such recommendations.

Let's hear from the field

As an Ed & Dev registrar working across both school and clinic settings, I deliver a wide range of interventions at a group level and an individual level. Within the school setting, I run class-wide social emotional learning programs with a focus on skills such as identifying emotions, coping strategies, perspective taking, and communication strategies. These programs then help in identifying students that may be eligible for more focused group-based intervention such as social skills groups which we also provide within the school context. Additionally, class-based programs are often run in conjunction with professional development for teachers and school staff. Working within the school environment enables me not only to provide intervention at group and individual levels but also to work within a "team around the learner" approach.

Within both school and clinic settings, I provide counselling and therapy to individuals using evidence based and developmentally appropriate approaches when working with issues such as anxiety, depression, family relationships, neurodivergence, and school related concerns. This can sometimes involve using a manualised treatment approach or formulating my own treatment plan for the client depending on my assessment of their presenting concerns, for which I mainly utilise the frameworks of CBT and ACT. While intervention occurs at an individual level, I believe it is still imperative to collaborate with families and schools, to ensure best outcomes for the young person.

—Shameema Saleem (School Psychologist,
Private Practitioner & Registrar)

(5) Research and evaluation

Due to the structure of psychology training pathways, psychologists possess highly developed research skills. As a result, they are ideally situated to integrate research knowledge and action into their work as *scientist-practitioners*. But what does this actually mean? The scientist-practitioner model is grounded in the belief that practising psychologists should be knowledgeable in both research and clinical practice and that psychologists who possess research knowledge and skills will provide more effective services (Jones & Mehr, 2007).

For educational and developmental psychologists, competence in research and evaluation includes the ability to identify questions that arise from practice and the subsequent development of research strategies to address these questions, effective communication of research methods and outcomes to non-psychologists, and the transformation of research evidence into policy development or program application.

What does this look like in practice?

As we have established, research skills are essential for educational and developmental psychologists. But what does it look like when applied to the competencies? The application of research and evaluation skills is illustrated in the following contexts.

- Testing and assessment: the accurate interpretation of psychometric tests requires a grounding in research methods and statistics. Knowledge of how to interpret base rates, factor analytic structures, population samples, error estimates, and confidence intervals are necessary skills in test interpretation.
- Intervention: the selection of evidence-based intervention strategies and programs requires psychologists to understand the evidence base. This may involve critical appraisal of the existing research and types of evidence for an intervention, for example comparing research designs such as randomised controlled trials, systematic review, quasi-experiments, and peer-review versus non-peer-review data. The psychologist synthesises this research data to make informed decisions on intervention selection.
- Evaluation: how effective was your group intervention? How much is a client improving? Answering these questions requires implementing evaluation measures to assess change over time. An understanding of research design and subsequent application of pre- and post-tests enables educational and developmental psychologists to make data-informed decisions about treatment effectiveness and future directions.
- Professional development: staying up to date with the latest research in the field or an area of interest forms part of the continuing professional development requirement for psychologists. Regular reading of peer-reviewed journals, academic articles, and professional magazines (like Monitor and InPsych) supports the maintenance of this competency. Some professional associations include access to journals and databases as a part of their membership. For example, membership to the Australian Psychology Society's College of Educational and Developmental Psychologist includes full access to the journal, *The Educational and Developmental Psychologist* (see Chapter 7 for more information on Professional Associations). Also, professional associations, such as the

APS, regularly provide members with updated evidence guides and position statements that support practitioners in staying cognisant of current research, for example, the *Evidence-based practice and practice-based evidence in psychology: Position statement.*

(APS, 2022c)

Let's hear from the field

In the Research Methods subject I teach, I emphasise the importance for educational and developmental psychologists to be able to synthesise, distil, and apply knowledge from research in the local context. This requires the ability to both value the knowledge that the people whom we work with hold (e.g., children, parents, teachers, policy makers) and offer recommendations drawing from published research and from practice-based experience that is relevant to their unique context.

In practice, when I am working with a teacher, say, to formulate the best way to support a child with autism, I would obtain background information about the child, what the child and the parents have tried and experienced and their preferences for intervention, and what the teacher and the school have done and are able to do. It is important to not undermine or override the knowledge and experience of the people involved, and to apply research- and practice-based evidence in a way that is appropriate to the local context and take into consideration the input from different stakeholders. The same principle applies to policy and program recommendations. Educational and developmental psychologists therefore hold a special and important role in the distillation and application of research evidence in practical contexts.

—Dr Man Ching Esther Chan (Educational and Developmental Psychologist and Lecturer in Educational Psychology)

(6) Communication and interpersonal relationships

The ability to effectively communicate psychological knowledge to others is a critical skill. For educational and developmental psychologists, such communication will often take the form of written reports and diagnostic statements. Communication is provided in written and oral formats to various stakeholders, including clients, their families, teachers and schools, government and medico legal agencies. The purpose for which the information is requested will inform the way it is prepared and delivered. Identify who your audience is and what you want them to know about the client.

The nature of psychological practice necessitates effective interpersonal relationships. Educational and developmental psychologists often work as part of complex systems and multi-disciplinary contexts. They perform consultative roles in providing advice about learning and developmental problems, well-being, and mental health promotion, conveying their professional opinion to ensure client needs are addressed and met. Consultation is a key competence of educational and developmental psychologists; it is a distinct professional practice skill and functions differently from direct service provision. As a consultant, the educational and developmental psychologist gives professional advice within their area of competence, in doing so, they may also need to clarify their role within a particular setting, for example, within a school or multi-disciplinary team. In situations where the educational and developmental psychologist is working with other disciplines, there may also be a need to communicate ethical obligations concerning shared files to ensure confidentiality responsibilities are upheld.

Effective communication is also essential when psychologists work alongside differently qualified professionals or psychologist peers. They may need to communicate and establish boundaries to ensure role clarity, especially when a client is engaged with multiple allied health professionals concurrently. The interdisciplinary context provides an opportunity for psychologists with different endorsements to work collaboratively in support of a client. Think of a scenario where a client requires acute or inpatient mental health care. An educational and developmental psychologist in the school setting may consult with a primary care psychiatrist or psychologist to support their shared client's case management.

What does this look like in practice?

Psychologists are often criticised for "psycho-babble" in reports and other written correspondence. In essence, "psycho-babble" refers to detailed test information and statistical language that often justifies our clinical judgement and diagnostic impressions; however to the layperson or non-psychologist, this language can be confusing and sometimes confronting. The ability to effectively communicate complex psychological information to various stakeholders is a competence educational and developmental psychologists must possess. Adjusting your communication for different audiences may be essential to ensure a client gets the support they need, and that the reader can operationalise and interpret your recommendations. For example, a teacher needs to understand a student's level of achievement in a psychoeducational assessment and the subsequent recommendations required to support a learning difficulty; does the communication you provide (i.e. the report) ensure this? Similarly, a government department or disability agency may review your report to determine a client's eligibility for funding or services. Does your language indicate the severity of the client's presentation and make clear statements about diagnoses and impact? Communicating effectively to stakeholders may mean the difference between a client receiving the support they need or not.

Let's hear from the field

In my work as an educational and developmental psychologist, I demonstrate competency in communication and interpersonal relationships by: working hard to develop strong and trusting relationships with clients, families and carers, members of school communities, and others, including health professionals; demonstrating active listening; having empathy for my clients and "walking in their shoes"; educating clients and families about the therapeutic process; exploring the expectations of my clients; inviting my clients to tell their stories; focusing on the coping skills, strengths, and personal resources of my clients; paying attention to the influence of the immediate environment as well as the broader environment; gathering information from a variety of sources; regularly providing updates to referral sources; keeping the wellbeing of my clients at the heart of any communication or decision-making; regularly consulting with trusted colleagues.

—Dr Michelle Andrews Luke (Educational and Developmental Psychologist and Lecturer)

(7) Working with people from diverse groups

Working as an educational and developmental psychologist, you will engage with clients who differ from you in several ways. That goes without saying. Competence in working with people from diverse groups is the ability to practise competently and ethically with people who may differ in age, culture, race, gender identity, language, ability, sexual orientation, socio-economic status, or religion (note this list is not exhaustive). The competent educational psychologist also demonstrates cultural responsiveness, including with Aboriginal and Torres Strait Islander peoples.

Psychology as a profession has not always worked respectfully with diverse groups. Awareness of the socio-political and historical context of the profession and the impact on educational and developmental psychology practice is important to understanding and ensuring ethical practice in the future. Examples of where the historical context has impacted current practice include The Australian Psychological Society's 2016 formal Apology to Aboriginal and Torres Strait Islander people for the role psychology played in their mistreatment and the APS position statement on the use of psychological practices that attempt to change or suppress sexual orientation or gender.

Educational and developmental psychologists respect client diversity and integrate this knowledge into assessment, intervention, and formulation decisions. Consideration of a client's socio-ecological environment, such as the impact of diversity factors, enables understanding of the client in context.

What does this look like in practice?

When looking at culture as an indicator of diversity, the goal of educational and developmental psychologists should be to create culturally safe and culturally responsive practice environments. A focus on cultural responsiveness as opposed to cultural competence creates space for the psychologist to respectfully acknowledge the impact of culture within the therapeutic relationship or interaction, be that their own culture as well as the clients. Being culturally reflexive means having respect for other cultures, being self-aware of one's cultural perspective, and showing cultural humility in understanding and respecting the client's cultural identity.

In working with clients from diverse groups, psychologists might ask themselves the following type of questions:

- How does my own culture and background impact my ability to work with this client?
- How do I demonstrate cultural reflexivity with this client?
- How can I be diversity affirming with this client?
- How am I being perceived by this client who has a different cultural background? What barriers might this create in developing our therapeutic relationship?

Let's hear from the field

Working as a psychologist (Educational and Developmental Registrar) means that I get to work with people from many different backgrounds, cultures, and life experiences. This brings an incredible variety to my work but also requires me to work with reflexivity and adaptability and to consider the influence of culture and diversity on the presentation, assessment, and support for client needs. Practising reflexivity as I work and support clients means that I constantly examine my own values, beliefs, and assumptions about issues clients may face. Knowing myself is as important as knowing psychological theories, tools and strategies. I often work through an ecological systems theory when formulating a client's case such as the interaction between support systems in the meso-system or the influence of policies in the macro system. Woven through this is consideration for culture, gender, socio-economic status, religion and spirituality. All of these factors are opportunities to bring rich, context specific and individually tailored support to the client.

—Dr Georgia Dawson (Educational and Developmental Psychology Registrar, Lecturer)

(8) Practice across the lifespan

A common misconception is that educational and developmental psychologists only work with children. It is true that many educational and developmental psychologists work in schools or may focus their practice on children. However, this is a limiting view. Educational and developmental psychologists can and do work across the lifespan. Throughout their lives, people go through various stages of development and transitions. Educational and developmental psychologists are interested in supporting people to grow, develop, and adapt at different life stages, such as childhood, adolescence, adulthood, and late adulthood.

What does this look like in practice?

The practice across the lifespan competency needs to be considered in terms of the context in which the psychologist provides services.

Figure 4.2 Working with diverse groups at different ages and life stages are competencies educational and developmental psychologists will develop throughout their training. Educational and developmental psychologist, Kirsty Vondeling says, "The perinatal period is a crucial time in which parent-child interactions have the propensity to significantly impact the trajectory of a child's mental health and development. Educational and developmental psychologists, with their knowledge of attachment and development, are much needed and well placed to positively impact parent and infant mental health outcomes"

A psychologist in a school, for example, may not have the same skill level in working with older adults but will likely have expertise working with clients in the childhood or adolescent stages of development. Having said that, it is crucial to recognise that client work often necessitates a multi-generational focus. Let's look at the following situations. Work with a child or adolescent client will often also involve work with the parent to support the mental health and well-being of the young person. Similarly, working with clients in later adulthood might also include working with an adult child seeking support with a parent's decline in functioning or healthy ageing. In addition, psychologists may provide family therapy, and in such cases multiple clients at potentially different life stages are involved.

Let's hear from the field

As Educational and Developmental Psychologists we use our knowledge and training to work with people across their lifespan and apply our skills in communication to provide a service that is effective, engaging and relevant to the individual, with consideration of the broader systems they belong to. In a typical day as a School Psychologist this may look like working with a primary school child to explain how emotions manifest in their body using picture books, "feelings bottles" of glitter to represent thoughts and emotions of varying intensity; paper and pencils to illustrate the physiological signs of anxiety in their body and beating a drum to model the changes in their heart rate when anxious. In working with adolescents, this competency could be shown in how we help them unpack the social and emotional consequences of the communication they had on TikTok and teaching them a problem-solving framework to resolve social issues with their peers. In working with parents or grandparents, this may look like actively listening to their concerns and providing evidence-based information and guidance about child and adolescent development, to enable them to understand their child's behaviour from another perspective. As Educational and Developmental Psychologists, we hold knowledge about a range of presenting issues across the lifespan and like artists, we creatively consider how best to share the tools we have to paint a picture and offer a perspective that can be understood by the individual or group we are working with.

—Keshini Niles (Educational and Developmental Psychologist, School Psychologist)

A New Zealand Perspective

Sonja Macfarlane

It is noted that the core competencies for Educational Psychologists in Australia, that are outlined in this chapter, are very similar to the those that are outlined in the New Zealand Psychologist Board's *Core Competencies for the Professional Practice of Psychology in Aotearoa New Zealand*, listed here, namely:

1 Discipline, Knowledge, Scholarship, and Research
2 Diversity, Culture, and The Treaty of Waitangi/Te Tiriti o Waitangi
3 Professional, Legal, and Ethical Practice
4 Framing, Measuring, and Planning
5 Communication
6 Intervention and Service Implementation
7 Communication
8 Professional and Community Relations, Consultation, Collaboration
9 Reflective Practice
10 Supervision (for those providing supervision)

The reflections that follow here emanate from my own cultural lens, as a *wāhine Māori* (Māori woman). I note that the word "competency" broadly refers to the awareness, knowledge, skills, abilities, and behaviours that an individual holds, subscribes to, and enacts. This immediately causes me to reflect on the "how" of enacting our core "professional competencies," versus the "how" of enacting our core "personal competencies," by asking myself; "Should this be a binary?"

I ruminate on the fact that a *te ao Māori* (Māori worldview) perspective maintains the view that our *tikanga* and *kawa* (cultural protocols and customs) require us to uphold and enact a particular set of core competencies, so that the *mana* (dignity), *mauri* (unique essence), and *oranga* (well-being) of the people with whom we interact will be respected and maintained. I therefore reflect further on the following questions: "Should the ways we enact our professional and personal competencies differ?" "Should we subscribe to particular ways of being, doing, and behaving in our professional life, that are different to, or at odds with, those in our personal life?" "Do our Māori elders and leaders espouse two sets of competencies; different ones, for different people, in different contexts?" I believe they do not.

As I further reflect on the "how" – or the enactment – of core competencies for Educational Psychologists in Aotearoa New Zealand, three Māori cultural concepts immediately spring to my mind, as they refer to the ways in which people should always behave and interact with others – in every setting, in every situation, and with any person. These three concepts (or core cultural competencies) – which are fundamental to *te ao Māori* – are those of *tika*, *pono*, and *aroha*. *Tika* refers to what we do, and how we do it, reiterating the importance of "doing the right thing," and "doing things right." *Pono* refers to what we uphold, and how we behave, reiterating the importance of being reasoned, just, fair, truthful, and acting with integrity. *Aroha* refers to what we feel, and how we connect, reiterating the importance of being respectful, compassionate, empathetic, kind, and caring.

I firmly believe that we must always enact our awareness, knowledge, skills, abilities, and behaviours by upholding the core cultural competencies of *tika*, *pono*, and *aroha*, so that we are working from the *ngākau* (the heart), and not from the *rākau* (ticking the box).

Concluding comments

In this chapter, we explored the eight competency areas of educational and developmental psychology and looked at how these competencies translate to practice in the field. The specialist capabilities of educational and developmental psychologists enable practice with a broad range of clients, groups and, organisations. There are many avenues where psychologists can affect change and use their psychological and scientific knowledge to improve outcomes for diverse groups of people.

In Chapter 5, we look closely at some key skills and attributes that educational and developmental psychologists display in their work and practice.

5 | Skills and attributes

> *"Akin to Paediatricians who are concerned with human development, Educational and Developmental Psychologists are trained to work across the lifespan leveraging both therapy and learning to live well and support people with making positive life transitions and adjustments."*
>
> —Dr John Roodenburg

Introduction

In Chapter 4, we learned about the competencies of educational and developmental psychologists and how these capacities are demonstrated and integrated into work and practice. But skills underpin competence. So, what skills does an educational and developmental psychologist need? How do attributes influence practice? In this chapter, we explore a range of skills and attributes that an educational and developmental psychologist may possess, the list is by no means exhaustive, but it's a great starting point for considering your future work as an educational and developmental psychologist.

The effective communicator: connecting with others, at any age

Educational and developmental psychologists are highly effective and articulate communicators. They are also reflective listeners who modify their language and approach according to the context and audience. Who is your audience and what do you want to convey?

DOI: 10.4324/9781003330974-5

Educational and developmental psychologists need to have the ability to articulate often complex psychological information to non-psychologists (i.e. clients, families, stakeholders, and organisations). Delivering a diagnosis to a parent, explaining intervention strategies to a teacher, describing a client's functional needs to a funding body, communicating test results to a young person in an age-appropriate way, advocating for a student's right to access accommodations in a setting, or negotiating program resources with a principal are all examples of when educational and developmental psychologists need to communicate to different audiences effectively.

Communication also plays a major role in one of the most fundamental things we do with clients, building rapport. Rapport building is an essential part of any therapeutic relationship, even espoused as the most important influence on treatment outcomes, therefore connecting with the client is central, setting the tone for future interactions with them. Many educational and developmental psychologists work with children and young people, and although building rapport with clients can sometimes be challenging with clients of any age, with younger clients, building rapport may take longer or put more demands on the psychologist's communication and interpersonal skills. This may mean spending time playing card games, watching funny videos on TikTok, or talking about your pets. Giving a relationship time to develop gently is an important skill and may be the difference between creating a strong therapeutic alliance or client disengagement.

Multi-disciplinary and interdisciplinary work: being a team player

Seldom does an educational and developmental psychologist work in isolation. Educational and developmental psychologists are often found working as part of a team. Psychologists working in schools, whether as a Department of Education employee, guidance officer, mental health practitioner or contractor, commonly work alongside other allied health professionals such as speech pathologists, social workers, youth workers, occupational therapists, or mental health nurses, not to mention school leaders and teachers. Knowing how your skills differ and intersect with the other professionals enables coordinated care and support for students and clients.

An increase in private practice work has also resulted in more educational and developmental psychologists working in clinical settings along with the emergence of more interdisciplinary psychology practices. Differently qualified psychologists can be found working alongside one another, an environment that provides a rich opportunity for supervision, secondary consultation, and referral. Consider a scenario where a combination of general, educational and developmental, clinical, counselling, or neuropsychologists may work in the same practice. Even if a practice is not interdisciplinary, psychologists may refer or consult with other psychology disciplines to support a client's needs.

The innovative problem solver: using a systemic lens

Educational and developmental psychologists are creative problem solvers. They seek to understand the issue from multiple perspectives and tailor recommendations to address needs. Sometimes, the strategy for a problem will be straightforward, such as removing an obvious

Figure 5.1 Problem solving is a key skill of educational and developmental psychologists

environmental stressor, but innovative solutions may be required for more complex problems.

Students experiencing school refusal or those displaying challenging behaviour often require comprehensive support and intervention at a systemic level. In such situations, educational and developmental psychologists will integrate their knowledge of child development and psychopathology, evidence-based interventions, functional behaviour analysis, and ecological systems to develop a multi-levelled response.

Educational and developmental psychologists are also well placed to deal with issues of an organisational nature such as those within schools. The psychologist brings knowledge of systems theory and skills in consultation, which, when combined, enables problem-solving on a broader scale. Think of a situation where a school wants to improve student well-being. The educational and developmental psychologist may do one or more of the following to address the problem and provide solutions; operationalise student well-being, investigate existing school data on well-being, administer surveys to students, staff, and families to collect additional information, review current well-being programing across the school, and provide professional development to school staff on improving well-being.

Networking skills: making connections

Ever heard the saying "working the room"? Well in your psychology training and career, learning the art of networking has many benefits. First and foremost, it may help you to get a job.

Let's start with the postgraduate years. From the minute students begin a master's program, they can immediately build a peer network. The days of competing with fellow students for university places are over. Instead, students develop supportive relationships with each other to become peers and, eventually, professional colleagues and associates. During the postgraduate journey, hours are spent in fieldwork placements working under the supervision of senior psychologists and supervisors. All students should consider each field placement as a potential job interview. Introduce yourself to the principal of a school or the practice manager of a clinic and start making connections with the workplace, it is not uncommon for postgraduate students to be offered employment before their course finishes.

Networking continues to be important as your psychology career progresses. At early or even established career stages, networks can operate as opportunities for career expansion or change. Word of mouth is powerful; many workplaces will head-hunt or seek recommendations from peers when recruiting. Workplaces frequently contact universities when seeking employees, asking placement and course coordinators if they can advertise vacancies to graduates.

Your professional network also serves as a mechanism for peer support and consultation, supervision, and referral pathways. The educational and developmental psychology community is small compared to other practice areas of psychology. Therefore, building a community of professional colleagues is integral and offers multiple benefits to your practice.

Networks allow us to be connected and stay connected. As you progress in your psychology career, you may be looking for opportunities to expand your network. Attending conferences on topics of interest or attending peer consultation groups are great ways to achieve this. Sometimes, it may be worth consolidating and reconnecting with old networks. Ask yourself, What are my current professional needs? Who in my network can support me? What support can I offer them? Chapter 7 has further information on professional networks.

Professionalism: respecting the role

Multiple relationships

Educational and developmental psychologists need to be astute in the management of multiple relationships. A multiple relationship occurs when a psychologist is in a professional role with a person while, at the same time, being in another role with that person or in a relationship with someone closely associated with or related to that person. Sounds complicated? It certainly can be. Let's break it down into some examples of when multiple relationships might occur.

- A school psychologist might be involved in extracurricular activities in the school (e.g., as a sport coach while also providing counselling to a student in the team).

- A psychologist in private practice might be treating multiple members of a family (e.g., siblings).
- A family friend asks you to assess their child or provide psychological intervention.
- A teacher in your school asks you for counselling for their own personal issues.

Multiple relationships are not inherently unethical; however, educational and developmental psychologists must assess the ethical appropriateness of professional relationships they engage in and consider questions such as: Is their professional judgement impaired? Or, is there a risk of harm or exploitation to the individual with whom the multiple relationships exist? There may be clear ethical concerns in managing multiple relationships, and the psychologist may decide not to work with the client. However, there will also be times where despite the ethical issues present, the multiple relationships cannot be avoided (e.g. in a situation where someone requires emergency support or where a psychologist practises in a small community with limited psychological services).

Dual service provision

On occasion, two psychologists might be involved in the care of a client. We touched on this scenario in Chapter 4 when discussing the *communication and interpersonal relationships* competency. The most likely situation where a client may be simultaneously involved with two psychologists is where a student receives support from a school psychologist and an external private practice psychologist. Ideally, the psychologists will work collaboratively to negotiate a shared care arrangement with clear intervention goals for each practitioner. Professionalism, in this case, would require informed consent from the client (if capable or those with parental responsibility) on an agreed treatment plan.

Dual professions

Another situation that requires a high level of professionalism and boundary management is the occurrence of dual professions. This is where an individual is qualified in two or more professions. This situation may be particularly relevant to psychologists working in schools who may also be registered teachers. In said situation, if the psychologist attempts to work in both roles (i.e. in providing psychological intervention to students and working as a classroom teacher, there may be a high likelihood of confusion for students and conflict of interest for the psychologist). The classroom teaching role has a disciplinary and classroom maintenance aspect that can set the dynamic of a student-teacher relationship. The therapeutic relationship however should not be a disciplinary one. Therefore, psychologists who are also working in a teaching role will likely encounter difficulty in managing this dual relationship. Many school psychologists will have been in the position where a student has been sent to them for misbehaving. In this scenario, the session with the psychologist is seen by the student as punishment and can rupture the opportunity for developing a therapeutic relationship. For this reason, the school psychologist must make it clear to the school and students that engagement with the psychologist is voluntary and not a disciplinary action. It is for this reason that school psychologists should not do yard duty!

Mentoring: having a mentor, being a mentor

A supervisor and mentor might be one and the same or you might have different people play these roles (see also Chapter 8). In your journey to becoming a psychologist, you will come across many potential mentors. In the educational environment, a lecturer or tutor may inspire you in an area of study or practice, or you may engage with them on shared research interests and as a result, seek to emulate a similar academic pathway. Academic mentors can support your progression through the higher degree process, becoming referees and advocates. The other avenue to finding mentors is in the field and most obviously, within practicum placements. Provisional psychologists encounter many supervisors during their training. Each of these supervisors may become a potential mentor. Who did you connect with on a professional level? Who worked in an area of practice that you seek to follow? Who can you learn from as you transition from provisional to registered psychologist? Who can be a career coach? If a person or persons come to mind when answering these questions, you have identified some potential mentors.

Typically, a mentor will nurture your skills and abilities, broaden your thinking, challenge your perspective, and help you construct a bigger picture. Mentors are the people to have capacity-building conversations with; they may inspire you to make a career change, take a risk on a new venture or begin that research you always wanted to do.

What about being a mentor to others? When we think of a mentor, we tend to automatically think of someone more senior, someone with many years of experience. This doesn't always need to be the case. Peers can be mentors to each other. Who in your student cohort or early career network is a mentor to you? Or perhaps you are a mentor to them?

Reflective practice: the why question

In Chapter 3, we learnt about the registration requirements of psychologists and the ten hours of peer supervision mandated per annum. This requirement highlights how critical reflective practice is in the psychology profession and the importance of engaging in this practice throughout your career, no matter how long you've been registered.

Effective educational and developmental psychologists engage in reflective practice, a process of self-reflection, self-rating, and self-regulation. Why do we reflect? To help provide optimal support to our clients. Why should we reflect? Because it makes us better practitioners.

The process of supervision typically necessitates a focus on reflective practice. Through the act of supervision, the psychologist actively reflects on their psychological practice using skills such as appraisal, analysis, and interpretation. This insightful look into professional practice informs practice-based decision-making.

Reflective practice brings into awareness our own implicit knowledge base and provides an opportunity for growth. It's an objective look at your practice and what you are doing and why. What worked well in the session with that client? What could I have done differently? I feel stuck in working with this client, what else could I try? Is there another way to look at how the client responded? These are typical questions that underpin reflective practice, and engagement with this skill supports continued learning and improvement.

Lifelong learners: curiosity

Being a scientist-practitioner means that there is an expectation to stay cognisant with current research and the translation of such research into practice. Just as the field constantly changes and evolves, so do the skills of educational and developmental psychologists. This means that educational and developmental psychologists need to be lifelong learners and commit to staying current with process and practice.

Educational and developmental psychologists are informed professionals who regularly engage in professional learning opportunities to grow and consolidate their skills but also to critically examine new and emerging trends in the field. Educational and developmental psychologists are curious about the human condition across the lifespan. They desire to seek and build knowledge and recognise there is always more to learn. Students at the end of their respective training pathways often comment that "they don't know everything yet" or "there is still so much to learn," and they are right, there is always more to learn. How exciting!

Interview with a Practicum Coordinator, Sophie Morris (Educational & Developmental Psychologist)

Q: In your opinion, what qualities do successful students possess?

A: Successful students tend to be the ones who are passionate and engaged about the field of Educational and Developmental psychology and are curious to learn all they can about the field and the many roles of Educational and Developmental Psychologist (EDP). I have found that these students are open to exploring the breadth that the role of an EDP can offer and will take up any opportunity while on placement to try out a setting or client group that they may not yet know much about.

Q: You liaise with a lot of field supervisors, what qualities are they looking for in a provisional psychologist?

A: Our supervisors always comment that they're looking for provisional psychologists who are proactive and take initiative in their work. These students will take the time to research client presentations and put together an initial formulation prior to supervision, will bring new research to their supervisor for discussion, and will be flexible in how they utilise their time and fit into the role. Clear and open communication and strong collegiality are also particularly important qualities our supervisors look for.

Q: What skills would you consider important when working in schools, hospitals, or private clinical settings?

A: Strong communication skills are highly relevant across these settings. This includes communicating clearly with others and taking the time to listen and understand other perspectives and roles. Provisional psychologists in these settings are often working as part of a larger team, and an understanding of systems theory and collaborative practice is imperative. EDPs must be flexible and understand that the demands of the role are such that what may be planned for a day may not be what eventuates.

Q: What skills are important when working with families?

A: EDPs are often working not just with the individual, but in the case of young people also with their family. A skilled provisional psychologist will approach family work in a person-centred and validating manner, taking the time to understand the family's own values and goals.

Q: What is your advice for educational and developmental psychology graduates? What skills will support their career as early career psychologists?

A: The profession of educational and developmental psychology is a rewarding one. I encourage graduates to commit to being self-reflective in their practice, being a lifelong learner and continuing to build their knowledge base and skills over a long career.

A New Zealand Perspective

Cathy Cooper

As is in Australia, educational psychologists in New Zealand conduct their professional practice in schools and in clinical and community environments, working across an increasing broad range of disciplines and settings. Skills required for New Zealand-registered educational psychologists include extensive knowledge of human development, family and group dynamics, disabilities and their implications for learning and behaviour, education organisations and ecological frameworks. A broad knowledge is required of Te Whaariki – the New Zealand early childhood curriculum, the New Zealand Curriculum Framework and Te Marautanga o Aotearoa – the curriculum for Māori immersion education.

Educational psychologists need to possess the attribute of being excellent communicators with strong interpersonal skills, particularly in the practice of developing and maintaining effective relationships with children and young people, and their parents, whānau (family) and caregivers. It is essential for the educational psychologist to be able to communicate well to work effectively in these relationships across a diverse range of settings. They need to be great team players as the work of an educational psychologist is seldom undertaken in isolation. Teamwork provides the opportunity for networking, mentoring and lifelong learning, all valuable tools to upskill the educational psychologist throughout their career. The ability to engage in reflective practice is paramount for the educational psychologist to be able to grow in their professional practice. Educational psychologists need to have the ability to translate specialist knowledge into practical information. In addition, they need to be reflective listeners who can consistently modify their language and approach according to the context and audience.

While all education psychologists undertake analysis, those working in contract and private practice settings particularly require the ability to undertake psychometric assessment. This is less likely undertaken in government settings and more often used in contract and private practice work. It is an advantage to be confident and competent in using the WISC-V,[1] the WIAT-111,[2] the Woodcock Johnson IV,[3] and the ABAS-3,[4] among other psychometric tools.

Educational psychologists work not only with individuals but also at a systems level. The Positive Behaviour for Learning (PB4L) programme, for example, which includes universal whole-school change initiatives, targeted group programmes, and individual student support services, is led in some New Zealand regions by educational psychologists. PB4L initiatives assist parents, whānau, early childhood centres and schools to address behaviour, improve children's well-being, and increase educational achievement. Psychologists who have developed the skills and attributes necessary for educational psychology professional practice in both Australia and New Zealand tend to be well placed to lead programmes of this nature as well as working successfully in a wide range of roles in both the public and private sectors.

Concluding comments

In this chapter, we have taken a deep look at some of the skills and attributes required of educational and developmental psychologists. We discussed being an effective communicator, working with others, problem-solving, networking, and making connections, professionalism, mentoring, reflective practice, and lifelong learning. As said at the beginning of the chapter, these are just some of the skills and attributes that educational and developmental psychologists may possess, but all will help you in your future or existing career. Now that skills and competencies are understood, Chapter 6 will discuss some practical considerations for preparing for a career as an educational and developmental psychologist.

Notes

1 Wechsler Intelligence Scale for Children Fifth Edition: Australian and New Zealand Standardised Edition (WISC-V A&NZ)
2 Wechsler Individual Achievement Test, Third Edition: Australian and New Zealand Standardised Edition (WIAT-III A&NZ)
3 Woodcock Johnson, Fourth Edition: Australian and New Zealand Standardised Edition (WJ-IV A&NZ)
4 Adaptive Behaviour Assessment System, Third Edition (ABAS-3)

6 | Work experience and getting prepared

"When I think about how I was on my very first day of my postgraduate studies, compared to the day that I received my full registration at the end, my skills were worlds apart. Did I know everything there was to know about being a psychologist? Absolutely not! But I certainly felt like I had developed the skills and competencies to get started, and to continue my learning along the way."

—Jennah Alonso

Introduction

Deciding to study psychology is an exciting and fascinating path that can lead in many rich and rewarding directions. The reasons for choosing this field of study are as varied as the number of individuals stepping on this path. Some people come to this area of behavioural science with set expectations of becoming a registered psychologist with broad and specific visions of helping others. Some people tap into their curiosity of people, and the reasons behind human motivation and behaviour. Some people are intent on gaining a better understanding of themselves, whereas other people are just interested in psychological research, data, and other influential factors playing a role behind the scenes on human behaviour and motivation. Whatever the reasons, studying this field of science opens many exciting career possibilities, particularly for those choosing the educational and developmental psychology pathway as there is versatility and richness to this stream of psychology. Like the versatility and richness in the actual role, preparing yourself to become

94   DOI: 10.4324/9781003330974-6

an educational and developmental psychologist through work experience is also vast and rich. This chapter will outline some of the things to consider when embarking on a career in educational and developmental psychology.

What is the area of educational and developmental psychology about and what service does it provide?

The area of educational and developmental psychology is an area that deals with the psychological needs, difficulties, and issues of individuals, as they transition from one stage to another throughout their life. Professionals working in this field use psychological skills to diagnose, treat, manage, and affect outcomes concerning learning, adjustment, and enhancing people's ability to tap into internal resources required at different stages throughout life. In this area of psychology, there are opportunities for working with children, adolescents, parents, educators, and adults. Educational and developmental psychologists can work independently, as part of different organisations, or as part of multi-disciplinary teams of speech pathologists, occupational therapists, general practitioners, developmental psychiatrists, and general psychiatrists. Work can span individuals, groups, and organisations, in educational, clinical, community, or private settings. Understanding the nuances and scope of educational and developmental psychology is your first step in preparing your career. It will also hold you in a good position when applying for jobs and coursework (see Chapter 1 for a detailed overview of educational and developmental psychology and Chapter 2 for preparing for interview).

As a distinct area of practice, educational and developmental psychology requires a deep understanding of psychology, developmental psychology, and education (Gilmore et al., 2013). It is deeply connected to several disciplines within psychology, such as cognitive psychology, motivation, behavioural psychology, and neuropsychology, as well as drawing from educational disciplines such as learning disabilities, working with gifted children, and educational design (Murphy & Benton, 2010; Miller & Defina, 2009; Fisher et al., 2010; Plomin & Walker, 2003). Professional educational and developmental psychologists use theoretical and practical knowledge from cognitive, organisational,

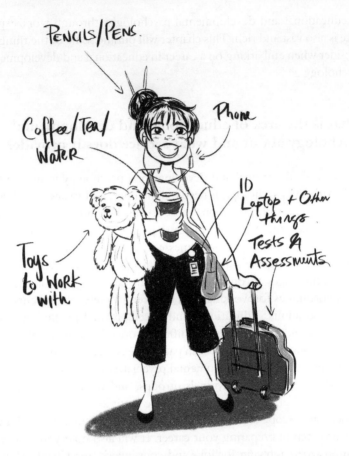

Figure 6.1 There are several ways to prepare for your career as an educational and developmental psychologist, and the first step is understanding the field

developmental, and educational psychology. They can diagnose disabilities and disorders, design and manage specialised plans (e.g. individualised education plans; National Disability Insurance Scheme [NDIS] plans), and educate and advise teachers, parents, families, and carers (i.e. support workers) on strategies for promoting well-being, behavioural management, transition, and learning. Educational and developmental psychologists also provide expert counsel on issues that arise at different stages throughout life, spanning mental health and well-being, neurodevelopmental and learning problems, psychological disorders, learning issues, and effective educational methods. Training in educational and developmental psychology can therefore be diverse and some may feel that the scope of the work becomes narrower as they progress through their career development. Much like the breadth of undergraduate degrees in psychology, educational and developmental psychology can also feel quite broad in the early stages. However, the later stages of training (e.g. master degree) will provide opportunity to practise, experience, and apply specific knowledge in this particular field of science, which in turn assists with fine-tuning the particular area of interest of psychologists (i.e. working with school-age children focusing on assessment and identification of learning difficulties). The next section will go into more detail on that particular subject.

Training as an educational and developmental psychologist

Becoming an educational and developmental psychologist is a long road that takes at least six years of continuous study to reach master's degree level, and another two years to complete the registrar program for Area of Practice Endorsement (AoPE) as discussed in Chapters 2 and 8. It will require hard work, thinking, and planning to map out the steps needed to pursue that goal. Preparing for the work ahead is essential, but most importantly, being open to what your journey may bring and embracing the learning is paramount. The first part involving the academic training is, in some ways, easier to accomplish as it relies on good organisational skills and work ethic to succeed at the higher education level (master's program). However, the second part involving the registrar program for professional endorsement is much harder to complete as it requires desire and passion to expand on one's existing credentials and dedication to further professional knowledge, practice, and competencies. Taking this path, you will embark on a new learning phase. It will demand willingness and desire to invest (time and money) in your learning as you step onto the path of specialisation. See Chapter 8 for a detailed overview of endorsement and endorsement supervision requirements.

During the path of psychological training, the first 4 years are spent being immersed in theoretical study and the development of the building blocks of psychology. This is foundational knowledge upon which psychological practice is based. In the 5th and 6th years of psychological training, students become more focused on the specific areas of interest (i.e. educational and developmental psychology). Some come to this stage straight from their Honours years. Others come after taking a break from study. Some experience roles as research assistants during their fourth year of psychological study. Others take time off from study and work for a few years before returning to complete a master's program. Those applying for master's programs with some gained experience in the helping professions, whether paid or volunteer work, tend to have an edge and are better prepared for the demands of the course. There are many opportunities for volunteering positions (e.g. Lifeline, Asylum seeker resource centre, hospitals, clinics, and aged care), jobs working in schools (e.g. school aid or kindergarten assistant), or within different community organisations. Getting involved in any work that involves research experience, clinical experience, or taking on roles that require administrative and/or leadership responsibilities, will demonstrate resourcefulness, passion, and interest in the field, and most importantly, the much-needed skills that support higher-level study, such as organisation and reliability. The diverse career options in educational and developmental psychology allow for many opportunities that, together with strategic work (i.e. volunteer or employment), add favourably to being competitive at interviews for a master's program application, course work, and future jobs.

Whatever path is taken, once you are a part of a master's program you may notice that the scope of your training becomes narrower (compared to Undergraduate degrees) and the progress of your career development begins. At the master's level trainees are first exposed to working directly in the field as a provisional psychologist. That is when the practical experience begins, and when working with "real" clients is first experienced (i.e. as a provisional psychologist). During this stage, the expectation is to accumulate practical experience and to apply theory into practice while acquiring the essential competencies of educational and developmental psychology practice. The educational and developmental psychology master programs structure the practicum requirements in a comprehensive and logical way with professional placements able to be completed in various settings working with a range of clients (diverse ages) and stakeholders (i.e. teachers, parents, and carers). This training reflects the variety of work that educational and developmental psychologists perform. Master students may complete part of their placements in University clinics that are adjoined to the individual programs (The University of Melbourne, ACU, Monash and Queensland University), schools (special schools, state, independent or private; within the primary, secondary, and tertiary levels), and various services such as Catholic Care, Child and Adolescent Mental Health Services (CAMHS), specialised settings (i.e. Irabina Autism Services or Aurora School for Deaf children), private practice settings, community organisations (i.e. Anglicare and United Connections), University clinics providing support to students and staff (i.e. RMIT and Swinburne Universities), and aged care (i.e. Vasey).

Preparation for practice

Discipline specific skills are usually addressed during postgraduate education (Schweinsberg et al., 2021). The postgraduate level is essentially where skills and vocationally based models of practice are developed (Tee et al., 2018). The Australian Psychology Accreditation Council (APAC) framework (2009) expects psychology graduates to possess a common set of skills such as industry-specific academic knowledge and clinically orientated skills. These skills form the base for an easy transition into the workforce (Hoare & Luke, 2022). See Chapter 5 for a detailed overview of skills required of educational and developmental psychologists.

Educating and training students to develop the necessary skills to practise is the function of educational organisations such as Universities. During a master's program, students must acquire practical skills as part of their training and accumulate 1,000 hours of work experience under the supervision of qualified psychologist with the essential credentials. Professional supervisors need to be psychologists registered with Australian Health Practitioner Regulation Agency (AHPRA), have board-approved supervisory status, as well as endorsement in educational and developmental psychology. The professional supervision is one of the most important components of the training of educational and developmental psychologists as it equips the provisional psychologist with the much-desired professional experience, as well as the knowledge and expertise of the professional competencies required in their field of study. Many psychology students look forward to the practical component of their training. However, success will be very much dependent on high-level organisational skills, grit, and mental toughness. The process of completing the professional placements is very intense, highly specialised, and requires malleability, discipline, specific knowledge, and the ability to put the learned theory into practice.

Books and resources that will help you get prepared

Books

- Making sense of interventions for children with developmental disorders, Caroline Bowen and Pamela Snow (2017)
- Brain-Based Parenting: The neuroscience of Caregiving for Healthy Attachment, Hughes and Baylin (2012)
- Make it stick: The science of successful learning, Brown et al. (2014)
- The handbook of school psychology, Thielking and Terjesen (2017)

Podcasts

- Mental Work Podcast
- Quantitude Podcast
- The testing Psychologists Podcast
- The Family Voices Podcast
- Two Shrinks Podcast
- Two peas in a Podcast – Mandy Hose & Kate Jones

Websites

- Raising Children network: raisingchildren.net.au
- Centre for Clinical Interventions: cci.health.was.gov.au
- Dementia Australia: www.dementia.org.au
- OPAN Older persons advocacy network: www.opan.oeg.au
- National ageing Research institute (NARI): www.nari.net.au
- OneMind PsyberGuide: https://onemindpsyberguide.org/

- BeyondBlue: www.beyondblue.org.au
- BeyondNow Suicide Safety Planning app: www.beyondblue. org.au/get-support/beyondnow-suicide-safety-planning
- CBT Techniques: https://positivepsychology.com/cbt-cognitive-behavioral-therapy-techniques-worksheets/
- ADHD foundation: www.adhdfoundation.org.au
- Psychology Tools: www.psychologytools.com
- Smiling Mind: www.Smilingmind.com.au
- Dr Furman explains kids' skills: www.youtube.com/watch?v=QhuY-WlgRGU
- Australian Research Alliance for Children and youth: www.aracy.org.au/publications-resources/area?command=record&id=96
- ProQuest Premium Medline (accessed through the APS)
- The College of Educational and Developmental Psychologists APA Division 15: https://apadiv15.org/

How do the competencies translate into practice?

Based on current research and data, Australia's need for professional psychologists is growing (APS, 2020). The need for educational psychology services in settings such as schools, hospitals, disability, and community organisations will continue to grow, and educational and developmental psychologists play a distinct role in supplying that need (Gilmore et al., 2013). Graduates from educational and developmental psychology master programs readily obtain employment in many of the aforementioned settings, often even before they have completed their training. They have access to those settings during the completion of their placements and that gives them the advantage of having potential employers getting to know them and identifying their distinct passions, interests, and strengths.

Education and developmental psychology training is unique. The distinct focus on prevention and the robust training in lifespan development, as well as focus on optimising learning from infancy to end of life, makes the educational and developmental psychologists well qualified for complex work that requires understanding of issues such as attachment, identity, and self-determination (Gilmore et al., 2013). Educational and developmental psychologists draw on concepts such as resilience, well-being, and quality of life, working proactively with vulnerable individuals and groups as a preventive measure. This focus demonstrates the discipline's uniqueness. There are many examples of educational and developmental psychology as a discipline focusing on preventive psychology. For example, the early identification and provision of appropriate interventions for young children with learning difficulties to improve school engagement, learning outcomes, and avoid risk-taking behaviours and mental health problems later in life (McNamara & Willoughby, 2010; Svetaz et al., 2000). The focus on early diagnosis and intervention is a significant feature during the training of educational and developmental psychologists. Educational and developmental psychology students receive unique and intensive training in psycho-educational assessment, diagnosis, and intervention. The process of early identification of learning and developmental disorders is well documented as a preventive measure which helps avoid other difficulties that may lead to further treatment and expense for the individual (Gilmore et al., 2013). Preventive interventions also significantly reduce social and economic costs to the community, through reduced welfare dependence, criminal justice system costs, and healthcare expenditure associated with supporting people with mental health concerns later in life (Knapp et al., 2011).

The distinct focus on early intervention, preventive psychology, and the application of theory and evidence-based interventions across the training and professional practice, provides the educational and developmental psychologist with a depth of knowledge and skills that surpasses the focus on education alone. Professional educational and developmental psychologists specialise in assessment and intervention for developmental, social-emotional functioning, learning and behavioural issues, diagnosis of learning disabilities and developmental disorders, counselling, providing interventions at the individual and organisational level, as well as consulting across a range of issues working with individuals, groups, and systems. The breath of these competencies is demonstrated by the range of settings and areas in which educational and developmental psychologists work, such as research, hospitals, schools, disability services, community organisations, as well as by the many different titles they may have (e.g. school psychologist, guidance counsellor, disability services officer, child and adolescent counsellor, and geropsychologist) (Gilmore et al., 2013).

Professional jobs and roles

Upon completing your 6th year, professional registration as a practising psychologist can be obtained. Various roles and positions within the field and sub-fields of educational and developmental psychology require carefully polished skills acquired and practised during formal training. Some of these fields are in the education system working in schools, the mental health space working in clinics or community organisations, private entities such as private practice settings, and much more. The vital component here is not only to match your skills and qualifications to the positions you undertake but also to focus on your strengths and passions. These are important considerations when choosing the professional roles you are likely to apply for and preparing for work as an educational and developmental psychologist.

Let's hear from the field

"Do you feel ready?" is a question that was asked over and over again around the time that I graduated from my postgraduate degree. At first, I wasn't sure. I knew that I had just spent the past six years studying psychology (eight if you count high school psychology!), but at first it was daunting to think about being a fully-fledged, registered, non-provisional psychologist. Reflecting back, just a few years prior before starting my postgraduate degree, I hadn't had a lot of experience in the field specifically. I had been a disability support worker for quite a few years which was a wonderful job, and all the theoretical learning in my undergraduate degree was great, but I did feel like the real learning began when I started my first placement. As part of my training, I had three placements across two years. I was first placed in my university clinic where I was primarily completing neurodevelopmental assessments, with a few intervention clients here and there. Here everything was a first, from my first clinical interview to my first cognitive assessment administration, to my first parent feedback session. My second placement was then in a primary school, where I had the opportunity to work within a school environment, completing educational assessments and running small group programs for social and emotional development. Following this, my final placement was in a private practice where I had a lot more intervention experience, working to manage my own caseload and work therapeutically with children and families. It certainly had been a steep learning curve, but a necessary one. The training that I acquired across those two postgraduate years developed my competencies across wide range of areas, including counselling, clinical assessment, case conceptualisation, intervention, ethics, and so much more. Supervision had been so important and had been so valuable to my learning. So, was I ready to go into work? I'd say yes. While I knew I still had a lot of learning to do, I felt prepared to give it a go.

Jennah Alonso (Psychologist, and Educational
and Developmental Psychology Registrar) (August, 2022).

A New Zealand Perspective

In the context of bicultural practice in New Zealand, two Educational Psychologist colleagues provide their views on work experience and getting prepared for both Māori and Pakeha (white) perspectives.

As Tangata Whenua mixed with Pākehā blood my return to university after 20 years to train as an Educational Psychologist was not what I expected. Familiar feelings of inadequacy, trying to culturally fit in and desperately trying to avoid being perceived deficitly resurfaced, leading to feelings of cultural unbalance and negative perception of my abilities. On top of these internal feelings I found myself navigating ignorance and biases of Tangata Whenua and Māori culture that is deeply engrained in the colonised world.

The experience of my training gave me a deeper understanding of the impact of the colonised environment not only with my life but also my whanau, Tīpuna (ancestors), and Te Ao Māori (the Māori world). It also highlighted several reflections regarding the role and practice of psychology through a cultural lens. For example: (1) how does one practise as a Māori Educational Psychologist while continually switching between two cultural worlds on a daily basis; (2) how can training programmes delve deeper into unpacking the colonised environment to help practitioners become well informed and gain confidence with working in a bicultural way; and (3) how does one or can one stay safe from the harm of a colonised environment?

The above reflections have been pertinent in my growth as a Māori Educational Psychologist and how I navigate my cases. Readings, researching information, professional development, and discussions with Māori practitioners have helped me with understanding the effects of colonisation and building up my cultural knowledge. Sometimes the knowledge gained is painful, other times it is refreshing, an affirmation of who I am.

Now that I am a fully registered Educational Psychologist, I have a Māori supervisor which has benefitted me greatly. There is a shared understanding of what it means to be Māori and experiences of what is faced in a colonised environment. If I have any wonderings about myself as Māori or about Te Ao Māori my supervisor is able to discuss it with me.

I continue to look for opportunities to up skill my knowledge around Māori approaches which would benefit my work as well as teach me about my culture. These experiences and interactions into Te Ao Māori acknowledge my Māori identity allowing to me feel culturally balanced and secure in who I am.

Ko taku reo taku ohooho, ko taku reo taku mapihi mauria
My language is my awakening, my language is the window to my soul
Sharnee Escott (Educational Psychologist)

In preparation for my journey as an Educational Psychologist I was for the very first time in my life required to explore my own cultural identities and the influences on my beliefs, values and practices. I started the journey of identity and considered the world around me from the perspective of a Pakeha (white) woman and acknowledging differences by my own eurocentric experience. I had not fully considered the history and impacts of colonisation on Tangata Whenua. I experience cultural shame.

Practising in a cultural safe way is a constant navigation of identity and power sharing so that the people I work with feel safe. *DiAngelo's (2018)* book "White Fragility" although North American in context should be essential reading for anyone who intends to practise psychology. DiAngelo sums up the reactions of white people when they are challenged on their views and interactions with indigenous and people who are culturally and linguistically diverse. The most important message is that it is not up to others to ensure white people feel safe in indigenous spaces. It is important to consider that indigenous people or people who are culturally and linguistically diverse are navigating white spaces all the time and that is not always a safe space for them.

Preparation for psychology training for me included reading and studying Māori frameworks and undertaking a Māori language course. Now that I am a fully registered Educational Psychologist I continue being a student of Mātauranga Māori not just to meet on the competencies required by the board but because it is my personal and professional choice, responsibility and commitment to Te Tiriti o Waitangi (The Treaty of Waitangi) as a citizen of and Psychologist in Aotearoa (New Zealand).

I now actively use the principle of Te Tiriti in my approach to my practice. For example, I incorporate Macfarlane's (2009) Te Pikinga ki Runga a kaupapa, a Maori framework for assessment and intervention. I apply this framework across all akonga (learners) because Māori models of health and well-being and ethical practice make so much sense to me and can be applied to everyone.

Rachel Drayton (Educational Psychologist)

Further Reading

DiAngelo, R. (2018). *White fragility: Why it's so hard for white people to talk about racism.* Beacon Press.
Elkington, J. (2014). A Kaupapa Maori supervision context-cultural and professional. *Aotearoa New Zealand Social Work, 26*(1).
Escott, S., & Abraham, Q. (2021). Colonisation in Aotearoa/New Zealand: Navigating two cultures of psychological being, education and wellness in educational psychology. *Educational & Child Psychology, 38*(4).
Macfarlane, A., Blampied, N., & Macfarlane, S. (2011). Blending the clinical and the cultural: A framework for conducting formal psychological assessment in bicultural settings. *New Zealand Journal of Psychology, 40*(2).
Macfarlane, A., & Macfarlane, S. (2019). Listen to culture: Māori scholars' plea to researchers. *Journal of the Royal Society of New Zealand, 49*(suppl. 1).
Macfarlane, S. (2009). Te Pikinga ki Runga: Rising possibilities. *Set: Research Information for Teachers* (Wellington), (2).
The New Zealand Psychologist Board. *Core competencies for psychologists.* https://psychologistsboard.org.nz/forms-guidelines/
The New Zealand Psychologist Board. *Guidelines on supervision.* https://psychologistsboard.org.nz/wp-content/uploads/2021/06/BPG-Supervision-June-2021.pdf
The New Zealand Psychologist Board Scopes of Practice. https://psychologistsboard.org.nz/looking-to-register/scopes-of-practice/
Savage, C., Macfarlane, S., Macfarlane, A., Fickel, L., & Te Hēmi, H. (2014). Huakina Mai: A kaupapa Māori approach to relationship and behaviour support. *The Australian Journal of Indigenous Education, 43*(2), 165–174.
Waitoki, W., Feather, J. S., Robertson, N. R., & Rucklidge, J. J. (Eds.). (2016). *Professional practice of psychology in Aotearoa New Zealand.* New Zealand Psychological Society, Te Rōpū Mātai Hinengaro o Aotearoa.

Concluding comments

Gaining experience and preparing for practice often takes place in your 5th and 6th year of study while completing a master's program. It is a time of high excitement and anticipation but also an incredibly intense period of juggling the demands of the coursework and those of practicums and placements. Educational and developmental psychology trainees come out of the master's program with unique skills and competencies that are desired and highly applicable to various contexts and settings. They are equipped with critical, creative thinking and strong reflective and reasoning skills. They possess psychological knowledge, information, and research skills and can assess, diagnose, and provide and design interventions. They can deal with complex problems relating to change and life transitions, learning and adaptation, educational attainment and difficulties, emotional and mental health matters, human behaviours, and behavioural change and wellbeing within schools, workplaces, and across the lifespan.

Professional associations and member groups

"It is crucial for psychologists to be active in their professional association and, where appropriate, the relevant union as well, to help advance our profession."

—Paul Bertoia

Introduction

Commencing employment as an educational and developmental registrar or psychologist can be a daunting task, particularly when you are a sole practitioner, the only psychologist working on a team, or have limited opportunities to receive support from your employer or supervisor. One important way to ensure you thrive and manage your career is to join relevant professional associations. Multiple professional associations support the work of Australian psychologists, and relevant associations are surveyed later.

The Australian Psychological Society (APS)

The purpose of the APS is to be the lead organisation for advancing the scientific discipline and ethical practice of psychology in Australia. First formed in 1944, the society now represents over 27,000 members (APS, 2022d). Within the APS, the Division of Educational Psychologists was established in 1967. In the early 1990s, the APS divisions were re-organised, and the current College structure was established

DOI: 10.4324/9781003330974-7

Figure 7.1 Professional associations can provide unique networking opportunities between colleagues and future friends

to recognise the standing of psychologists who hold additional education and work experience in specific areas of practice. The APS advocates for the psychological health of Australians across all sectors, including public education and health, private practice, academia, and non-government schools and organisations.

The College of Educational and Developmental Psychologists (CEDP)

The CEDP is the peak member organisation for psychologists who hold (or are working towards) an area of practice endorsement in Educational and Developmental Psychology with the Australian Health Practitioner Regulation Authority (AHPRA). APS Colleges help establish practice standards/competencies and focus on the processes and procedures that enable quality assurance of the profession. The CEDP organises regular professional development events relevant to members and provides practice resources. Various membership options are available. Fellows of the CEDP are members of the APS who also hold an AHPRA endorsement in educational and developmental psychology. Academic Members of the CEDP have attained a PhD degree in educational/developmental psychology, relevant post-PhD work experience, and have produced a notable body of published research in the area. Student subscribers to the CEDP are APS subscribers who are currently enrolled in an Australian Psychology Accreditation Council (APAC) accredited program in psychology.

The CEDP is run by an elected National Committee of members. State sections provide a focal point for delivering professional development, networking events, and they assist the National Committee meet its goals at the State/Territory level. Each state section has its own CEDP committee and elected Chair/office bearers.

Fellows and members of the APS benefit from:

- Competitively priced and regularly scheduled, professional development opportunities
- Access to resources including school, assessment, intervention and private practice resources
- Access to a professional advisory service to help clarify practice and ethical issues, regulatory requirements, and contracting/working arrangements that involve third party providers
- Competitive professional indemnity insurance (PII) incorporating limited access to a legal hotline. The Health Practitioner Regulation National Law requires all psychologists (or their employer) to hold PII
- A national, searchable *Find a Psychologist* (referral) service
- Access to APS publications including the *Australian Journal of Psychology, Australian Psychologist* and the College journal, *The Educational and Developmental Psychologist*
- Reduced rates for attending APS conferences and the CEDP conference
- Online recruitment and business opportunities listings via *PsychXchange* as well as student and early career resources.

In addition, Fellows of the CEDP are encouraged to use the post-nominal FCEDP after their surname to showcase their academic standing and status within the College. The CEDP has around 1,000 members and is the third largest APS College.

As well as the College of Educational and Developmental Psychologists, the APS has more than 40 interest groups (IGs) that assist communication between members with similar, more specialised interests. Examples of APS IGs include Acceptance and Commitment Therapy and Psychology, Perinatal and Infant Psychology, Psychologists in Schools, Psychology and Ageing, Psychology and Early Intervention, Psychology in the Public Sector, Psychology of Intellectual Disability and Autism, and Rural and Remote Psychology.

Paul Bertoia, past Chair of the College of Educational and Developmental Psychologists reflects:

> As an Educational & Developmental Psychologist working across schools and government health and community sectors, as well as in private practice, a consistent thread has been my professional group membership with the Australian Psychological Society. Collaborating with colleagues within the sectors I have worked in and learning about the breadth of our profession outside those sectors, while advancing our common interests, has been crucial to my own professional development across my career. I have learned a great deal through my APS membership, and volunteering has given me many opportunities for leadership outside my regular work. Working in the public service I have also consistently been a member of Education or Health Sector unions, which have provided important workplace advocacy for psychologists and their colleagues from other professions. It is crucial for psychologists to be active in their professional association and, where appropriate, the relevant union as well, to help advance our profession.

Similarly, Andrea Fairlie notes:

> I first joined the APS as a student, and found that it helped me gain a greater understanding of the many aspects of the psychology profession. Belonging to the APS has allowed me to meet so many

other psychologists, access high quality professional development, and stay up to date with the changing landscape of psychology. Throughout my career, I have had several jobs across metropolitan and regional Australia, and my APS membership helped me to stay connected to my field, and continually build my skill set. As a committee member of the College of Educational and Developmental Psychologists, and then as chairperson of my state section, I have felt I have been able to give back to my profession. My role has connected me with other psychologists with similar passions to my own, and allowed me to support others to enhance their skills. Plus, the networking opportunities within the College allowed me to get my current job!

The Australian Association of Psychologists Inc (AAPi)

AAPi was first established in 2010 to represent a united voice for psychologists and strongly advocates for fairer, more accessible, and more informed psychological practice (AAPi, 2022). The association emerged following long-standing dissatisfaction with funding for psychological services. The Commonwealth Medicare rebate scheme, for example, rebates private practice psychologists with an area of practice endorsement in clinical psychology at a higher level than registered psychologists. This results in psychologists who do not hold an endorsement in clinical psychology, but who often provide similar services under Medicare, receiving rebates that are up to 40% less than endorsed clinical psychologists.

The issue of Medicare rebates has become more important as many previously State funded psychological services have been withdrawn and Medicare item numbers have been extended. AAPi has around 6,600 members and offers a range of member services. Member benefits include:

- Competitively priced and regularly scheduled, professional development opportunities.
- Access to resources (including private practice, telehealth, Medicare, and specific practice resources).

- Competitive professional indemnity insurance (PII) incorporating limited access to a legal hotline. The Health Practitioner Regulation National Law requires all psychologists (or their employer) to hold PII.
- A national, searchable *Find a Psychologist* (referral) service.
- AAPi Career Centre.

Employee unions

Educational and developmental psychologists who are employed under an Australian industrial Award or Enterprise Agreement (EA) will have access to a labour union that can represent their interests in negotiations with their employer. This includes participation in sector or enterprise-wide negotiations and campaigns to improve wages and working conditions. Internationally, it is recognised that unionised workers earn better wages than their non-unionised counterparts, enjoy higher levels of job security, and have better health outcomes because of improved job security and safer workplaces (e.g. Muller & Raphael, 2021). However, the link between union membership and wage outcomes in Australia is complex.

Over recent decades, Isaac (2018) has demonstrated a clear association between slow wages growth and the decline of unions. Nevertheless, the extent to which declining union membership is a causal factor in poor Australian wage growth is contested. Bishop and Chan (2019) have concluded that the number of Australian workers covered by enterprise agreements (and who therefore have access to a union) has been relatively stable. Nevertheless, despite declining membership, unions have remained effective in extracting larger wage increases from employer organisations. Furthermore, Bishop and Chan note that *spill over* effects from union-led wage increases appear to support modest wage rises for other workers in similar jobs who are not represented by unions.

Psychologists working in the public, health, and non-government sectors in Australia are represented by different unions. The Community and Public Sector Union (CPSU), for example, represents most employees working for the Commonwealth, Australian Capital Territory, and Northern Territory governments. Other unions support public sector employees in each State. Psychologists working as public servants in NSW are represented by the Public Service Association, while in Western Australia, the Public Sector Alliance represents state government employees. The CPSU Victoria represents many public servants in Victoria. The Health Services Union (HSU) provides representation for health care workers across Australia. Employees in the non-government social and community services sector are often represented by the Australian Services Union (ASU).

Benefits of union membership often include:

- Opportunities to be actively involved in collective bargaining for improved wages and conditions
- Support for negotiating safe work policies and monitoring of unsafe work practices
- Assistance with making workplaces more inclusive and support for individual members who experience bullying, discrimination, redundancy or unfair dismissal
- Legal advice/representation on industrial matters including disciplinary meetings and processes
- Member benefits such as reduced banking and insurance fees, competitive credit cards, car hire, movie and travel benefits

Self-employed psychologists, independent contractors, and psychologists working for a private practice are unlikely to have an approved Enterprise Agreement lodged with the Fair Work Commission that specifies the terms and conditions of their employment. Consequently, the option to join a specific union in order to take advantage of collective bargaining to improve working conditions and seek support for industrial matters may not be available. Australian workplace laws are complex. Under Fair Work legislation, a safety net for minimum entitlements and laws to prevent discrimination against employees is in place; however, qualifying periods and salary caps can affect the right to appeal actions such as unfair dismissal. Unions assist their members negotiate this complex industrial landscape.

Psychotherapy and specific sector professional associations

Numerous Australian and international member organisations are available to support and represent members with practice specific psychotherapies (e.g. CBT, counselling, family therapy, mindfulness, and psychodrama).

Additionally, peak member organisations can support psychologists who are employed in specific sectors or who belong to specific cultural groups (e.g. aged care, early childhood intervention, Indigenous psychologists, intellectual disability, and mental health). The examples listed in the following showcase two examples of these more specific member groups.

Australian association for cognitive and behaviour therapy

The Australian Association for Cognitive Behaviour Therapy is a multidisciplinary group for health and other professionals interested in the practice, research, and training of evidence-based behavioural and cognitive therapies including traditional and emerging CBT, applied behaviour analysis, and mindfulness-based interventions (AACBT, 2022). The association has branches in New South Wales, Queensland, South Australia, Victoria, and Western Australia. Member benefits include:

- Discounted professional development opportunities including high profile workshops, master classes, pub discussions and free access to recorded webinars
- Reduced rates for attending the Association's annual conference and member rates for international CBT association conferences
- Free access to a range of CBT texts and treatment manuals from the Oxford Clinical Psychology series
- Free online access to Association's journal *Behaviour Change*

Australian Indigenous Psychologists Association

The Australian Indigenous Psychologists Association (AIPA) provides support and representation at a national level for all Aboriginal and Torres Strait Islander psychologists. AIPA aims to improve the social and emotional well-being of Aboriginal and Torres Strait Islander peoples and advocates for increasing the number of Indigenous psychologists in Australia. The association supports equitable, accessible, responsive, and culturally sensitive psychological care which respects and promotes the cultural integrity of Aboriginal and Torres Strait Islander peoples.

Full membership is available to all psychologists who are registered with the Psychology Board of Australia (including provisional psychologists) or retired psychologists of good standing who have had a significant relationship with AIPA. Members must be an Aboriginal and/or Torres Strait Islander people.

A New Zealand Perspective

Michelle Blick

The New Zealand Psychological Society (NZPsS; the "Society") is the largest professional association for psychologists in Aotearoa New Zealand. NZPsS was established in 1947 as a branch of the British Psychological Society and became a standalone incorporated Society in 1967. There are approximately 1,510 full members and 835 student subscribers (at the post-graduate level), with members representing a broad range of specialist areas of psychology including Educational and Developmental Psychology. The Society offers eight Branches representing geographic regions of the country and seven Institutes and Special Interest Groups. The aims of the Society include supporting excellent standards of practice in the interests of community well-being, providing benefits and services to support members, and advocating on professional and social justice issues. The Society is committed to developing and promoting biculturalism and cultural diversity as demonstrated through implementation of policies and practices that uphold the spirit and intent of Te Tiriti o Waitangi/Treaty of Waitangi, Aotearoa New Zealand's founding treaty document.

Educational and Developmental Psychologists belong to the NZPsS Institute of Educational and Developmental Psychology (IEDP), the only organisation in the country that offers professional membership for Educational and Developmental Psychologists. The mission of the IEDP is to support psychologists concerned with the learning, behaviour, and well-being of individuals, families, communities, and society. The work of members is primarily focused on the identification, assessment, and ongoing support of children and young people with learning support needs across the education, social services, and health sectors. The IEDP currently has 267 full members and 158 student subscribers. As a member of the IEDP, a psychologist is offered professional support and networking opportunities, access to professional development, advocacy to raise the profile of Educational and Developmental Psychologists, and representation of the profession to the public, media and government.

In addition to these services, IEDP members benefit from services offered to all NZPsS members and student subscribers. These include access to the following:

- Ethics Helpline
- Professional development including the annual NZPsS Conference
- Find a Mentor – for newly trained psychologists or those new to the country
- Find a Leadership Mentor – for those wanting to strengthen their leadership skills
- Find a Supervisor
- PsychDirect – "Find a Psychologist" service for the public
- Professional Indemnity Insurance
- Access to professional resources:

  o Professional books published by the NZPsS
  o NZPsS peer-reviewed journal *New Zealand Journal of Psychology*
  o Members' biannual publication *Psychology Aotearoa*
  o Monthly newsletter *Connections*
  o Webinars and professional practice videos
  o ProQuest – a research database

- Awards and scholarships
- Connection with international psychology associations through the Society's memoranda of understanding and opportunities to subscribe

Concluding comments

Professional associations provide an avenue for keeping your work fresh and dynamic. By joining relevant professional associations, you will have opportunities to learn and master new skills. Members of professional associations receive assistance with matters such as registration, clarifying ethical dilemmas, receiving referrals, and workplace rights. Help can be available for challenging practice matters. Most associations provide recognition and a range of rewards and other member benefits. Professional associations also provide opportunities to contribute or to give back to the field by publishing papers, mentoring new members, advocating for improvements or supervising intern and registrar psychologists.

Endorsement and supervision requirements for the registrar program

8

"Different people undertake endorsement for different reasons and to meet different needs. If you can do it now your future self will thank you. A bit like being in school and asking 'will I ever use this?'"

—Paul Garon Lan

Introduction

A common question that recent graduates of specialised master's degrees who have achieved general registration as a psychologist ask each other is: "are you going to become endorsed?" For some graduates, the answer is no, because there is a sense of not being ready to embark on another path of further intensive development. There is a feeling that the many years of study and training to register as a psychologist has taken considerable sacrifice and hard work, and some graduates either are too exhausted to think about it or want to enjoy the early years of their career without adding further responsibility, potentially to focus on personal goals that may have been pushed aside during the focused years of postgraduate study. For other graduates, there is a sense of "unfinished business," as the title general psychologist doesn't seem to describe their identity as a practitioner who has advanced training in the area of educational and developmental psychology. For other practitioners they may feel ambivalent about endorsement, but rationalise that if they are paying for regular supervision as an early career psychologist anyhow, they may as well be putting the investment towards something

 DOI: 10.4324/9781003330974-8

tangible, like an area of practice endorsement (AoPE). Lauren Brabham, an educational and developmental psychologist in private practice shared about the experience of endorsement:

> I was hesitant at first, but ultimately I'm very glad that I undertook the process. I had a brilliant supervisor who I genuinely feel supported me to further my competencies in a structured and more condensed way than I could have done alone. It was expensive, and time consuming- but a worthwhile personal investment for me.

The number of psychologists gaining endorsement in educational and developmental psychology increased 44% in the last 10 years nationally, and increased 53% in Victoria alone, where there are currently three postgraduate training programs. For comparison, the number of Clinical Psychologists grew by 57% nationally in the same 10-year period (PsyBA, 2022b). In the last five years (2016 to 2021), educational and developmental psychology was the third fastest growing endorsement area (21%) behind clinical psychology (28%) and clinical neuropsychology (23%). These figures demonstrate a strong interest in gaining an area of practice endorsement, particularly in regions where initial training programs are available. This chapter aims to help you understand the process of endorsement, the requirements of the registrar program, and to reflect about whether you want to take this next step in your career as a psychologist now or in the future.

Who is eligible for endorsement as an educational and developmental psychologist?

Approximately 35% of registered psychologists in Australia have gained endorsement in at least one area of practice, with less than 2% being in the area of educational and developmental psychology (PsyBA, 2022b). This figure is largely due to the availability of postgraduate programs currently operating in only two states of Australia. A psychologist can choose to become endorsed by undertaking a registrar program, if they have completed the required prior training. Unlike other aspects of psychology training, the registrar program does not involve completing a formalised course of study or degree.

Rather, the registrar program involves a period of professional practice that is undertaken with the regular support and guidance of an accredited supervising psychologist. The registrar program is typically undertaken over a two-year period (minimum) but can be shorter or longer depending on prior study (see further down later). Generally registered psychologists with PsyBA who have also completed Level 4 training accredited by APAC (see Chapter 2) are eligible to undertake the registrar program. Such psychologists have already completed a postgraduate degree focusing on the relevant area of practice such as Master of Educational and Developmental Psychology.

Until the most recent update to the APAC accreditation standards in 2019, there was only one pathway to gain eligibility for endorsement, through completing a postgraduate degree in the specific area of practice (minimum of two years). The new standards enacted a significant change and enabled a broader range of registered psychologists to become eligible to commence the registrar program. Psychologists who have held general registration via a Level 3 pathway for at least 12 months (i.e. the now retired 4 + 2, or 5 + 1 internship), or generally registered psychologists who have completed Level 4 training in one of the other eight areas of practice endorsement (e.g. counselling psychology, or clinical psychology), are now able to undertake a stand-alone course (sometimes called a "bridging course") to complete Level 4 training in an additional area of practice. There is currently one stand-alone bridging program in Australia in the area of educational and developmental psychology, the Master of Educational and Developmental Psychology Advanced at Monash University. To see the current list of programs, head to the APAC website (https://psychologycouncil.org.au/). The Master of Educational and Developmental Psychology Advanced stand-alone program is undertaken over 1 year (or part-time equivalent) and involves coursework and professional experience (750 hours minimum), there is no thesis requirement or major research project. Graduates of these programs are still required to complete the registrar program to gain the AoPE. Overseas-trained psychologists who are registered in Australia will require their postgraduate qualifications to be assessed for equivalence for entry into the registrar program.

What are the benefits of an endorsement in educational and developmental psychology?

A central benefit of undertaking the registrar program is the development and achievement of the area of practice endorsement competencies in educational and developmental psychology (PsyBA, 2022a). These competencies, discussed at length in Chapter 4, extend upon and complement the Level 4 competencies (APAC, 2019) developed during postgraduate study and are summarised in Table 8.1.

Table 8.1 Area of Practice Endorsement Competencies in Educational and Developmental Psychology

Competency	Selected components (see guidelines for full outline)
1	Knowledge of the discipline A broad understanding of development across the lifespan including knowledge of paediatrics, child psychiatry, neuropsychology, gerontology, and the behavioural and brain sciences in addition to knowledge of theories of learning, teaching, and education among others.
2	Ethical, legal, and professional matters Understanding ethical issues in educational and community settings, how to manage them and communicate them to others, for example, balancing ethical obligations while working with families or within schools.
3	Psychological assessment and measurement Knowledge and competence with assessment and measurement for learning and developmental problems across the lifespan, for example, career and work preferences and abilities, psychopathology and structured diagnostic tests and tests of specific learning difficulties.
4	Intervention strategies Competence to deliver evidence-based psychological interventions for learning and developmental problems at individual and group or systems level (e.g. policy development).
5	Research and evaluation Identifying and formulating appropriate research strategies for questions that arise from educational and developmental psychology, communication of methods and findings to others in educational and developmental settings and transforming research/evaluation into policy and practice.

(Continued)

Table 8.1 (Continued)

Competency	Selected components (see guidelines for full outline)
6	Communication and interpersonal relationships Provision of oral/written reports, consultancy advice, communication and education to stakeholders including clients, families, government departments and institutions, and for medico-legal purposes.
7	Working with people from diverse groups Applying knowledge and understanding how the practice of educational and developmental psychology is influenced by social, historical, professional, and cultural contexts, in addition to practising sensitively with diverse clients.
8	Practice across the lifespan Competence with clients across the lifespan including childhood, adolescence, adulthood, and late adulthood as relevant to the context of practice.

As mentioned in Chapter 1, the title of educational and developmental psychologist is legally protected in Australia and may only be used by registered psychologists who hold an AoPE in the area. Furthermore, under National Law, it is unlawful for an individual to advertise themselves in a way that suggests they hold endorsement when they do not, by using a title and/or other means under section 133 of the Guidelines for Advertising a Regulated Health Service (AHPRA, 2020). Unlawful breaches may attract a financial penalty of up to $60,000 per offence or imprisonment of up to three years per offence (or both). Thus, a key benefit of gaining endorsement is the ability to use the protected title as part of your professional branding and correspondence, such as on a business website, business card, email signature, and on psychological reports. By becoming an educational and developmental psychologist you are bringing further strength to the identity and visibility of educational and developmental psychology in Australia, particularly if you are working in a jurisdiction with low numbers of psychologists with this kind of training or a rural/remote location.

There are additional benefits of becoming an educational and developmental psychologist, including eligibility to become a *Fellow of the College of Educational and Developmental Psychologists* (CEDP) with the Australian Psychological Society and use the post nominals "FCEDP" in professional correspondence and branding. For those who wish to become involved in advocacy and policy, this also provides the opportunity to nominate as a committee member of the CEDP in your State/

Territory or even at the National level (see Chapter 7 for more information on getting involved in professional organisations).

Given only 2.4% of registered psychologists in Australia hold an endorsement in Educational and Developmental Psychology (PsyBA, 2022a), gaining an endorsement in this area may support individual salary negotiations, promotion to senior roles, and/or contribute to increased employment opportunities, both in practice and in academia where minimum numbers of staff must hold endorsement in the relevant area of practice under APAC accreditation requirements for Level 4 programs. These employment opportunities may be particularly notable in jurisdictions that do not offer initial training pathways in this AoPE, as supply of similarly trained psychologists is likely to be very low. At this stage, there are not clear paths of international recognition of endorsement aside from trans-tasman mutual recognition with New Zealand; however, that does not mean that holding one may not have its benefits.

A final benefit of holding endorsement is *future-proofing*. There may be other benefits to gaining endorsement which are yet to be realised by the profession. This is because the regulatory and policy environment is dynamic both in Australia and internationally. While there are no financial benefits currently for clients of psychologists who hold an endorsement in this area of practice, it is unknown whether this might change in the future. There is also the potential that psychologists who do not hold an endorsement may find their scope of practice reduced. For example, there have been instances recently where National Guidelines and white papers have advocated to limit certain professional activities to specific groups of psychologists (e.g. undertaking developmental neurocognitive assessments; APS, 2019). Furthermore, the Australian Autism Research Council (AARC) guidelines on Autism assessment identified Educational and Developmental Psychology as one of three AoPE's with requisite skills to independently assess and diagnose neurodivergence (AARC, 2018).

Taken together, as educational and developmental psychologist Kate Crosher says, "The whole point of endorsement is to build one's competency. To learn. To educate oneself."

Becoming an educational and developmental psychologist is a visible and tangible way to demonstrate that you have advanced and verified qualifications in educational and developmental psychology.

Figure 8.1 Holding endorsement carries multiple benefits and many educational and developmental psychologists consider the registrar program to be an important source of career development

The "nitty gritty" details of the registrar program

The requirements of the registrar program can be grouped into three broad areas; psychological practice, supervision, and active continuing professional development (CPD). Depending on the pathway to registration, registrars have different minimum requirements for each of these areas. Table 8.2 summarises the minimum hour requirements based on the current endorsement guidelines (PsyBA, 2022a). The specific requirements for each of the three areas of the registrar program are discussed later.

Table 8.2 Minimum Requirements for the Registrar Program Based on Qualifications of the Applicant

Qualification type	Minimum duration of psychological practice	Total hours psychological practice	Required hours of supervision	Required Active CPD
Level 4 training (Master's degree)	88 weeks (approx. 20 months)	3,000 hours	80 hours	80 hours
Level 4 training (Combined MPsych/PhD)	66 weeks (approx. 15 months)	2,250 hours	60 hours	60 hours
Level 4 training (DPsych/PsyD)	44 weeks (approx. 10 months)	1,500 hours	40 hours	60 hours
Level 4 training (Stand-alone AoP program) First endorsement	88 weeks (approx. 20 months	3,000 hours	80 hours	80 hours
Level 4 training (Stand-alone AoP program) For attaining second and subsequent endorsements	66 weeks (approx. 15 months)	2,250 hours	60 hours	60 hours

Psychological practice

This term refers to any tasks undertaken by the registrar that utilise their skills and knowledge as a registered psychologist (regardless of remuneration) during the registrar program period. The registrar must perform a minimum of 176 hours per year of direct client contact providing psychological assessment, intervention, prevention, consultation, and management planning. In addition to these minimum hours of direct clinical care, the registrar program can also include the use of professional knowledge in a range of activities both with clients, but also as part of managerial responsibilities, administration tasks, education, research, advisory, regulatory or policy development roles. In this way, a registrar may gain their hours of psychological practice through their clinician role as part of paid employment, but also through volunteering on a committee with a professional organisation and undertaking paid work as a research assistant where knowledge in educational and developmental psychology is required.

Supervision

An essential component of the registrar program, a registrar may have one or more supervisors overseeing their psychological practice. Supervision costs vary, but often mirror the prices for client sessions. Some supervisors offer discounted supervision as part of their service to the profession and support of early career practitioners. Undertaking a mix of individual and group supervision sessions can reduce the cost of the registrar program, as well as provide an opportunity for peer connection and shared learning. Table 8.3 summarises specific details about the rules for supervision during the registrar program.

Table 8.3 PsyBA Requirements and/or Recommendations for Supervision of Registrars

	Summary of Requirements
Board-approved supervisor (BAS)	A registered psychologist who has undertaken the PsyBA approved training to gain approval to act as a supervisor. This may be providing supervision of provisional psychologists undertaking internships (5 + 1), university placements as part of a postgraduate degree, or supervising registered psychologists as part of a registrar program. To be eligible for BAS, the psychologist must have also held general registration for at least 3 years.
Principal Supervisor	All applicants for the registrar program must have a principal supervisor. This supervisor is board-approved and has held an endorsement in the area of practice relevant to the registrar for at least two years. The principal supervisor provides 50–100% of supervision to the registrar during the program.

	Summary of Requirements
Secondary Supervisor/s	An optional secondary supervisor who is also board-approved to provide supervision. Where the secondary supervisor holds endorsement in the same area of practice as the registrar program, they may provide up to 50% of the total supervision in the program. Secondary supervisors can provide up to 33% of the total supervision if they are endorsed in a different area of practice, or if they are a general psychologist who does not hold an endorsement. All secondary supervisors must have held general registration for at least 3 years.
Frequency of supervision	Recommended to occur at least fortnightly (excluding annual leave), however this may vary in frequency across the course of the registrar period ensuring both adequate support and that the required hours are met prior to the completion of the program.
Duration of supervision	Majority of sessions should be at least 1 hour, however up to 25% of the total hours may be accrued in shorter supervision sessions.
Individual versus group supervision	Individual (one-on-one) supervision sessions should comprise 66% of the total supervision, with up to 33% of the supervision hours allowed to be completed as part of small group supervision.
Annual minimum	At minimum, at least 40 hours of supervision should be accrued for each year of psychological practice (or part-time equivalent). For those taking leave of absence for part of the year, a minimum of at least 10 hours should be accrued.
Mode of supervision	Supervision is synchronous (occurs in real-time) but may occur through web conference or telephone as relevant to the competencies being addressed. There are no minimum requirements for in-person supervision; therefore, it is possible to have a supervisor in a different state/territory, or country as long as they are accredited appropriately.

Carrie Parratt, an educational and developmental psychologist registrar, reflects on being a supervisee:

My journey to be an Educational and Developmental Psychologist has been a long one. I completed my Master of Counselling at Monash as a mature-aged student in 2007. I was lucky enough to complete a placement in a Catholic school where I secured my first job as a School Counsellor. I then moved on to work in an independent school here in Melbourne. I realised that I wanted more knowledge, so I decided to continue my studies, and began my Graduate Diploma in Psychology in 2008. I finally graduated with my Masters of Educational and Developmental Psychology in 2019.

I had always undertaken supervision as a School Counsellor and found it rewarding and helpful. A turning point for me and my confidence as a psychologist, however, was during my placement at the Krongold Clinic at Monash University. I was fortunate enough to meet several supervisors who supported me throughout my placement and beyond. It was an amazing opportunity to experience regular supervision and the richness of discussion with other interns and supervisors each with a different slant on assessment, report writing, and therapy.

At times supervision was a challenge, I would sometimes feel a bit anxious about what I would talk about or worry as to how prepared I should be for the session. Funnily enough, I always ended the sessions thinking about how much I had gained from participating and feeling more confident in my ability to share and to reflect on my own practice. I have met many wonderful clinicians on the way during group supervision sessions and have learnt so much from their insight and the discussions that would evolve.

Sometimes I felt so tired from a day of work and was reluctant to go to sessions, however there was always some pearl of wisdom that I could take away which would inspire me to become a better clinician myself.

Sadly, one of my supervisors died a couple of years ago. I think of her often and feel blessed that she was able to mentor me on my journey. At the time, I was not sure where to find a new supervisor, so I went back to the Krongold team. True to form they pointed me in the right direction. I considered availability, experience, cost, and compatibility when finding someone suitable and of course since the COVID-19 pandemic, being able to undertake supervision online via video conferencing has made a convenient difference.

From my perspective, it had taken me so long to become a general psychologist, there was no way I was going to stop there. Working with children and families in the educational sector was what I loved, and so as soon as I graduated, I put my application in to enter the registrar program. I have finally obtained my endorsement and am grateful to all those who helped me to persevere on this amazing career path.

Active CPD

As described in Chapter 3, all registered psychologists must undertake CPD as part of maintaining their registration (30 hours including 10 hours of peer consultation/supervision). Those psychologists who are undertaking the registrar program must undertake a required amount of active CPD (see Table 8.2). Active CPD engages the psychologist through written or oral activities that aim to strengthen and measure learning such as a written test, undertaking prescribed readings, role plays et cetera. If CPD activities do not involve an active component, the supervisor can set additional activities such as written tasks to provide an active learning activity.

Finding a supervisor for the registrar program

Before you can apply to PsyBA to commence a registrar program, you need to have arranged a supervisor. In an ideal world, you would create a short-list of potential supervisors, weigh up their desired skills and knowledge, as well as how well you would work together in a supervisory relationship, and then select your first preference/s to be your supervisor/s. It is not uncommon for psychologists in the registrar program to have more than one supervisor, each with expertise in different areas of practice. Unfortunately, only 22.3% of psychologists nationally are board-approved supervisors (PsyBA, 2022a) and this can make it difficult to find a supervisor who has the capacity and/or the qualifications to undertake supervision for the registrar program in Educational and Developmental Psychology. To generate a list of potential supervisors, the PsyBA website also has a "find a supervisor" function which allows you to search for board-approved supervisors and registrar program principal supervisors in each area of practice. There are currently 341 principal supervisors listed in the directory for educational and developmental psychology across Australia. The directory also enables you to email supervisors directly to enquire about their potential availability. For "warm leads" on potential supervisors, it can be useful to contact the academic staff at the university where you undertook your final years of training for suggestions, or to use professional networking forums on social media (e.g. Facebook and LinkedIn) to source recommendations. For example, if a LinkedIn contact has posted to celebrate that they have recently gained endorsement, you are able to message them privately to seek the name of their supervisor and ask them about their experience with that supervisor, as they may still have a free place available. With the increase in interest for gaining endorsement in recent years, some supervisors may even have a waitlist for their availability, so it is advised to plan before contacting potential supervisors.

Changing a supervisor

Adding or removing a supervisor does happen and it is more common than you think. Changes can be supervisor or registrar led; for example, it may be that the supervisor becomes unavailable due to a career break, change in role, or workload issues. Sometimes, the supervisory relationship may come to a premature end during the registrar program because of a mismatch of some kind. The supervisory relationship is a bit like finding the right hairdresser. Some hairdressers may have the skills and expertise, but their fit with what you are seeking at that point in time isn't quite right. Rapport, connection, approachability, and helpfulness are some of the other factors you might want to consider when seeking a supervisor. Ask yourself: *Do you hit it off?* If you don't, it is okay to look elsewhere, but also appreciate, your relationship with your supervisor, like any relationship, can take time to grow. As psychologists we understand that supervisees, like clients, may change psychologists. No supervisor will take it personally, but as a courtesy do let them know your intentions. There is nothing worse than a host and ghost! If you realise that things aren't working part-way through your registrar period, it can be beneficial to discuss with peers before having an honest conversation with your supervisor. If the relationship is working well but you require support outside of your supervisor's competence area, consider adding a secondary supervisor to your team. To add or remove supervisors, you will need to access the appropriate documents from the AHPRA website.

Tips for managing the supervisory relationship

The supervisory relationship is a professional relationship akin to the client-practitioner relationship, in that there are professional obligations to consider yet it has more of a collegial tone. It is important to choose a supervisor with whom you feel comfortable, but also someone who has skills experience that you would value learning from throughout the process. See the tips given here for getting the most out of your supervision experience.

- At the outset of supervision, discuss boundaries and expectations for both supervisor and supervisee to ensure you are on the same page. Consider the set frequency of supervision, modality of supervision (in person or via web conference/phone), structure of supervision sessions and supervisory style and preferences, whether sessions will be group or individual (or a mixture of both) and costs/payment options (if relevant). Ideally, this should all be documented and agreed in a supervision contract.
- Be organised for supervision sessions, plan the topics you wish to discuss ahead of time and ask your supervisor if they would like an agenda beforehand.
- Take time at the outset of your registrar program to set competency-based goals that you wish to achieve, ensure the goals are measurable and specific. Review these regularly.
- Ask your supervisor if they will set a review date to discuss how the process of supervision is going for you both. This gives an opportunity to discuss preferred approaches and adapt as necessary.
- Discuss potential CPD opportunities to complement your goals for the registrar program.

Kate Crosher, an educational and developmental psychologist at Enfys Psychology and Supervisor since 2008, reflects on her role as a supervisor.

Many years ago, as a teenager, my parents took me to a vocational psychologist to explore my future career options. I am eternally grateful as this one morning changed my future.

I think from that moment I always knew I wanted to work with children. So started my journey into Educational & Developmental Psychology. At the time, I was also given the suggestion of primary or tertiary teaching. I poo-pooed the idea at that time. There was no way I wanted to teach adults!!

Little did I know!

I scraped through undergraduate training. It took 3 years before I realised what my own style of learning and studying looked like. But I did eventually get my registration!

My journey as a supervisor started with a random conversation with a colleague who worked in another school in our network. Having been contacted by the University I attended, somehow, I reconnected and took on my first two students.

The first two years seemed difficult – it was the style of the placement that was difficult to fit within the dynamic of my role. But I really loved working with students. So in consultation with the Uni I managed to make it work and took on my first 6th year placement. She will always hold a special place in my heart. She taught me how to mentor and inspired my own reflection and learning. Gave me opportunities to support her, without any expectations other than providing her with opportunities. I am very grateful my first foray into supporting a 6th year student on placement went so well.

Over time I branched out and started supervising for endorsement, and CPD. People at every different level of experience and training. These days my job is 95% supervision.

Like most of us, sometimes, I am unsure whether I am doing a good job. I question myself and second guess my advice or decisions. Being a supervisor does not make you immune to self-doubt and imposter syndrome!

Most of the time I think I do an okay job. I am, however, always aspiring to be "better." Some of my key values and the messages I would give new supervisors are:

1   Be yourself. Be real. Genuine. Don't try to know it all.
2   Show supervisees HOW you made your decision, or what your thinking process sounds like. Don't just give them the answer.

3   Reflect. Always think about the why. Why do you do things the way you do? Why is your way of doing something important to you?

4   Recognise that the things they learn academically may not look the same in practice. Aspire for a certain level, but also show them the reality.

5   Be kind. Be flexible. They are adults. They don't need you to be their parent or teacher. You are also their colleague, their role model, their advisor, their support person.

6   Be a good role model. You don't have to be perfect. But at least try to show the way things "should" be done as much as you can.

7   Always remember that you are your supervisee's professional attachment figure. Apply the Circle of Security in your work. Be a safe place for them to land after they explore their professional capabilities.

So many students have come and gone over the years. Some are friends, have been colleagues, some are like passing ships in the night, but all are memorable in their own way. Even if there have been challenges, I have been inspired by their willingness to be vulnerable. To take a risk and trust me. To trust the process, and I am so very honoured to be part of each and every single supervisee's journey.

A New Zealand Perspective

Rachel Drayton

Whaiwhia te kete mātauranga
Fill the basket of knowledge (Māori Proverb)

In the final year of study, Intern Psychologists, those accepted on to the programme, are provisionally registered with the New Zealand Psychologists Board. They must have a Master of Educational Psychology degree from one of the three universities mentioned in Chapter 2. They must have been offered a scholarship or work-based training option and be nominated by a registered Psychologist to obtain provisional status.

Intern Educational Psychologists are required to complete 1500 hours of supervised practice, collate an e-portfolio that includes case study submissions, complete professional development and self-evaluation of how the core competencies are being met. The core competencies for New Zealand Psychologists are:

- Discipline, Knowledge, Scholarship, and Research
- Diversity, Culture, and Treaty of Waitangi/Te Tiriti o Waitangi
- Professional, Legal, and Ethical Practice
- Framing, Measuring, and Planning
- Intervention and Service Implementation
- Communication
- Professional and Community Relations, Consultation, Collaboration
- Reflective Practice
- Supervision

As mentioned in Chapter 2, each of the three Universities, structure courses differently and students may be required to undertake a number of the following tasks:

- complete a community placement
- design and deliver professional training for education teams
- undertake an addition research projects
- delivery of group intervention
- complete a final oral examination at the end of the academic year.

As part of a Ministry of Education scholarship, intern psychologists are provided with two hours of professional supervision per week by a principal supervisor. They will also receive supervision and support from a University Professional Practice Advisor who is Board registered Educational Psychologist.

New Zealand has small educational psychology workforce population. Therefore, it is unlikely that interns will be given the opportunity to select and interview a principal supervisor and make a preferred choice independently. Intern Psychologists will be allocated a trained supervisor in close geographical proximity to the regional Ministry of Education office they are based in. The supervisor will be familiar with the culture, people and specific service delivery of the team their supervisee is placed in.

Intern Psychologists who receive a Ministry of Education scholarship may also be provided with opportunities to:

- Network with practitioners from other disciplines such as physiotherapists, occupational therapists, speech language therapists, advisors on deaf and hard of hearing, advisers on refugee and migrant student and specialist teachers.
- Receive cultural supervision and work alongside Māori cultural advisors (Kaitakawaenga).
- Participate in group supervision with more experienced psychologists.
- Attend regular professional practice days with other psychologists in the region.
- Develop skills across early intervention (0–5), severe behaviour, and support students with more complex needs who receiving the Ongoing Resourcing Scheme (ORS).
- Be offered opportunities to receive case referrals across different teams.

In addition to the core competencies, Intern Educational Psychologists are required to demonstrate additional **Core Competencies for Psychologists Practising within the "Educational Psychologist" Scope of Practice**. These are:

- Discipline, Knowledge: Theoretical Foundations and Research (Practice within systematic problem solving and solution – building frameworks)
- Diversity, Culture, and the Treaty of Waitangi/Te Tiriti o Waitangi (completion of culturally safe assessments).
- Framing, Measuring, and Planning: Assessment and Formulation (situational analysis)
- Intervention (identifying contextual variables that influence practice).

The supervisor's main role is to support the Intern Psychologist to meet their University and Psychologist Board requirements. They are required to support case work using a situational analysis framework (Annan, 2005) for assessment and formulation. They ensure that supervisees are developing skills and are guided by a set of practice principles: family entered (whānau); culturally affirming; strength-based; collaborative; inclusive; evidence-based and ecological (He Pikorua).

Supervisors provide an evaluation of the supervisees progress throughout the year and sign off on the criteria at the end of placement so that full registration can be applied for with the Psychologist Board. Registration is also contingent on successful completion of the University programme.

Further Reading

Annan, J. (2005). Situational analysis: A framework for evidence-based practice. *School Psychology International*, *26*(2), 131–146.

He Pikorua. *Ministry of education practice framework*. https://hepikorua.education.govt.nz/

The Institute of Educational and Developmental Psychology (IEDP) New Zealand. www.psychology.org.nz/members/networking/institutes/institute-educational-and-developmental-psychology-iedp#:~:text=The%20Institute%20of%20Educational%20and,families%20and%20in%20learning%20environments

Johnson, J. (2015). *Case work in education: Planning and decision-making for specialist practitioners*. Dunmore Publishing.

The New Zealand Psychologist Board. *Core competencies for psychologists*. https://psychologistsboard.org.nz/forms-guidelines/

The New Zealand Psychologist Board Scopes of Practice. https://psychologistsboard.org.nz/looking-to-register/scopes-of-practice/

Waitoki, W., Feather, J. S., Robertson, N. R., & Rucklidge, J. J. (Eds.). (2016). *Professional practice of psychology in Aotearoa New Zealand*. New Zealand Psychological Society, Te Rōpū Mātai Hinengaro o Aotearoa.

Concluding comments

If you have decided it is the right time to undertake the endorsement program and take your psychology career to the next level, here is a handy checklist of considerations before you begin:

- Will you be able to undertake 176 hours per year of direct client contact given your current work role and personal circumstances?
- Have you found a principal supervisor to oversee your registrar program? Have you checked that they are board-approved on the PsyBA website as a supervisor and have the required AoPE?
- Have you considered whether a secondary supervisor may be beneficial? Either to support targeted competency development or to supplement the frequency of supervision sessions with your principal supervisor?
- Will your supervisors collectively provide a minimum of 40 hours of supervision per year of the registrar program?
- Will you be able to meet (and budget for) the minimum required amount of active CPD?
- Have you considered the feasibility of costs associated with the registrar program? (supervision costs, CPD costs, and processing fee at both commencement/completion of program).
- Will your employer offer any support as you undertake the registrar program? (e.g. release time, budget for CPD, financial support, and assistance in locating a supervisor?)

In Chapter 9, we explore what the real-life work of the educational and developmental psychologists looks like with some reflections from members of our community.

9 | A day in the life

"It is a rewarding career that can be energising as much as it is exhausting. I am constantly reminded of the privilege it is to walk alongside families at really difficult times in their lives."
—Dianne Summers

Introduction

Being an educational and developmental psychologist entails hard work and diligence. Nevertheless, this profession provides endless opportunities and worthwhile experiences. Educational and developmental psychologists work in different contexts and their practices vary depending on their role and workplace. This chapter provides a glimpse in the daily life of educational and developmental psychologists from six different contexts.

A day in the life of an academic educational and developmental psychologist

By Associate Professor Vicki McKenzie, University of Melbourne

What are the best features of working in a university as an academic Educational and Developmental Psychologist? For myself it is the people and the creativity. A university context is rich with happenings, opportunities, and resources. You can investigate any topics that interest

140   DOI: 10.4324/9781003330974-9

you. There is encouragement to link with other academics here and in other countries and present your work wherever it is relevant. Teaching in a postgraduate psychology program is challenging, the students have already worked very hard to gain a place in an advanced degree, they are conscientious, hardworking, and keep us on our toes.

The tough stuff when you work as an academic is the workload, which is substantial, and includes the importance of publishing and disseminating your work. Many of my work hours are spent sitting or standing at a screen, or in collaborative work groups addressing current issues in teaching or the workplace. The need for self-care is evident, the intensity of the work can at times take over and you must ensure you look after yourself and maintain other aspects of your life.

Training in educational and developmental psychology clinical practice has been my theme activity which underpins a wide range of my work: teaching, running master classes, supervising practice, overseeing the teaching program. I also work outside of the University in a small private practice as it is a professional responsibility to maintain my clinical skills. Underneath all of it is my motivation to support young people, the schools where they study, and improve the professional services needed. This is where I see the opportunity to make a positive difference to child and family well-being.

My day typically begins with checking the inbox for any urgent matters. This can take considerable time as I receive queries from would-be students, from various organisations and other academics, and from various committees with minutes and agendas. Working in a University places you in an amazing stream of information and opportunities. As with many other professionals it is always a challenge to balance immediate demands and the longer-term tasks.

My first appointment is with a research student who is studying ways to help students with autism maintain their engagement with their tertiary studies. Many students with autism find the university context difficult and leave early in their course, and this study proposes some interventions that might help with their stress. Working with a PhD student involves keeping up with the field of study, regularly meeting and discussing progress, and reading work that needs reviewing. As a positive benefit I keep on top of the latest data in this area, and I enjoy working with the students as they clarify the research issues and improve their writing. The PhD is a 3-to-4-year process and 6–8 years for part-time students, so obviously along the way many life issues arise – weddings, babies, illnesses, breakups, part-time work demands, self-doubt. . . . Hence, it is important to offer support while keeping the long-term outcome in mind. It is such a buzz when a student submits their work, after so long with such effort it is a wonderful achievement. Of course, I will have read thousands of words in the process!

My next task is to prepare teaching, and my greatest interest has been teaching students in counselling and psychotherapeutic work applied with children, adolescents, and their families. Teaching at a master's level with smaller classes allows for vibrant interactive lectures. As a practising psychologist I have worked with both adults and young people as they address issues that impede their growth and development. The challenge in class is to teach these processes to students so that they can learn how to use this knowledge and skill to work for positive outcomes with their clients.

The purpose of the overall course is to develop competent educational and developmental psychologists, so its focus is both the theoretical and practical elements of psychological practice in educational contexts. The practicum allows students to go into the field and test their skills while still relying on the support of their supervisor. Tertiary teaching is challenging, as at university level lecturers are expected to be current and expert, up to date with technological change, and responsive to changing environmental factors. University level teaching has its satisfactions, as students are keen to learn, and sessions can be tailored to include a high component of participant interaction and feedback. It is very pleasing to watch students develop over the two years into competent professionals.

Working as Course Coordinator, I have been doing less direct teaching, I work with our team to select, train, and accredit the postgraduate students over their two-year program. On any day I might be delivering a lecture, consulting with the staff, mentoring new staff, working on course changes, supervising student research projects, and interviewing students on issues they raise. Again, with post graduate students, our students are adults with adult issues, many trying to work and study. Many students need special support, which may be solved in a meeting or might be referred on to support structures within the University. I am asked to advise on difficulties with a specific staff/student relationship, ethical matters, personal matters and academic difficulties. So, this may require a counselling hat, a tough line, or at times a kind friend.

Attending meetings is next, most days there is a meeting, particularly in times of reorganisation or difficulty, but also to keep programs running well and inform staff. My favourite meetings are our Educational Psychology team meetings where our team discusses current issues for students and their studies. Running a course of study in psychology in an education faculty requires collaboration across two quite different Schools – Graduate Education and Psychological Sciences. Today's meeting is with the Post Graduate Psychology Programs Committee where I meet with Clinical and Clinical Neuropsychology and Applied Psychology staff who are running master programs. This collaboration has grown during our participation in this committee which has produced better understanding of the commonalities and differences between courses and allowed us to run cross-stream case conferences, and offer master classes.

Later in the day we have a discussion on promotion tasks. Educational and Developmental (Ed & Dev) Psychology programs are focused on advocacy for our area of study to improve access to funding and meet community needs for psychological services. The integration of education, psychology, and developmental studies is embedded in the development of educational psychologists, who draw on this wide body of knowledge relevant to the learning of individuals across the lifespan. Community understanding of this area of work could be improved, hence it is important to clarify the specific set of skills our graduates can offer so that clients can access the specific services they need. Beyond working in schools, our graduates can be found in government agencies, research positions, in private clinical and educational practice as well as in schools and educational services. So, our challenge in promotion is to show how educational and developmental psychology academics and practitioners are well placed to make a broad contribution to educational and health policy and school practice – so that we can gain more places in university courses to expand in this area! This can be frustrating, sometimes exciting, and is always engaging because there is always more to be done.

To conclude, a day, any day, as an academic in this field is complex, challenging, and rich with important and worthwhile interactions with many clever and interesting people over many thought-provoking issues.

A day in the life of an NDIS provider

By Marianne Bishop

The National Disability Insurance Scheme (NDIS) is the funding pro-vided to individuals with life-long disability that require support in their daily living. Working as a psychologist for an NDIS provider involves working with the team around the participant – a multidisciplinary team of allied health professionals, support workers and coordinators, and sometimes their family. The assessment and therapy needs of NDIS participants varies widely, but any work with participants must directly assist with their primary disability, relate to their NDIS goals and must have funding allocated to provide the service.

The participants I see have a variety of disabilities such as autism, intellectual disability, substance use disorders, acquired brain injury, and dementia. As such I work across the lifespan. As participants' fund-ing is limited it is important to develop specific and succinct interven-tion plans that meets the participants' needs and also fits within the budgeted hours allocated by the NDIS plan.

My week starts with a team meeting to discuss any new process or business updates. Working in the community with participants can be isolating, so it is nice to see some colleagues on Monday mornings. Mondays are also new referral days when new participants are added to your caseload. My employer allows clinicians to manage their own case-load to meet their Key Performance Indicators (KPIs). Weekly work-flow reports are provided, so you can monitor your KPIs and plan your work to meet the target for billable hours. Being able to self-manage my caseload and calendar allows for some flexibility in my calendar and working hours.

After the morning meeting, I get out on the road for my first appointment of the day. Most participants are within a half hour drive from my home as the amount of travel that can be billed is limited by the NDIS pricing guide. When seeing participants face to face, I try to schedule several appointments in the one area to save on costs to the participants plan.

The first participant I see today is a 9-year-old girl whom I visit at school. We are working through regulating emotions using a Cognitive Behaviour Therapy (CBT) framework. After the appointment I call her mum and provide psychoeducation so that the family can support her using the strategies that we have discussed in session. Fortunately, her NDIS goals allow for family therapies as her goals clearly state the inclusion of the family in planning strategies to help her. Unfortunately, not all participants have clearly defined goals that allow this to happen. This participant also has funds allocated for further assessment. It is important to note that assessment is not often included or allowed with NDIS funding unless it specifically relates to providing further information to better support the individual's primary disability. As such, assessment is not a core component of the workload in the NDIS space.

My next client of the day is a 35-year-old lady with Autism who is also struggling with social anxiety. Since leaving school and disengaging from work she is having difficulties engaging in society through meaningful activities. Again, having clearly defined goals is really important for this participant. The NDIS does not support intervention for mental health conditions such as anxiety therefore the work I do with her relates to improving her daily living skills and developing strategies that help her to engage in society. This participant also receives occupational therapy (OT) through my organisation. I call the OT to discuss some things that he may be able to help with in their next session. Working in a multi-disciplinary team can help to support participants' needs utilising the skill and expertise of other allied health providers.

I head to the office for my next appointment which is a telehealth appointment with a participant in South Australia. I have a few participants interstate, particularly from rural areas, as their access to psychological services is often limited due to remoteness and the cost of travel. This participant is a 38-year-old indigenous man that has PTSD. His NDIS goals centre around emotional regulation and anger management. My client did not arrive for his telehealth appointment. I contact his support worker to check in on his well-being and discuss options to help him to remember to attend sessions. We develop a plan that includes enlisting the help of a support worker to help him attend sessions.

My afternoon is scheduled to work on progress reports and letters of support for two other participants. As a participant's plan comes to its end date, I am required to write a progress report and recommend the number of hours of support that the participant needs in their next plan. This can be the hardest part of the job as the NDIS works on a deficit model. I am required to highlight the negative impacts of the participants' disabilities on their life with little room to celebrate the successes and the positive outcomes they have achieved. I am also required to justify why the participant should receive further funding for psychological services, including how the recommendations provide the best value for money and that the services could not be better provided by another support service. Reports are also required to be written to meet the high-quality standards of my organisation, including the look and feel, grammar and writing style. Although challenging to write the report, it is very rewarding when your request for funding is approved and allocated for future service provisions.

The first letter of support is for a participant in Tasmania to purchase a tablet device to access telehealth appointments. Currently a support worker brings a device to their house which means for every hour of psychological service they also have to pay an hour of support. This is not good "value for money" which is a key criterion for requested supports from the NDIS. The other letter of support I am writing is for a 4-year-old boy who has funding for psychological support, but he really needs a positive behaviour support (PBS) plan. This is a frustrating situation for the family supporting the young boy and requires a fast turnaround so that support can be provided as quickly as possible as the boy has challenging behaviours that require the use of restricted practices.

My day ends with a review of my calendar for the upcoming days. I send appointment reminders to my participants and log off for the day.

A day in the life of work in the state school system

By Cathlin Sheridan

As a psychologist working in the state school system, I support schools and families by identifying the educational, social, and emotional needs and strengths of students, ensuring the inclusion of all students by understanding their various and diverse experiences and promoting practices that improve student's outcomes.

I provide services to multiple public schools including primary, secondary and specialist school settings, and as such are not attached to a particular school. I am fortunate to be part of a multidisciplinary team of psychologists, social workers, and speech pathologists. As a team we regularly consult on complex cases and work collaboratively on referrals. We each bring different perspectives and skills on how to best support a school or student. This provides me with an opportunity to develop knowledge of other disciplines which assists me in developing the best possible strategies and recommendations to support students, teachers, schools, and families. Working closely with my colleagues allows opportunities for peer consultation and support.

There is no typical day in my work, and we must be responsive to the needs of schools as they arise. For example, if a school requires support with crisis intervention this takes precedence and less urgent plans I had for the day may need to be postponed.

The COVID pandemic changed the way we worked significantly. Currently I am working in a hybrid model, meaning that a lot of the face-to-face meetings, professional development, and team meetings are held online, and part of my day is working from home. However, I continue to attend onsite at schools to provide a service as needed.

During the week I consult with members of the school leadership and/or well-being staff. On any given day I will have at least one or two of these meetings, during which we discuss the needs of the school. We work together to identify priorities including at the whole school level, targeted small group level, and individual student level. A significant amount of my work is providing consultation and therefore I need to have knowledge of best teaching practices, disability inclusion, evidence-based interventions, trauma informed practices, and mental health and well-being supports and initiatives. Often, I will refer the school to other services if appropriate. From these meetings I will take a number of referrals back to our team for allocation.

My work is diverse and often challenging. I may be allocated a referral to provide a school with Professional Development to staff on managing challenging behaviours and writing Positive Behaviour Support Plans or developing Individual Education Plans. I may be asked to complete a psychological assessment to identify a student's strengths and weaknesses and identify possible barriers to why the student is not progressing as expected. I find assessing students to be one of the most rewarding aspects of my job as it allows me to directly interact with the student, identify areas where the student is struggling and make recommendations that will make a positive difference to that student and enable them to receive the most appropriate support.

Sometimes a referral may be to see if a student is eligible for additional support due to a disability. A school may request assistance in supporting a student who is displaying challenging behaviours. This may include interviewing parents and teachers, observing the child on numerous occasions to identify under what circumstances the problem behaviour is likely to occur, and to identify why the child may be displaying these behaviours. I then work collaboratively with the school to identify what skills the child is lacking and therefore requires teaching, and I support the classroom teacher to implement interventions.

I am sometimes referred students living in Out of Home Care where the school is requesting support in implementing strategies to support their social, emotional, and educational needs. I will consult with the student's case managers, carers, and staff supporting the student at school. I undergo professional development in trauma and regularly consult with my social work colleagues on trauma informed and strength-based teaching strategies.

I often receive referrals to attend a Student Support Group meeting to collaborate with a student's family and the school regarding a student's attendance concern. This may include identifying barriers to the student attending (e.g. anxiety) and to discuss strategies and develop a plan to support the student to increase their school attendance.

While no two days are the same, an example of my day could include the following. I start my day by checking and responding to emails for urgent referrals. At 9 am, I arrive at a primary school and meet with the Wellbeing Coordinator and discuss referrals for the next hour. We discuss at length a student who is displaying challenging behaviours and the impact the behaviours are having on staff and students. I then attend another primary school for a planned observation of a student with a disability. The school may have requested support identifying adjustments that the teacher and support staff can implement to best include the student. Following the observation, I speak briefly with the teacher to gather further information. I travel home to write up my behavioural observations and recommended adjustments. I consult for an hour with a Speech Pathologist colleague who has been requested to review a Positive Behaviour Support Plan. We email the school with our recommendations and forward resources on evidence-based strategies to support and include students with Attention Deficit Hyperactivity Disorder. At the end of the day, I check my emails and calendar and prepare for the next day where I have organised a parent and teacher feedback following from completing cognitive and academic achievement assessments for a student with literacy difficulties.

Every day I come across a new experience where my skill set is needed to support schools, families, and teachers in their endeavour to improve student outcomes in academic achievement, engagement, and well-being.

A day in the life of an educational and developmental psychologist working in an independent school

By an independent school psychologist

The day starts bright and early at 8 am with a return to school meeting with Jana and her mother. Jana has spent some time in hospital, having overdosed during the holidays after breaking up with her boyfriend. She has missed the first two weeks of term and is nervous about returning. Her boyfriend is a former student, and his younger brother Kyle is in year 11 with Jana, so she believes the cohort all know about the breakup; Kyle had been cautioned by his parents to be discreet about her hospitalisation, but Jana can't be sure he hasn't told anyone where she's been these past two weeks.

The meeting addresses Jana's safety plan that has been worked on with her by her CYMHS team and we go through how we can support Jana with her coping strategies and identify some safe spaces for her to use on days that she is feeling upset or unsafe. We also draft an email for Jana's teachers to explain that she may at times need to leave class for a while and asking for their cooperation in letting her leave when she needs to. Jana is nervous about responding to questions about where she has been and the breakup from her peers, so we agree that she will spend some time with me after the meeting to talk about this. That means the first planned client of the school day will need to be rescheduled, so I quickly shoot them an email to apologise and promise to be in touch later in the day with a new appointment time.

Jana and I go to my office and I listen to her concerns. She identifies her best friend, Hilary, as the person she trusts most and we decide to see if she's able to join us, as Jana knows she has a study session this period. Jana messages Hilary, who is already in Reception; she knew that Jana was coming in for a meeting today and planned to meet her and walk with her to the lockers. Hilary is amazing: I listen quietly as Hilary tells Jana that she's already fielded a lot of questions from concerned (and some nosey) peers and has made it clear that no one is to ask Jana anything! Jana leaves with Hilary to get ready for the rest of her day and I get on with emailing her teachers. We agree to a quick check in before school tomorrow if she needs it.

Session two is Andrew, who is in year eight and struggling with his behaviour in class. He was initially referred by his Head of House, who was getting weekly complaints from subject teachers about Andrew's disrespectful attitude, calling out and disrupting other kids' learning. When we met last week he became very emotional describing how hard it is when he can't sit with his friends; he feels that the teachers are always telling him off and that no one else gets as much scrutiny. We had agreed today that we would have a look at his experiences a bit more using a checklist, so I have set up the CBCL self-report for him to work through during the session. We agree that I'll have a look at the numbers and then make another time to talk about what it might mean and plan what we do next. I'm suspecting ADHD, and make a mental note to check which paediatricians are taking on new referrals at the moment just in case.

At recess a grade four teacher drops past to ask my advice about how to score some items on a rating scale she has been sent by a student's external psychologist. I've spent quite a bit of time observing the student prior to suggesting the external referral, so she wanted to check whether some items were a two or a three. I commended her for not just circling both, which makes these really hard to score; this is why I prefer online forms!

I grab a quick cup of tea and am delighted to see that there are leftover snacks from some meeting somewhere this morning. Being in the same building as the Principal pays off some times.

After recess I see Jordan, who is in Year 12 and starting the process of his application for special consideration for Uni next year. Jordan has a complex history and lots of trauma, and has found themes in this year's English text particularly challenging. We are working together to write his statement of impact so I can help manage any triggers. Today we focus on some dot points to make sure the most important elements are captured and make a time in a fortnight to keep going.

It's now midday and I head up to the ELC to visit the three-year-old group for some observation. There is a child in the room who has been experiencing some explosive tantrums and the teachers have noticed that they most often occur after lunch. I want to see what the period leading up to lunch looks like, in case it sheds any light on the tantrums. I get up there and find out that the student in question is away today, so we will need to reschedule; I stay for a while and chat to the educators while the children play outside.

After 30 minutes of drinking countless cups of tanbark tea, I return to my office to catch up on some emails. There is an assessment report that has come through for a year five student who has finally been assessed; concerns have been flagged since she was in Prep but parents had not been receptive to recommendations for assessment. It could have been easier to get the assessment done if we did it at school, but we refer these assessments out because my colleague and I don't have the time to manage these with the counselling and consultation load. The report is 36 pages long, so I make myself a calendar note to set aside some time to look at it thoroughly tomorrow afternoon.

At lunchtime I have arranged to go for a walk with a colleague who is struggling to support her daughter, who is starting to display problematic eating behaviours. She wants some advice about what actions to take and how to talk to her daughter about her concerns. I direct her to some parent resources and give some advice about bringing the topic up. She has been emotional as we have walked, so we agree to change tack, talk about our weekend plans and grab some sushi on the way back to school.

I get back to my office ten minutes before the end of lunch and there is a ruckus outside my door, which is next to the health centre. There has been a fight at lunchtime: one student is nursing a black eye and his friends are milling about, talking animatedly about what has happened. I sneak past them and into my office and hear enough to realise that the perpetrator of the black eye is Nathan, a year seven student who is on his final warning. This is likely to result in a meeting with parents to discuss his ongoing enrolment, which has been flagged as one I might be asked to attend if it arose, in case Nathan is prepared to accept any psychological support. I have been clear that he needs to be agreeable and that seeing the psychologist is not a consequence for poor behaviour, which everyone seems to be on board with. I quickly check my family calendar in anticipation of a later finish than expected.

After lunch is Bella, who is in year 9 and has been seeing me on and off all year with concerns about her place in her friend group: while she is part of a group, she doesn't have a best friend but everyone else seems to. She really struggled during lockdown, as most of her group caught up in pairs which never included her. She has been experiencing persistent low mood and some social anxiety and has recently been telling her mum that she feels sick in the mornings to avoid school. She had been reluctant to share with her mum what is really going on, but this afternoon agrees that I can give mum a call to start the ball rolling.

Last period rolls around and I am having a check-in with a year 10 student, Harvey, who has recently started attending family therapy; his older brother has a drug addiction and has been in and out of the family home with some periods in jail. He lets me know that it has been awkward talking about his brother with his parents, because they've always tried to shelter him from the issues by not talking about him that much. Harvey is optimistic that it will help to be able to talk to his parents about his worries about his brother and his fears that he'll come to the house in the night to get money, as has happened so many times before. We wrap up earlier than planned, as all seems in hand for now, and agree to check in again in a month. I remind Harvey that he is welcome to pop in any time if he needs a debrief and that his mentor is also always happy to have a chat too.

I take advantage of the "bonus" time to call Bella's mum, Fran, who is relieved that Bella is talking to me, as she had suspected something was going on with her friends. Fran acknowledges that it must be hard for Bella because all the mums in the group are close, but can see that maybe it's not the right group for her. We agree to stay in touch as I continue to work with Bella on building some confidence connecting with other students.

It's nearing the end of the day and I pop into the aftercare room to make sure that the staff have received an updated behaviour support plan for Elliot, a grade one student with autism who has been having meltdowns in the program. They have assigned a staff member to stay with Elliot for the time being and agree to let me know if they need any more help.

I go back to my office to see where I can fit this morning's bumped appointment in; it's pretty busy this week but I do some shuffling and send her the new time. I remember that I haven't heard anything about Nathan yet, so I call Head of Senior School to ask if there is anything I need to know. She lets me know that Nathan has been sent home and the plan is for him to stay home for the rest of the week while they plan what to do next. I've got enough on without volunteering myself, so I ask her to just let me know if she needs anything.

Time to catch up on notes from the day and clear some emails. I need to get better at deleting the emails that I don't need but are a consequence of being on most distribution lists in the school so I don't miss anything. I check tomorrow's schedule before I leave to make sure there's nothing I need to prepare. It looks pretty straightforward, but I know that any day can throw up anything.

A day in the life of a Take Two clinician

By Melissa O'Halloran

It's 8 am and I'm checking my schedule for the day when I hear the familiar tone of an incoming email. There has been an incident overnight at a residential home involving one of our young people. Katie is a 15-year-old who is currently living in the home with three other young people. Her behaviours are classified as "high risk" by the Department of Families, Fairness and Housing (Child Protection). She has experienced considerable trauma since her early infancy and there are concerns about her escalation in risk. Katie has been in out of home care for 3 years and a court case is scheduled to be heard in the Victorian Children's Court next month for which I have been subpoenaed. The incident report for the previous night indicates that after Katie argued with her carers she left the house. When she returned later in the evening the carers called police as Katie was aggressive and appeared substance affected.

When I arrive at the office, I check in with my colleagues and in particular my supervisees. I quickly consult with my supervisor regarding the incident last night and update Katie's risk assessment. Given the escalation in risk, we agree that I should follow up with the residential home, case manager, and DFFH worker. This results in me sending out several emails to Katie's care team. To make sure there is consistency in how we support Katie I suggest we schedule a care team meeting. Care team meetings ensure services supporting a young person are integrated and share information. Young people like Katie often seek attunement and connection in subtle ways that can be easily missed. As such, it is important that care teams are supported and grown to provide trauma-informed care to the children, young people, and families across the day and week. In addition, I arrange to provide reflective practice with Katie's carers next week. Reflective practice provides an opportunity for the residential carers to slow down and think about what Katie might be communicating through her behaviours. Supporting care teams and carers is a significant component of my role and is just as important as the individual therapy with the young people.

After I complete my case notes, I prepare for two telehealth sessions with adolescents referred to me via a partnership with the Navigator Program. This program supports adolescents who are disengaged from their education and my role is to support the case workers and provide mental health consultations. After the sessions I drive to a primary school for an outreach intervention session with Thomas. Thomas is a 9-year-old boy who is in a foster care placement. Although this is a stable placement, Thomas has had over 27 placements within the past 12 months and within that time frame there have been changes in his mood and behaviour. My primary goal is to provide a safe relationship and space where he can talk about his worries, and we practise strategies to help build his affect regulation. Today is my fourth session of child-led play with Thomas and he is becoming familiar with me and my suitcase of toys, games, books, and sensory items. Although the intervention is child-led play all items in my suitcase have a purpose and allow Thomas to express what he needs to communicate. They also allow me to be creative when things don't go to plan and to match what Thomas needs from the session. This week Thomas seems a little "tuned up" and asks to play "balloon tennis." It seems important for him to be in control today, so he takes the lead and makes up the rules as we play. Hitting the balloon back and forth is rhythmic and physical and we're not sitting face-to-face with eye contact. There's no pressure on Thomas to talk and the sense of control he has on our time together seems to calm him. It's not long into the game that he tells me that he got into a fight this morning with another student. As the game progresses, we end up drawing what happened on a white board to try and understand what Thomas and the other child were thinking and feeling during the incident. In addition to sessions with Thomas, I see his foster carers fortnightly to provide them with psychoeducation and career guidance; we have a session booked for next week.

My next appointment for the day is with a father and his baby. Caleb, a 16-month-old infant, was referred to Take Two after being presented at the DFFH high-risk infant panel. He has recently been returned to his father's care and there are concerns about Caleb's safety given his father's history of substance misuse and potential risk of placement breakdown. We have been using Theraplay (Booth & Jernberg, 2010) as a dyadic model to strengthen their attachment relationship. Caleb and his father have been making progress. Their play is more sustained this week and they delight in each other as Caleb's dad blows bubbles.

I head back to the office to prepare for supervision with one of my supervisees. Jessica is a new graduate, and we spend time discussing her cases, review an assessment report together and discuss strategies to help her keep on top of her administration. I spend the final hours of the day catching up on emails, writing case notes from my sessions, and finalising recommendations in an assessment report. On my way home from the office, I begin my routine for self-care which is to unwind by listening to music. I find the ritual helps me transition from work to my home.

Melissa is employed as Senior Clinician with the Berry Street Take Two program www.berrystreet.org.au. Take Two is a Victoria-wide therapeutic service helping address the mental health impacts of trauma on vulnerable infants, children and young people aged 0–17 years of age (Berry Street, 2022). The names and stories of staff and clients have been de-identified to protect their identity.

Hi! I'M KATHRYN!
YOU MAY HAVE NOTICED THERE ARE
SOME DRAWINGS IN THIS BOOK.
I DREW THESE! FUN FACT: I AM
ALSO AN EDUCATIONAL &
DEVELOPMENTAL PSYCHOLOGIST!

I DON'T REALLY LIKE WRITING
(THAT'S WHY I DRAW PICTURES!)
BUT I THOUGHT IT WOULD BE FUN
TO CONTRIBUTE TO A CHAPTER.
SO I THOUGHT IT WOULD MUCH MORE
FUN TO EXPLAIN MY ROLE AS AN
ED&DEV PSYCH IN A COMIC FORM!
(AND IT'S A LOT EASIER AND FUN TO READ!)

SO LET'S LEARN WHAT IT IS LIKE TO
BE IN "A DAY IN THE LIFE" OF AN
ED&DEV PSYCH IN PRIVATE PRACTICE!

7.00 – 7.40am

I WORK iN A SMALL TOWN AS I PREFER TO PROViDE SERiViCES TO PLACES THAT HAVE LESS ACCESS COMPARED TO THE CiTY. I LiKE TO START EARLY TO AVOiD TRAFFiC & ENJOY A COFFEE & A CROiSSANT.

Email check

Social Media, Memes & News.

Curating playlists:
"Old Millenial Indie"
"Supermarket Radio"
"PG Hits"

Self Care

8.15–8.30am

MY SUPERViSEE ARRiVES & WE REViEW WHAT iS AHEAD FOR THE DAY.

Today is busy! Like every other day.

Hoo-boy... but looking forward to it.

MORNiNG!

MORNiNG!

8.30am

OUR PRACTiCE MANAGER & OCCUPATiONAL THERAPiST FiONA ARRiVES! WE DEBRiEF SOME MORE!

9.00am – Our first Client arrives

I WORK DIRECTLY WITH THE PARENTS WHILST MY SUPERVISEE WORKS WITH THE CHILD (WE WORK TOGETHER!)

AFTER THIS SESSION, I QUICKLY TOUCH BASE WITH MY SUPERVISEE TO SEE HOW THEY ARE GOING. LATER IN THE DAY, WE ALLOCATE MORE TIME FOR FORMAL SUPERVISION.

THIS ENABLES A SPACE TO REFLECT & UNDERSTAND THE PSYCHOLOGICAL WORK WE ARE DOING.

(FORMAL SUPERVISION USUALLY OCCURS IN THE AFTERNOON).

*To be honest EVERY moment is a teaching moment — When working with me, I always like to find teaching opportunities!

10.00am – 1.00pm – Neurodeveloptmenal Assessment

IT'S TIME FOR THE EARLY YEARS (2–7 YEARS) NEURODEVELOPMENTAL ASSESSMENT CLINIC. WE ARE A MULTIDISCIPLINARY TEAM WHERE WE ALL COMPLIMENT EACH OTHER'S SKILLS TO HELP UNDERSTAND THE CHILD & CONSIDER THEIR NEEDS IN ACCORDANCE TO THEIR DIAGNOSIS & CIRCUMSTANCES... SO WHO IS THE TEAM??

Occupational Therapist
Fiona conducts the developmental history with the parents

Child Psychiatrist
Our consulting Psychiatrist Bruce oversees the case and assists with formulation, diagnosis and recommendations

Special Educator
Avril has outstanding expertise in early childhood, parenting programs and autism.

I help too!

I assist Kathryn and hone in on my observations skills and note-taking!

AND ME! THE ED&DEV PSCYH! I WORK DIRECTLY WITH THE CHILD & COMPLETE A DEVELOPMENTAL ASSESSMENT (i.E. WPPSi/WiSC/PEP3). I ALSO COMPLETE INDIRECT ASSESSMENT SUCH AS PLAY, DRAWING & WRITING

Bubbles

Drawing Paper

Toys

Play-Doh

10.00am – 11.30am – Neurodevelopmental Assessment

I WILL TYPICALLY CONDUCT A COGNITIVE & DEVELOPMENTAL ASSESSMENT WHILST FIONA INTERVIEWS THE PARENTS.

11.30am – 12.00pm – Case Conference

THE CHILD PSYCHIATRSIT, OT, SPECIAL EDUCATOR & MYSELF GATHER TOGETHER TO DISCUSS & REVIEW OUR FINDINGS. WE COLLABORATE OUR IDEAS FROM THE INFORMATION GATHERED, MAKE DIAGNOSES & PROVIDE RECOMMENDATIONS FOR THE CHILD & THEIR FAMILY.

12.00pm – 12.30pm Feedback*

WE PROVIDE IMMEDIATE FEEDBACK TO THE FAMILY SO THEY HAVE AN IDEA ABOUT OUR FINDINGS & IMMEDIATE RECOMMENDATIONS. DON'T WORRY, WE SEND A REPORT WITH ALL THE DETAILS.

*(FEEDBACK CAN GO LONGER THAN 30 MINUTES … WE TAKE TIME WITH OUR FAMILIES IF REQUIRED).

1.00pm – 2.00pm Lunch

WE FAREWELL THE FAMILY, THEN, SANITISE & CLEAN THE ASSESSMENT SPACE. WE ARE THEN REWARDED WITH LUNCH WHERE WE SHARE STORIES, REFLECT & LAUGH.

2.00p.m - 6.00pm

THE DAY IS CERTAINLY NOT OVER!
THERE IS STILL TIME TO...

FOLLOW UP ON PHONE CALLS &
EMAILS.

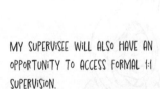

...TIME TO PROVIDE THERAPY. I TAKE
PRIDE IN PROVIDING PLAY THERAPY,
BUT I ALSO ASSIST IN PROVIDING
PSYCHOTHERAPY TO CHILD &
ADOLESCENT CLIENTS EITHER FACE TO
FACE &/OR TELEHEALTH.

MY SUPERVISEE WILL ALSO HAVE AN
OPPORTUNITY TO ACCESS FORMAL 1:1
SUPERVISION.

6.00pm – Closing time

THEY ARE LONG DAYS BUT, THEY ARE GOOD DAYS. I JUST HOPE THAT I HAVE
MADE A DIFFERNECE TO THE CLIENT'S WELLBEING FOR THE BETTER.
(EVEN IF IT IS JUST A SMALL CHANGE).

A SUPERVISOR ONCE TAUGHT ME THAT
OUR ROLE AS A PSYCHOLOGIST IS
THAT...

"WE TEACH COURAGE"

EVEN IF MY CLIENT WALKS OUT
WITH THE TINIEST BIT OF COURAGE
THAT CAN MEAN A LOT.

I AM EXTREMELY FORTUNATE AND PRIVILEGED TO BE IN THIS ROLE. I HAVE TO
THANK MY MENTORS AND SUPERVISORS FOR THEY CONTINUE TO HELP ME & MAKE
ME THE PSYCHOLOGIST I AM TODAY ... & FOR THE FUTURE.

I ALSO NEED TO THANK MY CLIENTS AS THEY TOO KEEP ME MOTIVATED
& CONTINUE TO TEACH ME LESSONS FOR MY LIFE LONG LEARNING.

PERSONAL THANKS TO:

KELLY ANN ALLEN
FIONA LENEPVEU
PROF BRUCE TONGE
DR AVRIL BRERETON
JACQUI ADLER
KIM MURRIE
JO ROGERS
SALLY ARMSTRONG
MAREA MAVRIDIS
KIRSTY FINTER
CAMELIA WILKINSON
JASON SKUES
ANITA GARDNER

TO ALL MY PEERS TO WHOM I CONSULT AND...

THOMAS SAUNDERS

ALL DRAWINGS & WRITING CREATED AND COMPLETED BY
KATHRYN KALLADY
EDUCATIONAL & DEVELOPMENTAL PSYCHOLOGIST   2022

10 | Finding work

> *"When workplaces first accept an educational and developmental psychology student for a placement they recognise the value that this approach adds to their service, and often ask for more of our students. In recent years, our students have been approached with multiple job offers before graduating, as the demand exceeds supply."*

—Claire Ting

Introduction

You've done it. You're an Educational and Developmental Psychologist. Time to translate Vygotsky (Langford, 2005; Vygotsky, 1978) into practice and find a job that helps you identify your proximal zone of development. In other words: time to find a job that complements who you are, the unique skills you have learned, and what you have yet to learn with the clients you want to support.

In this chapter, you will find everything you need to know about finding work. While the strategies and approaches may also suit psychologists more generally, this chapter aims to specifically tailor job hunting to prospective or existing educational and developmental psychologists. This chapter presents several techniques for finding employment opportunities including targeted approaches for specific job listings and making sure you effectively promote yourself in the best possible light.

DOI: 10.4324/9781003330974-10

The search for a job

Analysts are projecting *psychology* as a profession will continue to grow by more than 20% over the next three years (Seek, 2022). You can use three broad techniques or sources for job hunting: Established channels, social media, and targeted solicitation.

Established channels

Finding a job using established channels involves using specific search terms in online employment marketplaces. Established channels can be broad or involve sector-specific search engines. A broad list of channels is detailed in Table 10.1.

Mystique surrounds the title *psychologist* in Australia; mind reading abilities one of the common misconceptions. As frustrating as this can be, it also offers flexibility – after all, who wouldn't want a mind reader working for them? This is an important reality for

Table 10.1 Channels for Finding Work

Established job-seeking channels for psychologists in Australia		
Name	*URL*	*Category (broad/ specific)*
Seek	Seek.com.au	Broad
Indeed	Au.Indeed.com	Broad
LinkedIn	Linkedin.com	Broad*
PsychXchange	PsychXchange.com.au	Specific: Psychologists
Careers.Vic	Careers.VIC.gov.au	Broad (Public Service)
Jobs Western Australia	Search.Jobs.WA.gov.au	Broad (Public Service)
Northern Territory Jobs	Jobs.NT.gov.au	Broad (Public Service)
Careers Jobs Tas	Careers.Jobs.tas.gov.au	Broad (Public Service)
ACT Careers and Employment	Jobs.ACT.gov.au	Broad (Public Service)
Service NSW	Service.NSW.gov.au	Broad (Public Service)
Smart Jobs Queensland	Smartjobs.QLD.gov.au	Broad (Public Service)

Note: *LinkedIn can also be used as part of a networking strategy

Figure 10.1 Early Childhood is context where educational and developmental psychologists work and can offer great expertise

educational and developmental psychologists to be aware of as it means you need to be able to both educate others about the profession while presenting yourself to potential employers who may not know what value your training and advanced competencies add to their organisation.

The benefit of searching for work using established channels is the breadth of advertisements available across various industries. Our competencies are advantageous across several conventional and unconventional settings. Traditional workplace environments include private practice, early childhood intervention services, academia, hospitals, aged care services, early learning settings, schools, and tertiary institutions. Positions in more novel spaces are also on the rise, such as government roles shaping health-related, disability, and inclusion policy, and in HealthTech or EduTech organisations alongside multidisciplinary teams with developers, designers, and data analysts (Pappas, 2022).

Job searching, when using established channels, follows a similar approach to conducting a literature review: keywords need to be considered as they dictate the breadth and accuracy of job opportunities generated. Although "Psychologist" is going to be your "go to" search term, keep in mind outside of clinical settings such as private practice, employers don't always know they want a psychologist, let alone an educational and developmental psychologist. Employers often only know what responsibilities a candidate needs to fulfil. Here is a list of popular keywords that can be used to filter relevant job opportunities:

Useful Search Terms and Keywords for Job Hunting

Psychologist	Psychology	Psychological
Educational psychology	Developmental Psychology	Therapy
Mental health	School Psychologist	Counselling/Counsellor
Well-being	Disability	Early intervention
AHPRA	Development	Assessment
Cognitive	Research	Brain

Social media

Australia's social media advertising market is estimated to be the fifth largest advertising market in the world (Interactive Advertising Bureau, 2021). Of over 21 million active Australian social media users, almost 20% cite following influencers and other experts (Ramshaw, 2022).

The opportunity for health promotion, publicity, and advertising is not lost on psychology, with psychologists, psychology practices, and businesses increasingly investing in a social media presence. Having a social media presence as a practitioner can be a rewarding and ethically challenging experience (Diamond & Whalen, 2018; Drude &

Messer-Engel, 2021; Smith et al., 2021). Social media platforms to investigate for professional use include LinkedIn, Facebook, Twitter, LinkedIn, Instagram, Tik Tok, and ResearchGate (Tutelman et al., 2018). Certain platforms are more relevant than others when looking for work, such as LinkedIn, with data indicating increased use of this platform benefiting job seekers' visibility and perceived professional connectedness (Davis et al., 2020).

Although there is no official rule book to follow when using social media to find work, some general steps to follow may include:

- Ensure your profile(s) is complete and relevant. Before attempting to identify work opportunities using social media channels, remember to audit your social media profiles to ensure alignment with regulatory and professional expectations (PsyBA, 2022a; Smith et al., 2021; Tutelman et al., 2018). This type of audit should be considered an ongoing process to maintain compliance. In these cases, it is acceptable and recommended to *Google* yourself! (Gamble & Morris, 2014).

- Identify and follow companies, organisations, professionals, and colleagues. Company pages can be *followed* on LinkedIn, enabling Company-specific news and employment updates. The chances of identifying opportunities increase when following and engaging with online content shared by aspirational colleagues and organisations of interest.

The list of channels relevant to finding work offered in this book will invariably change with time as social media platforms are regularly discontinued – do you remember MySpace, Vine, or Google+? Remaining in sync with trending social media channels is an additional challenge for psychologists using or relying on social media for work, advertising, and health promotion.

Targeted solicitation

Connecting with peers, attending workshops, professional development activities, and similar professional events often organised through membership organisations such as the APS (Chapter 7) are all highly relevant for psychologists. Targeted solicitation describes a process of purposefully identifying and contacting peers, colleagues, professionals, organisations, or companies of interest to express interest and enquire about employment. That adage "it is more about who you know than what you know" is alive and well.

Do you want to work in the developmental unit of a hospital? A targeted solicitation approach to finding work would involve researching hospitals with developmental units or wards, identifying the professionals that work in these teams, and reaching out via email, phone, and/or social media. The interaction is purposeful: self-introduction, understanding of the unit and service, existing roles and responsibilities, and the scope for your employment working as an educational and developmental psychologist on the team.

Applying for work

Whichever technique or set of techniques used to find work as an educational and developmental psychologist, applying for work requires submission of a resumé or curriculum vitae (CV) and often a cover letter. This process can share many similarities to those described in Chapter 2 when applying for an accredited higher education program. Both are an exercise in communicating who you are, what you know, and what you can offer. The key difference is that although your audience and the potential employer may know what a psychologist is; they may not know what your advanced skill set in educational and developmental psychology means. This is highlighted by the proliferation of positions advertising roles for a *General or Clinical Psychologist*. In reality, the position needing to be filled is by a psychologist capable of providing clinical services to a specific client group.

With Educational and Developmental Psychologists encompassing only a relatively small percentage of registered psychologists in Australia (see Chapter 8 for statistics), finding work becomes as much about educating employers about your unique competencies and advanced training as it is about marketing yourself. Having developed and submitted a CV to AHPRA to gain registration, the focus of this section will be on the importance of a cover letter.

If you come across an advertisement for a role describing your professional competencies and skill set, interests, preferred client group, and career goals, apply! The significance of an articulate cover letter showcasing your advanced training that is tailored to the job opportunity and industry should never be underestimated; in short, know thy competencies and skills (see Chapters 4 and 5). This also applies to Key Selection Criteria (KSC) where there is more scope to detail how competencies and experience relate to advertised job requirements.

Cover letter examples

- Ensure you have researched the employer and role
- Highlight unique competencies
- Avoid duplication – offer information that complements your CV
- Proofread thoroughly for spelling, grammar, and clarity

Educational setting: School

Re: School Psychologist position

I am writing to apply for the advertised position of School Psychologist at [School Name].

I believe I am a strong candidate for the position as I have a keen interest in psychoeducational assessment and counselling. As an Educational and Developmental Psychologist, I have undertaken additional training and supervised practice to develop advanced competencies in educational and developmental psychology that are highly relevant to the advertised position. As an endorsed psychologist in this area, I bring the necessary background and understanding of school psychology and broader educational systems.

Evidenced in my response to the key selection criteria and my curriculum vitae, I have a strong belief in the science-practitioner model and apply this to my everyday practice. My experience and training focus has been across the life span, with a focus on primary and secondary school students (from Foundation to late adolescence) where I have developed a solid understanding of the funding eligibility criteria and application processes required to access support for students with additional learning and behavioural needs. Through implementation of the Response to Intervention (RTI) framework, I offer services across all three tiers: whole school, small group, and individual levels.

I have worked with children and adolescents providing individualised counselling and therapy, providing diagnostic assessments for specific learning disabilities, autism spectrum disorder, and attention-deficit hyperactivity disorder.

Enclosed is a copy of my resume to support my application for this role. I have a current Working with Children Check and professional indemnity insurance. I would appreciate the opportunity to talk more about this position, and how I could use my skills to the benefit of [School Name], its students, teachers, parents, and families.

Thank you for taking the time to consider my application.

I look forward to your response.

Private Practice

Re: Psychologist/Clinical Psychologist

I am writing to apply for the advertised position at [Clinic]. After reviewing the key selection criteria and position requirements, although the advertisement doesn't specify you are seeking an Educational and Developmental Psychologist, I believe my area of endorsement and experience are highly relevant and make me a strong candidate for the position.

As an Educational and Developmental Psychologist, the postgraduate training, additional professional development and supervised practice I completed helped me to advance my competency across the lifespan. This includes child, adolescent, adult, and older adult development, behaviour, mental health, developmental disorders, the teaching and learning process, educational leadership, prevention programs, evidence-based individual and group intervention.

I draw extensively on therapeutic methods such as CBT, ACT, DBT, Reminiscence Therapy, and play therapy to provide best treatment approaches to meet each client's needs. I have developed a solid understanding of Medicare and the National Disability and Insurance Scheme (NDIS) for compliant practice in private settings.

In support of my application, I have addressed key selection criteria and attached my current curriculum vitae. Proof of my current Working with Children Check and professional indemnity insurance can be provided upon request.

Thank you for taking the time to consider my application.

Dr Jake Kraska, Educational and Developmental Psychologist, Director of Level Up Psychology offers some advice:

Having worked for and with schools, research institutes, private practices, defence, tech companies, and tertiary institutions, it has become clear to me the unique perspective an educational and developmental lens offers to both clients and organisations. Working from the perspective of prevention, strengths, and systems, rather than a reactionary and individualistic diagnostic standpoint, enables you to think about problems in a different way than many other mental health professionals. This unique perspective and area of knowledge is a skillset that you can leverage in interviews, job applications and even advocating for a pay rise!

Many organisations may not understand your unique skill set, and it's up to you to educate them. You can do this in a professional manner in your CV or your job interviews. Linking your knowledge of schools, development, ageing, and neurodevelopment to the individual challenges an organisation can put you ahead of other candidates. Whether it's considering how to manage a particular mental health challenge across a cohort of students at a school level, using your knowledge of systems and behaviouralism to assist an organisation in managing change, or using your knowledge of neurodevelopment to support a tech company in developing diagnostic and treatment tools for families. The list goes on!

Given the variety of workplaces your skillset is applicable to, it's important to consider a variety of sources for job listings. While PsychXChange and Seek are common you should also be reviewing the specific recruitment pages for government agencies (both federal and state), LinkedIn, and organisations own websites – many organisations don't list their job on typical job listing pages. Or they don't know they need an educational and developmental psychologist (and it's your job to tell them why they need one)!

Don't think that just because you are working towards being an educational and developmental psychologist, you should only work in a school, early intervention centre, or aged care facility (although these are also great settings if you are interested). Your skillset can be applied to a range of settings. Consider the type of work you want to do (or even the type of organisation you want to work for) and think about how you can apply our unique approach and way of thinking to the challenges that industry is experiencing.

A New Zealand Perspective

Cathy Cooper

As in Australia, New Zealand registered educational psychologists offer a valuable, unique, and currently under-represented perspective to the discipline and practice of psychology. On completing their internship, some educational psychologists are offered roles in the organisation they undertook their internship in. This can be common, for example, in the Ministry of Education Learning Support service, in the Explore Specialist Advice Behaviour Support service and for registered teachers who undertook an educational psychology internship with the Resource Teachers of Learning and Behaviour service (RTLB). For other new psychologists or those more experienced psychologists seeking change, they have on hand the three broad techniques or sources for job hunting also available in Australia: established channels, social media and targeted solicitation. Frequently utilised in New Zealand are a number of well-known websites listing psychologist jobs. In addition, word of mouth can be common in New Zealand due to the small population where it is common that someone knows someone who knows something useful.

Established job-seeking channels for psychologists in
New Zealand

Name	URL	Category (broad/ specific)
Seek	www.seek.co.nz/ psychologist-jobs	Broad and specific
TradeMe jobs	www.trademe.co.nz/a/ jobs/healthcare/ psychology-counselling	Broad and specific
Te Whatu Ora (previously known as individual District Health Boards)	www.tewhatuora.govt.nz/ about-us/jobs	Broad and specific
New Zealand Psychological Society	www.psychology.org.nz/ members/supporting-our- members/psychologist- vacancies	Broad and specific
LinkedIn	www.linkedin.com/jobs	Broad and specific
Ministry of Education	https://jobs.education. govt.nz	Broad and specific
Department of Corrections	https://mahi.corrections. govt.nz	Broad and specific
Oranga Tamariki – Ministry for Children	https://mahi. orangatamariki.govt.nz	Broad and specific
New Zealand Defence Force	www.defencecareers.mil. nz/army/careers/browse- roles/psychologist	Broad and specific

Other employers of psychologists in New Zealand include:

- Employment Assistance Programmes (EAP)
- Rehabilitation services – for people affected by physical and/ or mental injury. Frequently these services are provided by contractors or psychologists in private practice
- Community organisations
- Kaupapa Māori services – which are owned or governed by Māori and apply Māori language, philosophy and principles in their provision of services to people of all ethnicities and backgrounds

- Universities and polytechnics – for roles in tertiary teaching and in student well-being hubs

Psychologists are frequently self-employed in private practice, contract, and consultancy roles. In the past, these tended to be held by psychologists who had been registered for some years however there is now an increasing tendency for psychologists, particularly those who returned to study after some time away, to move straight into these roles upon or soon after registration. It can be tricky finding out "how to do" private practice work however this is where supervision, including peer supervision, becomes particularly valuable.

Cover letters seem to be of similar format in both countries: one page in length and listing an overview of how the psychologist could be a good fit for the role advertised, with an invitation to the reader to delve into the applicant's resume for a more in-depth study of the applicant's professional qualifications as well as their professional and personal attributes and skills. The experience in research gained through study becomes beneficial in finding out about an employer and the role advertised so as to tailor each cover letter specifically and succinctly!

Educational psychologists are an important resource in New Zealand and in Australia. Increased awareness and understanding of their role and their value is creating broad and diverse employment opportunities in both countries.

Concluding comments

Educational and developmental psychologists offer a valuable, unique, and currently under-represented perspective to the discipline and practice of psychology. Applying for work can be a frustrating and arduous experience for this very reason, as the search for employment extends beyond selling yourself and the profession to include advocacy for a growing area of practice. Take the opportunity to celebrate the breadth and depth of advanced knowledge and skills represented by your endorsement so that clients of all ages and stages can benefit from working with a professional focused on lifelong learning.

A career as an educational and developmental psychologist

"Working with the 'human condition' isn't for the faint hearted. It requires a great amount of empathy, common sense, and academic smarts."

—Doug Scott

Introduction

Many of the same challenges experienced as a provisional and generally registered psychologist hold true when transitioning to the field as an educational and developmental psychologist. These can include feelings related to the imposter syndrome, balancing continuous learning needs, and managing risks associated with isolation. In fact, some of these concerns occur well after the transition period. There is also the ongoing challenge of advocating for educational and developmental psychology competencies; we are more than psychologists who only work in schools or with children. Although our area of practice is the only area to specifically include training in the delivery of school psychology services, educational and developmental psychologists have the skillset and flexibility to work with the Australian public across the lifespan and to apply models of learning and development to a broad range of contexts. In this chapter we will discuss the varied roles of educational and developmental psychologists, important issues for private practitioners, special considerations for working overseas, and for early career psychologists.

DOI: 10.4324/9781003330974-11

Varied roles and contexts

From the historical accounts of educational and developmental psychology outlined in Chapter 1, it is not surprising that the work of an educational and developmental psychologist is often misconstrued as being only school focused. When we look at the positioning of educational and developmental psychology in the discipline of education, in addition to over half of the educational and developmental psychologist population working in schools, it can be easy to see how people can view that work with schools, children and adolescents is all that we do.

Jessica Carroll, an educational and developmental psychologist and clinic coordinator at Queensland University of Technology, says,

> the understanding of the scope of educational and developmental psychology practice beyond the school is indeed fairly limited, but in fact, educational and developmental psychologists are well equipped to provide evidence-based intervention to a range of populations including adults. In this way, they are well situated to pivot to online mediums for therapeutic delivery. I successfully ran a private practice entirely online for several months during the pandemic, seeing children, adolescents, adults, and families in an effective way.

Working as an educational and developmental psychologist in schools

Although educational and developmental psychologists see clients of all ages, an evaluation of CEDP members revealed that their typical client base consists of primary school-aged children (5–12 years). According to CEDP members, their clients most commonly present with problems concerning school and education, including learning difficulties, autism spectrum disorders, gifted and talented issues, and behaviour management problems (Fletcher et al., 2010).

Studies of Australian school psychologists have shown that the main roles of educational and developmental psychologists in schools are consulting stakeholders about student well-being, conducting diagnostic psychoeducational assessments for developmental or learning needs,

Figure 11.1 The work of psychologists in schools has varied roles

Source: Image created by Simone Gindidis and supplied with permission from the College of Educational and Developmental Psychologists National Committee.

and counselling to support students and improve their mental health (Ding & Swalwell, 2018). But working with school-aged populations does not provide a homogenous role for psychologists. The way one psychologist works in a school (e.g. involvement with whole school supports, restorative practices, and curriculum-based preventive interventions) can be very different to the way another psychologist works.

Systemic work by educational and developmental psychologists routinely involves collaboration beyond the level of the individual student. For example, collaboration with schools often requires providing professional development and support programs for teachers, meeting with a wider range of school personnel to develop and review learning or behaviour plans and well-being supports, and assisting parents/families with children who have been suspended or who are disengaged from educational contexts.

Whether employed directly by a school/educational authority or consulting with schools as an external practitioner, educational and developmental psychologists working with children and adolescents seek to support young people's emotional, mental, social, and educational needs. Young people, especially adolescents, are frequently affected by mental health problems and developmental disabilities (World Health Organisation, 2022). Young women have reported unprecedented levels of psychological distress since the COVID-19 pandemic was declared and two out of five young people aged 16–24 in Australia recently reported experiencing a mental health disorder (ABS, 2022). If these issues are not addressed through early intervention (Ding & Swalwell, 2018) and if appropriate curriculum accommodations and adjustments are not provided, learning and development are likely to remain significantly compromised into adulthood.

Dr Nerelie Freeman, Course Leader of the Graduate Diploma of Professional Psychology and Educational and Developmental Psychologist at Monash University, reflects on what it is like to work in a school as an educational and developmental psychologist:

> What I love most about being an educational and developmental psychologist is working in schools. While psychs with other training (counselling, clinical) can work in schools also, I feel that ed and dev really gives you a solid grounding in child development, assessing and providing interventions to young people, and working in

Figure 11.2 A high prevalence of mental health issues among adolescents and children means that the educational and developmental psychologists can play busy roles especially within schools

school settings. I love the opportunity to see young people thrive in settings outside the classroom, such as in the pool, as a leader, on stage, or in a helping role such as a peer mentor. I don't feel like you get that when you work in private practice because often you only get to see them within the context of your office. I also love getting the unique perspectives from teachers – not just from completing a checklist, but from building a relationship, becoming part of the community. Psychology can be an isolating profession but when you work in a school you always feel like you're part of a team.

Due to the high prevalence of mental health issues among adolescents and children, the American National Association of School Psychologists (NASP) and the Australian Psychological Society (APS) recommend at least one psychologist for every 500 students. Psychologists who work to support large groups of students can become less satisfied with their work and are less likely to have time to deliver preventive interventions and services.

The services educational and developmental psychologists provide to schools are determined by the priorities of the school/educational authority and the type of service delivery model that is adopted. Traditionally, service delivery models have been broadly divided into systemic models and student-centred models.

Systemic models view a student in the context of their home, school, and community. It is commonly agreed that mental health and psychological well-being is dynamic and impacted by a variety of factors within a student's world. Therefore, therapeutic work may focus not just on one-on-one sessions with the student, but also consultations with teachers, friends, and parents (Bell & McKenzie, 2013). Systemic work can also take place by educational and developmental psychologists who work with parents, extended families, and the broader community in which the school is situated (e.g. government departments, non-government welfare organisations, and courts). The systemic model aims to engage with these broader systems in intervention and prevention programs for mental health and to foster and maintain student well-being.

Individual student-centred models focus on one-on-one sessions with a student. This delivery model does not always include prevention. Although a student/client-centred model is the most common approach for school psychologists around the world, there is evidence the approach is changing. However, it has been argued that this model does not adequately address the needs of schools (e.g. Bell & McKenzie, 2013). Often when schools require a student-centred model of service delivery from psychologists (i.e. working one-on-one with students experiencing issues) workloads can feel unmanageable unless there is a low student to psychologist ratio.

Debate exists about whether individual student-centred or systemic models are more effective. However, evidence from developmental science (i.e. children are influenced by context and systems) provides strong support for the use of broader, systemic interventions and including families and community agencies in intervention work is likely to improve outcomes.

Contract services by educational and developmental psychologists

A major shift in some Australian school sectors has been the intro-duction of contract psychologists to conduct psychometric assessments for students. That is, educational and developmental psychologists are working for third party organisations outside of the school/educa-tion authority but conduct the psychological assessment work within schools. Rather than the traditional arrangement where school psychol-ogists work under school management, contractor arrangements have become more common in both public and private schools (Ding & Swalwell, 2018).

Jesse Diggins, educational and developmental psychologist and founding director of *Psychs in Schools*, acknowledges that educational and developmental psychologists are also needed in schools.

> I've started a couple of companies with the mission of putting more psychs in schools. Since it's incredibly hard for schools to recruit psychologists, we do this by putting master's degree students (Ed & Dev and Clinical) in schools for 6-month and 12-month placements. Since launching at the start of the year, we've put prov psychs in seven schools around Geelong and we hope to keep expanding. We've been able to leverage off the Schools Mental Health Menu funding and the higher degrees of flexibility with NCCD funding in Catholic schools and the Disability Inclu-sion Profiles in public schools. With the demand so great at the moment, I like to think Psychs in Schools is helping by just getting more numbers on the ground and catching the kids that want sup-port and can't get it.
>
> Many Principals tell me it's a huge relief having a psycholo-gist in their team even if it's only part time. Since the pandemic, the existing supports like Student Support Services (SSS) and Child and Adolescent Mental Health Services (CAMHS) have been harder and harder to get into and the threshold for referral has crept up. To me it seems like schools are left holding many of the mild to moderate cases that aren't severe to be accepted elsewhere. I think the recent ABC mental health survey found that two in five young people had experienced a clinical disorder

since the pandemic. This coupled with one in three private clinics having their books closed means the issues have to be surfacing at schools. They probably feel like a bit of a front line for mental health issues surfacing.

The principals I've talked to are really appreciative to have someone to work directly without students, but also provide a clinical lens and indirect support to teaching staff. While the pro-visional psychologists I supervise might work mainly in those two tiers, when psychologists can work on whole school initiatives that incorporate evidence-based practices and research, then there's scope for school wide early intervention. I think that's what the government wants to happen with their recommendations to put one psychologist in schools for every 500 students, as well as cre-ating the schools mental health menu that promotes mental health literacy.

Contract arrangements represent one mode through which educa-tional and developmental psychologists may work with schools while maintaining a base in the private sector. There are also numerous other roles in private work for psychologists with this training.

Educational and developmental services in private practice

Increasingly many endorsed educational and developmental psycholo-gists work in private practice. Services offered by private practitioners often extend beyond educational assessment and counselling to include perinatal mental health support, developmental and cognitive assess-ments in the early years (children aged 0–5), parenting support and intervention for attachment, counselling for life transitions (career change and retirement), capacity assessment and therapy for older adults, to name but a few.

Educational and developmental psychologists working in private practice navigate public national and state funding bodies including Medicare, the National Disability Insurance Agency (NDIA), and National Disability Insurance Scheme (NDIS). Other third-party funders of psychological services include private health funds, insurance companies, and statutory agencies that provide compensation for psychological injuries.

Medicare

The Medicare Benefit Schedule (MBS) lists relevant services for which the Australian Government subsidises, generally through reimbursement, medical services. The issue of Medicare and the MBS in relation to psychological service provision is fraught with controversy and difficulty.

Controversy historically stems from the way in which the MBS items for mental health and psychological services were introduced into Medicare. There have been a myriad of unforeseen repercussions for the profession and the Australian public in response to how MBS items are reimbursed. The first is that of unequal reimbursement for psychologists with one specific area of practice over all others; followed closely by the impact this division has on the profession as well as public perception of psychology. This reinforces the need for advocacy by educational and developmental psychologists in private practice to dispel any misunderstanding regarding our role providing and charging for services commensurate with the time and our own advanced capabilities.

The difficulty for educational and developmental psychologists when navigating Medicare is also that it places the practice of psychology within a medical system. The adoption of a medical model can conflict with a developmental, educational, and/or systemic evidence-based approach to sustainable positive change. Assisting clients and their families with co-occurring presentations including neurodivergence, mental health, learning difficulties, or attachment, is complicated when conceptualised from a medical lens (Elkins, 2009). An example of this incongruence relates to the allocation of Medicare funding to individuals. A narrow focus on reimbursing individual "treatment" circumvents the ability to deliver client-centred services incorporating influential agents within a person's microsystem (Langford, 2005; Vygotsky, 1978) such as parents, caregivers, educators, schools, or workplaces.

Although contributions from educational and developmental psychologists on the debate surrounding these contentious issues is much needed, the purpose of including this information here is to highlight the need for educational and developmental psychologists working in private practice to be:

● Aware of the political climate within which they provide services rebated by Medicare
● Undertake requisite training to provide services reimbursed under the MBS according to mandated Medicare requirements.

Relevant Medicare schemes for educational and developmental psychologists to review at the time of writing include MBS items falling under Better Access to Mental Health initiative (Mental Health Treatment Plans), Helping Children with Autism (assessment and treatment items), and Chronic Disease Management (treatment items).

A variety of options are available and continue to be developed for educational and developmental psychologists to access training in this area, including from the Australian Institute of Medical Administration and Compliance (AIMAC) and professional organisations such as the Australian Psychological Society (see Chapter 7 for further details).

The national disability insurance scheme (NDIS) and the national disability insurance agency (NDIA)

The NDIS was established under federal legislation in 2013 (The National Disability Insurance Scheme Act, 2013) and services were rolled out nationally in 2016. The NDIS supports Australians diagnosed with permanent and/or significant disabilities and connects participants with the community. Australians funded through the NDIS (referred to as NDIS participants) collaboratively formulate Plans with NDIS representatives to support their needs, which may include increasing independence and funded opportunities to pursue personal goals.

There are currently three ways NDIS participants manage their support allocations:

1 **Self-management**
Participants are responsible for managing their own NDIA funding allocation.
2 **Plan management**
A Plan Manager (company or organisation registered with the NDIA) is responsible for tracking and approving appropriate NDIS funding expenditure.
3 **NDIA management**
The NDIA directly manages and pays service providers on a participant's behalf. Providers must be registered with the NDIS to provide services under this model.

Limited psychological services (e.g. capacity building funding for positive behavioural support to reduce challenging behaviour and improve relationships) can be provided to eligible NDIS participants; however, the NDIS was not designed to fund mental health interventions or psychological services that are available from existing health services. Psychologists working under NDIS funded arrangements often work for a registered NDIS provider. Under the current scheme, specific funding criteria, access to allied health professionals, and the range of services provided under a participant's plan, is limited and complex. Further changes in how the scheme operates, including changes to early childhood early intervention services, have been announced.

Other considerations for psychologists in private practice

Educational and developmental psychologists who work in private practice draw from or learn skills not necessarily covered at university. Logo design, marketing, and drumming up clients were not inherently taught in a psychology degree. Making yourself known to the local community, and professionals who are likely to refer become essential for growing and maintaining a client base. Sending our letters of introductions or flyers with infographics explaining like the ones in the following) are helpful in articulating the role to others.

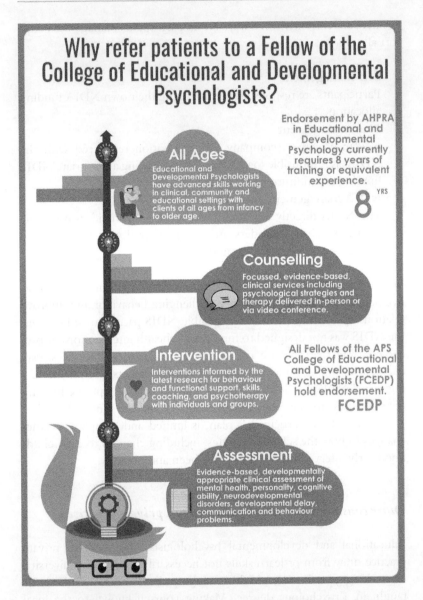

Figure 11.3 Advocating and educating others about educational and developmental psychology: making yourself known

Source: Image created by Simone Gindidis and supplied with permission from the College of Educational and Developmental Psychologists National Committee.

Letter of introduction for a Private Practitioner

Dear,

My name is Maria Ainsworth. I'm an educational and developmental psychologist in private practice. I am a member of the Australian Psychological Society's College of Educational and Developmental Psychologists.

When you have patients with a wide range of issues across the lifespan, you are likely to find expert, skilled assistance by referring your patient to an educational and developmental psychologist because they have advanced knowledge of:

- concerns about a child's cognitive, behavioural, or emotional development
- Assessment of a developmental delay
- Assessment of specific disabilities or learning difficulties (e.g. Intellectual Disability and Autism Spectrum Disorders)
- Assistance with feeding, sleeping or behaviour problems or disorders (e.g. Attention Deficit Hyperactivity Disorder)
- Assistance with attachment issues
- Parenting
- Assessment of school readiness
- Separation anxiety or school avoidance
- Psychoeducational assessment
- Poor peer-relationships
- Specialist behaviour management planning
- Low self esteem
- Well-being issues
- Mental health problems (e.g. depression, anxiety, and mood disorders)
- Assessment of giftedness
- Family relationship issues
- Physical or sexual abuse
- Assistance with treatment planning and specialist support
- Alcohol and other drug problems and dependency issues
- Divorce/separation
- Work stress
- Healthy ageing
- Adjustment and transition issues
- Issues of loss or grief

As you can see, these issues are likely to affect a number of your patients. An educational and developmental psychologist is an expert in using empirically driven proactive and preventive frameworks, and referral will be of tremendous benefit for your patients.

I have attached for your perusal an infographic which clearly demonstrates a few facts about educational and developmental psychologists.

Thank you for taking the time to understand the services which educational and developmental psychologists can offer your patients.

Warm regards,

Maria Ainsworth

Educational and developmental psychologists in early childhood early intervention (ECEI)

Educational and developmental psychologists play an important role in prevention and early intervention with employment opportunities in this space spanning private and public settings. Educational and developmental psychologist Janene Swalwell was an incredibly knowledgeable practitioner, researcher, supervisor, and lecturer, who passionately advocated for the recognition and inclusion of more educational and developmental psychologists in early childhood and disability settings. She also founded the APS Early Childhood Intervention Interest Group.

In addition to extensive research on the implementation of social-emotional-behavioural (SEB) learning strategies in preschools and early learning centres using the Pyramid Model (Swalwell & McLean, 2021), Janene articulated how educational and developmental psychologists contribute to ECEI in this 2018 APS CEDP infographic:

Educational and developmental psychologist and Chair of the APS Early Childhood Intervention Interest Group, Caroline Keating, reflects on her experiences working in the ECEI and Disability sectors:

Finding employment in a transdisciplinary key worker model early childhood intervention team working with children with

EDUCATIONAL AND DEVELOPMENTAL PSYCHOLOGISTS

EXPERTS IN EARLY CHILDHOOD

ASSESSMENT & DIAGNOSIS

Formal assessment and diagnosis of intellectual, mental health and developmental conditions. Identification of circumstances that promote positive development and wellbeing (e.g. attachment, developmental trauma and neglect)

REPORTING & PLANNING

Creating reports, plans, guides and intervention strategies about children's development and learning, family and social circumstances, often in collaboration with families, carers and service providers

EDUCATION

Providing information on how children develop and learn, how trauma, neglect, delays and disabilities impact on development and functioning. How to promote positive parent-child relationships, self-regulation and social-emotional competence.

COUNSELLING

Individual and group play-based therapy for children. Families as a whole, parents and other professionals in understanding and managing developmental and mental health problems in children and their caregivers.

INTERVENTION

Development of strategies to address problems such as toileting or unsafe behaviour, interventions to promote skills and functioning, and coaching in relevant intervention practices.

CAREGIVER SUPPORT

Supporting families and caregivers to process reactions to diagnosis, living with, and supporting a child with a disability. Promotion of family functioning, promoting strengths and addressing challenges.

CONNECTION & INCLUSION

Support to promote children's inclusion in family, education, care and community activities and services. Connection to Eary Childhood Services, Schools and Communities.

Educational and Developmental psychologists are trained to design, develop and deliver Early Childhood and Early Childhood Intervention (ECI) services. They provide support for all young children (0-6 years) especially those experiencing developmental challenges, delays and disabilities, their families and service providers. They work with and through families and other professionals to develop children's skills and functioning in all aspects of their daily life, now and for their futures.

Figure 11.4 Educational and developmental psychologists can be experts in early childhood

Source: Image created by Simone Gindidis and supplied with permission from the College of Educational and Developmental Psychologists National Committee.

developmental delays is where I found my perfect home as an educational and developmental psychologist. Working with young children and their families calls on such a broad range of skills and knowledge, and in the key worker model there is flexibility that as a clinician can be both daunting and exciting.

Early childhood is where I found stimulating work that required knowledge about child development and learning, child and family mental health, attachment theory and practice, inclusion, life transitions, as well as the professional skill to meet families where they are at and collaborate with a wide range of professionals in the "team around the child." I have loved working in local communities where children are – be it in homes, kindergartens or often the local playground – as a wonderful way to support child development and assist with what matters most for children and family day to day.

Early childhood intervention is about supporting families and caregivers to understand the unique needs of each child, to optimise their learning, relationships, and mental health. It requires understanding the systems and pressures children and families experience, and helping to ensure caregivers have evidence based knowledge early in their child's life to support their child where they are at. A transdisciplinary model of early childhood work has also given me a richness of collaborative practice and lifelong learning from wonderful colleagues in education, speech pathology, occupational therapy, and physiotherapy.

I have always been drawn to considering the ways in which development and learning are central to our wellbeing and mental health. For my career, this has meant a focus on the mental health across the lifespan of children and adults with a developmental disability. Service systems often struggle to cater to the needs of both disability and mental health concerns despite evidence of this being an area of significant unmet need. Siloing of services that somehow expect humans to either have a disability or a mental health concern are part of the problem.

Educational and developmental psychology is in a unique position to help bridge this gap, to understand people's developmental and mental health needs cannot be separated and that a holistic approach is essential. As an educational and developmental psychologist I can apply a holistic assessment lens to understand how developmental level, learning capacity and communication needs may contribute to the presenting issue and to effectiveness of certain interventions. Adapting and applying evidence based approaches to suit the learning, communication and developmental needs of my clients is something I am passionate about to ensure that everyone has access to appropriate mental health care.

Special considerations for working overseas

Working overseas with Australian credentialing as an educational and developmental psychologist

Opportunities for Australian trained educational and developmental psychologists to work internationally are widely available (see Chapter 3 for an overview of Australian registration requirements). One of the easiest options is to consider working in New Zealand. Under the New Zealand and Australian Trans-Tasman Mutual Recognition Agreement (TTMR), Australian endorsement as an Educational and Developmental Psychologist is compatible with the New Zealand scope of practice in educational psychology. Furthermore, Australian citizens and residents do not require a work or residency visa and demand for psychologists is strong.

A second and growing source of employment for educational psychologists is within international schools. International schools are well recognised as a rapidly emerging sector in global education. For example, in China, and Asia more generally, international schools are one of the fastest growing school sectors. Established international schools serve highly mobile, global expatriate students and their families as well as students and families from the local jurisdiction. Historically, international schools have been committed to education for global citizenship and they have been open to diverse cultural groups (Wurf, 2018). However, with recent growth, the quality and regulation of international schools is more varied, and an increasing number of schools are now operated by for-profit, corporate entities.

Larger, globally connected cities across South East Asia, China, Europe, the Middle East, and South America host international schools.

Curricula and accreditation are most likely to follow either a U.S. State-based school district or the UK National Curriculum (GCSE and A-Levels). Increasingly, the International Baccalaureate (IB) is available as an alternative curriculum. Overwhelmingly, the language of instruction in international schools is English.

Subject to the vagaries of exchange rates, local taxation settings, and Australian international taxation agreements, remuneration packages for international school employees can be extremely attractive. For applicants applying from their home country (expatriate appointees), employee benefits often include return air fares, housing allowances, health insurance, pension fund contributions, and an end of contract gratuity. Assistance with working visas and fee relief for employee's children who attend the school is frequently available. School fees for quality international schools are expensive. If you are considering work in an international school, the UK Times Educational Supplement www.tes.com lists global opportunities. Most northern hemisphere schools conduct a recruitment drive during the latter part of the year and information about upcoming job openings is often available on school websites. For experienced Australian candidates with an internationally competitive academic and employment history, specialist recruitment agencies (e.g. the U.S.-based Search Associates) offer a fee-based service to help secure an international position as a school counsellor/psychologist.

Australian international schools offer Australian curriculum and are accredited by an Australian State jurisdiction. Larger Australian international schools are located in Bali, Bangkok, Ho Chi Minh City, Hong Kong, Jakarta, Kuala Lumpur, and Singapore. One advantage of working in an offshore Australian international school is that holding Australian qualifications and registration with AHPRA is likely to allow you to practise as an educational psychologist within the school. Students attending Australian international schools sit Australian school examinations. The identification processes and provisions for special needs students follow the requirements of the Australian accrediting State.

More generally, the regulatory framework for the registration of educational and developmental psychologists varies widely across international jurisdictions. Where local registration requirements for psychologists are particularly onerous, international schools often advertise related, generic positions (e.g. school counsellor). Individuals holding international qualifications who work in the role of a school counsellor in jurisdictions where local regulatory frameworks for the practice of psychology are in place, would not be permitted to use the title "psychologist" or administer restricted psychological tests without first seeking local registration/licensing as a psychologist.

Outside of the international school system, finding work opportunities, seeking recognition for overseas qualifications, and registering as a psychologist with an international qualification can be complex (and expensive). In both the United States and UK, most post-graduate psychology programs require completion of a PhD/doctoral-level training for practice. Nevertheless, specialist-level master degree qualifications in school psychology are accredited in the United States. The *National Association of School Psychologists* (NASP) maintains accessible information on *State School Psychology Credentialing Requirements* for each U.S. State. Specialist graduate training programs in school psychology in the United States require a minimum of 60 graduate semester hours, and programs must include an internship year (1200 hours completed on a full time basis or at least a half time basis over two consecutive years). No U.S. state requires a doctoral degree to practise as a school psychologist (NASP, 2019), but U.S. states often require a review of international qualifications by an agency specified by the State to establish equivalency. Most U.S. States also set licence examinations for school psychologists and fees to obtain the appropriate standing can be high. Furthermore, completion of additional coursework may be necessary.

Similarly, in Scotland (unlike England, Wales, and Northern Ireland), professional master degree programs in educational psychology are still a standard pathway for practice as an educational psychologist. Nevertheless, irrespective of the practice jurisdiction, to work as an educational psychologist in the UK you will need to be registered with *The Health and Care Professions Council* (HCPC). The HCPC considers international applications for registration and extensive documentation is required (international application route). This includes certified copies of Australian coursework degrees, specifying the content of the coursework units/subjects, certified copies of logbooks documenting the hours and activities completed during psychology professional experience/internships, and practice activities outside the UK. Again, scrutiny fees for UK registration as a psychologist are expensive (around £550). It is therefore crucial that the application is carefully prepared to include all the required documentation and the requested certifications. See Chapter 3 for additional information about register-ing as a psychologist in international jurisdictions.

Working in Australia as an educational and developmental psychologist and coming from overseas

Moving to Australia from another country, any country presents chal-lenges around adjustment and transition for most people. Transferring credentials and professional expertise add additional complexities. Edu-cational and developmental psychologist Dr Pascale Paradis, who is the practice Director of 3P Psychologies, describes her experience:

> From the age of 15, I worked with children in a range of roles, swim-ming coach, summer camp and scout leader, homework helper, and subsequently completed my first degree in psychology in Quebec, Canada. I have always been passionate about working with children in educational settings and in the community so it felt very natural to continue my career working with children. In my initial years of training in Quebec, I did assessment work in schools and really enjoyed this role to inform further strategies and support to meet children's needs. I then moved to Scotland where I taught children with additional needs and also psychology, and this really helped shape my desire in becoming an educational psychologist. I contin-ued learning in a Masters in Psychology and Education program at Cambridge University and then the Institute of Education where I completed my doctorate in Educational, Child and Adolescent Psychology. I felt very proud of this incredible journey of entering a fascinating profession that enabled me to support many. During my doctorate, we were also very encouraged to work at a systemic level and not solely at a therapeutic level so that educational psychology is deployed across systems to facilitate change. This really stayed with me as an important message for the profession.
>
> When we relocated to Australia as a family, due to my husband's international career in maritime signalling, it was hard initially to resettle my career in new systems, particularly as I had to start at the provisional psychologist status level, engage in supervision and do the national exam. It felt like starting a career again but I am glad

I did all of this as it helped me gain confidence and knowledge to better support clients. As a result of practising in different countries, I became curious about the differences in the delivery of theoretical frameworks across educational psychology programs worldwide as I found myself noticing different models of practice i.e. medical, behaviourist, social constructionist models. This move to Australia also inspired me to ensure the psychologists of the future are well trained in supporting children, families and schools as I was finding the specificity of training programs in Australia not necessarily aimed at supporting children only (i.e. training being more across the lifespan) like in the UK. I then became a board approved supervisor and continue to train many in gaining their skills in working with children, families and schools. I am now also enjoying being the director of a paediatric psychology private practice, having a team working with me and helping them learn and thrive, doing ongoing counselling and psychoeducational assessments.

The profession of educational and developmental psychology is diverse with immense scope in working at different levels, with children, with families, in a therapeutic capacity, as well as with schools and community organisations to promote inclusion, support skills development and ensure appropriate strategies are implemented to meet needs. At the same time, supervision and training continues to be required to equip psychologists of the future.

I recently embarked on a journey of developing a range of resources when working with children for psychologists aiming to help them develop skills and also ideas for therapeutic activities. These resources and a book are part of a concept called The Therapist Backpack where all resources needed for the day of work are included in a backpack.

Overall, my educational psychology practice continues to evolve in supporting others across systems.

Special considerations for early career psychologists

Starting your career as an educational and developmental psychologist can be a time where you might have a ton of questions. Here are some frequently asked questions we have prepared in advance.

Question 1: I have imposter syndrome – is it just me?

Imposter syndrome (IS) is what is commonly referred to as the experience of professional self-doubt. Many professionals experience IS (Bravata et al., 2020; Clark et al., 2021; Freeman & Peisah, 2022) and in addition to it feeling terrible, IS can negatively impact mental health and lead to professional burnout. Quite simply: no, you are not alone.

Some evidence informed suggestions for how to approach combating IS were summarised succinctly by a psychologist in a recent APA blog post (Palmer, 2021). It may also be helpful to quantify and monitor your professional self-perception using established tools such as the Professional Self Doubt Scale (Nissen-Lie et al., 2010) and the Counselling Self Estimate Inventory (Larson & Suzuki, 1992).

Hannah Yared, PhD candidate at Monash Education, reminds us:

> It's incredibly important for people of colour who are wanting to pursue a career in psychology to see there is space for us – because we have a unique perspective to offer. It's just as important that clients see themselves represented too.

Question 2: I'm the only educational and developmental psychologist on my team, how do I avoid burn-out?

All sectors and professions are vulnerable to burnout and educational and developmental psychologists are in a good position to prevent this. This is because we have strong training in preventive mental health and personal well-being. However, being equipped with knowledge on coping, resilience, and well-being may not be enough. Understanding the field of psychology, the team you are working with, and the types of clients you may be working with can be a major help. The following are a few tips to think about should you find yourself in a team as the only educational and developmental psychologist (although some of these tips apply to those not in teams also).

- **Know your scope.** It is important for educational psychologists to educate team members on the AoPE competencies of educational and developmental psychologists and ensure that they have access to a diverse and varied caseload in line with their professional areas of competency. As described in Chapter 1, there are a lot of misconceptions about the role and capabilities of educational psychologists and professionals from other fields of practice may require information to understand the true scope of our role.

- **Create a support network.** The benefit of working in multidisciplinary teams is the opportunity to learn from others, share knowledge, and develop professional relationships and support systems. Early career psychologists in particular can benefit from these interactions. Make sure you also have a bank of support options up your sleeve – colleagues, peers, a supervisor, a professional body, or helpline. Building a professional network can occur through university peers, psychologists in the local area and also professional associations or networking events. You might find networks online – like on Twitter or Facebook. Terrific educational and developmental psychology communities on Facebook are: Educational & Developmental Psychology Networking Australia (EDPNA) www.facebook.com/groups/EDPNA and the Educational & Developmental Psychology Networking NZ (EDPNNZ) https://www.facebook.com/groups/205783553161757.

- **Maintain supervision.** Supervision is important for all psychologists (regardless of their area of specialisation, stage of career, or their place of work). Supervision can help psychologists to gain perspective about their work and ways to navigate challenges. See Chapter 8 to learn more about the benefits of supervision. Psychologists seeking a supervisor can use the AHPRA search tool available here: www.psychologyboard.gov.au/registration/supervision/search.aspx

- **Keep up professional development.** CPD Planning is important to maintain (see Chapter 3) and joining a professional association can be a good source for further learning (see Chapter 7) as well as creating a network mentioned previously.

- **Prepare for challenges.** New situations will arise and sometimes scenarios you are faced with can feel stressful. Make sure you are prepared for the unknown. Reassure yourself that you do not always need to know the answers to everything, you just need to know where to find them. Also remember that each experience contributes to a richer understanding of the field. Next time the situation arises you are better prepared. The most unexpected and challenging situations can help improve your skills as a psychologist. A current student undertaking placement experiences, Jessica Rodaughan says, "Even the most challenging experiences will ultimately help you to learn something new and become a better practitioner."

Question 3: *I have been working in a school and am wanting to move into private practice. How can I prepare?*

There can be a lot to consider when moving from a school position (which typically does not require complex systems for scheduling appointments, billing, and business expenses), to private practice. The following is a list of the types of software and funding systems, and support advice that can help educational and developmental psychologists when navigating the shift from school to private practice.

- Examples of practice management software for booking appointments and billing include Halaxy, Cliniko, Power Diary, and Core Plus.

  o There is also the APS Member Resource: Practice Management Software for Psychologists in Private Practice

- An understanding of funding/rebate systems is essential, such as Medicare Compliance/NDIS/Private Health Insurance

  o Medicare: www.servicesaustralia.gov.au/private-billing-procedures-for-health-professionals
  o NDIS: AHPA training https://ndisregistrationsupport.ahpa.com.au
  o NDIS: APS training: https://psychology.org.au/event/
  o Private health insurance information (insurer-specific)

A common challenge is becoming comfortable with discussing fees with clients and recognising the value of your time/work. Following up with clients who have failed to pay for a session or charging non-attendance fees when clients fail to arrive for their scheduled appointment are commonplace for psychologists in private practice. Supervision from a psychologist experienced in private practice can help you to overcome these issues and develop systems to avoid these issues occurring in the first place. Part of our ethical responsibility of creating boundaries is that we provide clear expectations to our clients about billing and attending scheduled appointments. However, because many educational and developmental psychologists work with children, establishing firm boundaries can be problematic. We need to balance our desire and ethical responsibility to act in the best interests of our clients, while also not undervaluing the work and services of educational and developmental psychologists. For all of the reasons outlined earlier and throughout this book, it is essential that educational psychologists reach out to colleagues and others already in private practice.

Question 4. How do I communicate what an educational and developmental psychologist does to different audiences?

Communicating to different audiences about the work of educational and developmental psychologists is important to help different stakeholders understand the role. There are likely to be multiple ways you can do this. Here are some ideas:

- Use infographics like the ones you will see throughout this book.
- Create a letter of introduction or generate marketing material
- Create a professional social media profile

Remember to avoid terms like "specialist," conveying you hold a specialist title (as this is not possible in psychology in Australia), or implying superiority over other psychologists. Testimonials (i.e. real or fabricated client stories and experiences that make a recommendation about a service or its quality) are also not permitted as these violate advertising guidelines for regulated health professionals (AHPRA, 2020). Additional guidance summarising AHPRA regulations is also available from the APS.

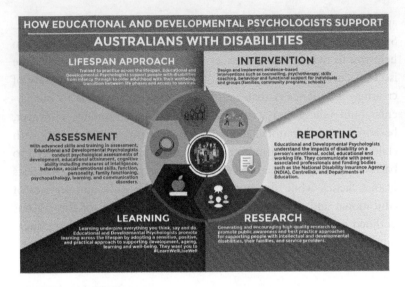

Figure 11.5 Educational and developmental psychologists can use infographics as a tool to articulate the work they do such as supporting people with disabilities

Source: Image created by Simone Gindidis and supplied with permission from the College of Educational and Developmental Psychologists National Committee.

Question 5. Now that I am an educational and developmental psychologist do I need to read peer-review papers?

Educational and developmental psychologists should continue to draw from evidence-based practice throughout their careers. This means accessing research through sources such as professional blogs and magazines (e.g. InPsych, Monitor, and Psychology Today) and journals. Here is a list of journals you might like to consider (see Chapter 6 for other sources of research like podcasts and books). **Journals:** Educational and Developmental Psychologist; British Educational Research Journal; Child Development; Comparative Education Review; Developmental Psychology; Developmental Review; Developmental Science; Early Childhood Research Quarterly; Educational Administration Quarterly; Educational Psychologist; Educational Psychology Review; Journal of Educational Psychology.

A New Zealand Perspective

Cathy Cooper

As in Australia, educational psychologists in New Zealand play an important role in prevention and early intervention, with employment opportunities covering private and public settings. Educational psychologists in New Zealand tend to begin their professional practices with government (e.g. the Ministry of Education) and community (e.g. Explore Specialist Advice Behaviour Service) organisations and then branch into other employment which can include contract work and private practice work. Frequently, educational psychologists working outside of government organisations provide psychometric assessment, and most provide intervention at an individual and/or a systems level.

It is interesting to note that the American National Association of School Psychologists (NASP) and the Australian Psychological Society (APS) recommend at least one psychologist for every 500 students. While this may happen in Australia and in large New Zealand cities, in New Zealand provincial areas the ratio can be far different. For example, in an east coast central North Island district, there is one educational psychologist employed by the Ministry of Education for a district of 35,700 people where 23% aged below 15 years. There is much scope in districts with low psychologist to student ratios for educational psychologists to work in private practice and to be contracted by schools.

As the work experiences of educational psychologists become broader, peer supervision is particularly important those working in contract and/or private practice work. Groups of 6–8 educational psychologists meet regularly to discuss issues which arise for them in their professional practices. This can be online or in person, however due to the geographical spread of educational psychologists and the use of Zoom made more popular in COVID-19 lockdown times, online peer supervision is becoming more popular. Peer supervision is used alongside personal one to one supervision that all psychologists are required to undertake by the New Zealand Psychologist Board. Educational psychologists working as contractors and/or in private practice are required to pay for their own supervision while those working for government and community organisations have this funded. An advantage of paying for your own supervision is that you can choose your own supervisor.

Professional development is particularly important, to ensure that educational psychologists continue to gain up to date relevant evidence-based knowledge throughout their careers. Professional development opportunities become more carefully chosen and subsequently more meaningful when the cost comes out of the private practice psychologist's own budget! The New Zealand Psychologist Board has a Continuing Competence Programme, the purpose of which is to uphold the Board's responsibilities under the Health Practitioners Competence Assurance Act 2003. All practising educational psychologists participate in the Continuing Competence Programme and are required to declare that they have done so when renewing their annual practising certificate.

The practice of psychology in New Zealand reflects the paradigms and worldviews of both partners to te Tiriti o Waitangi (the Treaty of Waitangi). Regardless of where or how they conduct their professional practice, all New Zealand educational psychologists are expected to adhere to the three principles of te Tiriti o Waitangi – partnership, participation and protection – to uphold the well-being of Māori and to ensure they work in a culturally competent manner with all cultures.

As in Australia, working with the human condition as an educational psychologist in New Zealand requires empathy, common sense and academic smarts!

Concluding comments

A career as an educational and developmental psychologist is a rewarding endeavour that can be varied based on interests and passions. In this chapter, we considered the varied roles of educational and developmental psychologists as well as considerations for private practitioners, working overseas, and early career psychologists. In Chapter 12, we will consider the future directions of educational and developmental psychology as the profession enters a new era with benefits associated with a diversified profession and technology.

Future directions of educational and developmental psychology

"The issues psychologists work on aren't going anywhere. In fact, the prevalence and help-seeking is increasing. Many psychologists are so overwhelmed they are turning people away."
—Jesse Diggins

Introduction

As discussed earlier, educational and developmental psychologists are in high demand in Australia. Once you have obtained a master's or PhD level qualification, with a view of becoming endorsed, many opportunities will be available. You might wonder, what is in store for the future of educational and developmental psychology? Experts in the field have raised some concerns and made some exciting predictions. We will discuss national challenges, such as the Medicare rebate system and the general public's limited understanding of our profession. Then we will move on to international trends, including the effects of COVID-19, implications of technology, evidence-based practice, Indigenous psychology, transdisciplinary collaborations, and prevention and well-being. We will conclude with a discussion of future roles for educational and developmental psychologists.

Future challenges of educational and developmental psychology

The first concern about the future of educational and developmental psychology is the lack of knowledge or misunderstanding of the field among students, employers, and the general public (Gilmore et al., 2013).

DOI: 10.4324/9781003330974-12

There is a need for more awareness about the diverse roles of educational and developmental psychologists to attract future students and inform those seeking psychological services. While educational and developmental psychologists can have a role to play in building advocacy and awareness of the profession through using their professional title in public domains (such as on letterheads and in media opportunities), challenges emerge at a national level. Thus, political leaders and policymakers must understand educational and developmental psychologists' role in advocating for the profession. A deeper understanding among government officials will help enhance service delivery and work to implement structural changes at a state and national level.

A second concern is Australia's lack of educational and developmental master's/PhD programs. There are only four, APAC accredited professional educational and developmental psychology programs in the country. Gilmore et al. (2013) suspect the scarcity of programs is partly due to a lack of understanding of the field by university decision-makers. The unique skills of educational and developmental psychologists, particularly in prevention and early intervention, may be disregarded in favour of other, more generic programs that offer training in mental health.

A second issue is that educational and developmental psychology, along with other non-clinical areas of psychological practice, experience challenges related to the government's health rebate system, known as Medicare. The current Medicare rebate system divides psychological services into two tiers – clinical psychology services and general psychology services. Higher rebates are provided for mental health services offered by a clinical psychologist above other endorsed psychologists (Gilmore et al., 2013). Taking effect in 2006, this two-tiered rebate model marked a critical moment in Australia's psychology health rebate history. Public perceptions of psychology started to change, and people began to prioritise clinical over other areas of psychology. This turning point is arguably responsible for students' increased interest in studying clinical psychology over other areas of practice. This is despite the considerable overlap in course content and opportunities for similar placement experiences across the different practice areas.

For educational and developmental psychologists, the Better Access initiative and associated Medicare rebate system has significantly affected the profession. Many educational and developmental psychologists are experts in mental health yet receive less remuneration for offering the same services as a clinical psychologist. Psychologists across all specialisations have felt the effects of the 2006 healthcare reform. The Australian Association of Psychologists Inc (AAPi) was formed in 2010 to represent a voice for psychologists. Part of their mandate is to "advocate for the removal of the two-tier funding system and reinstate one Medicare rebate for the clients of all psychologists" (AAPi, 2021).

Due to COVID-19 restrictions and school closures, many children lost access to school-based mental health support when they needed it most. Students experienced a host of pandemic-related stressors, such as family financial concerns and the loss of social interaction with peers (Reupert et al., 2021, 2022). In a study of American school psychologists, 56.5% of participants indicated that the pandemic would moderately impact students' overall mental health, and 22.4% indicated that it would severely impact students' overall mental health (Schaffer et al., 2021). As these results suggest, there is increased concern for children's mental health following the pandemic. Educational and developmental psychologists have stepped forward to help address the negative social, emotional, and mental effects of the pandemic. Additionally, educational and developmental psychologists can assess and address how online schooling has impacted students' learning. In a sense, now is an opportune time to advocate for our distinctive area of practice.

In 2010, Fletcher et al. raised concerns about the demographic makeup of Australian educational and developmental psychologists. In their 2010 survey, at a time when there were more educational and developmental psychology courses than today, concerns were raised about the ageing population of practising educational and developmental psychologists and universities not turning out new graduates quickly enough to replace ageing practitioners. Ten years on, we see educational and developmental psychology as a thriving practice area. As mentioned in Chapter 8, educational and developmental psychology is one of the fastest-growing endorsement areas. The current demand on the profession and call for greater psychological support in the community highlights that educational and developmental psychology has a hopeful future going forward.

Figure 12.1 Many advocates are calling for more educational and developmental psychologists in schools

Dianne Summers, Senior Teaching Fellow (Professional Practice), educational and developmental psychologist, and supervisor for over hundreds of registrars and provisional psychologists, is optimistic about educational and developmental psychology in the future.

My career began as a registered primary and secondary teacher with an undergraduate major in psychology and a passion for student well-being and inclusive teaching pedagogy. It soon became apparent that to make a real difference for the many students who were disengaged and disenfranchised from learning I needed to complete my journey to become an educational and developmental psychologist, so followed a master's degree and 2 years of supervision. My career in psychology commenced as a guidance officer (psychologist with teacher registration and 4 years of teaching experience) for the Victorian Education Department and I have since worked as a psychologist in all three Victorian education sectors in addition to private practice supporting children, adolescents and families.

Fast forward 25 years (and it has flown by) and I am now a Senior Teaching Fellow at Monash University, in addition to maintaining independent professional practice. My work is focused on teaching, training, supervising and supporting provisional and early career psychologists. The interest and demand for intake into the Master of Educational and Development Psychology program at Monash University continues to grow; from the 6 students that commenced with me in 1995 to a current postgraduate student intake of approximately 50 in 2022, from 300 applications.

Why the increased growth and interest in Educational and Developmental Psychology? The work is varied, energising (while at times exhausting) and affords the opportunity to make a real difference in the lives of people and families via influencing positive change in the schools and communities they live, work, and play in. I have been privileged to support families, schools, and communities to develop environments where children and people are understood and supported to be able to function at their best.

My career highlights now centre around seeing psychologists I have had a part in training make a difference to the lives of children and families they work with and to the school communities they work in. The demand for Educational and Developmental psychologists in schools, government agencies and other settings continues to grow as the specialism is recognised for its uniqueness in being able to work at the interface between education systems, family system, and disability services to support individuals through the challenges of transition across the lifespan.

Implications of technology

One significant change, which many psychologists see as positive, is the advancement of technology. Australian practitioners have been at the forefront of integrating technology into mental health services (Gindidis et al., 2019). Online counselling has grown in popularity, as well as applications and online programs. These services have existed for years, but their implementation grew exponentially during the COVID-19 pandemic as many psychologists transitioned to virtual modes of service delivery.

When COVID-19-related school closures forced school staff to transition their services online, technology became an invaluable tool. School psychologists worldwide pivoted to virtual or hybrid services during the pandemic's peak in their respective countries (Reupert et al., 2021). School psychologists reported using webcams or phones to deliver telehealth interventions and telecounselling to students. They also used web-based platforms to provide resources for parents, such as videos about behavioural, social-emotional, and academic issues (Reupert et al., 2021). Online service delivery was necessary, but it also introduced new ethical implications such as data privacy and the security of web-based platforms.

Further technological advancements include assistive technology for individuals with learning disabilities, for example, advanced assistance for vision and hearing impairments. There are also exciting new possibilities for electronic assessment and intervention for various psychological issues such as using biofeedback and artificial intelligence tools or virtual reality.

Christine Grové, Educational and Developmental Psychologist and Fulbright scholar, says:

> Using technology to address some of the challenges the profession has been critical in continuing services for clients during COVID-19. Significant changes were required overnight. There are many young people who experience mental health and well-being challenges. A potential negative mental health trigger for some youth

is a struggle to cope with stress at school, feelings of depression and anxiety and availability of adequate help for these stressors. In response to youth needs we co-developed a mental health and well-being Chatbot with youth, technology partners and expert stakeholders (Grové, 2021; Grové et al., 2020). An element of the Chatbot is powered by artificial intelligence using rules-based AI and natural language processing. It was developed to share evidence-based resources, well-being support, educational mental health information, and adaptive coping strategies. Digital tools such as Chatbot applications could support the mental health of young people in secondary schools or health care settings in conjunction with the well-being or health care team. It is hoped that by co-developing such a digital tool we will address some of the challenges of youth accessing accurate mental health information while waiting on long lists for services. Feedback from our youth reference group has provided suggestions on the Chatbot development, such as its name, identity, and persona. Overtime we will measure its effectiveness and whether this tool has long-term benefits and is sustainable for professionals and youth to use.

Concerns have been raised that technology may also have negative implications for children's learning and development. Concerns include cyberbullying and the overuse of social media and video games (Gilmore et al., 2013). However extensive syntheses demonstrate little impact on overall well-being (Best et al., 2014; Orben et al., 2019). Ultimately, the effects of technology are more likely to depend on the user, the amount of time spent using technology, and the specific type of technology (e.g. social media, television, and video games).

Biofeedback tools

Biofeedback is an unobtrusive process that measures physiological activity and enables individuals to monitor and change their physiological state to improve their well-being (Schwartz, 2010). Biofeedback tools measure physiological activity such as breathing, brainwaves, heart function, muscle activity, and skin temperature. For example, users can monitor their own physiological responses to stress (e.g. breathing rate) and be prompted to take steps to regulate these physiological systems. Once mastered, users can learn to self-regulate with little or no help from a biofeedback tool (Kennedy & Parker, 2019).

Seligman (2011) suggests that well-being is like the weather. Without the ability to measure things like temperature, rainfall, and wind patterns, the weather is ambiguous and poorly understood. The ability to accurately define and measure well-being and cognitive abilities is important for educational and developmental psychologists. Ultimately, biofeedback and other technological devices may more objectively capture physiological markers for well-being and cognition, providing advantages over traditionally derived informant or self-reported psychometric data.

As one example, the Personal Input Pod (PIP) provides a tangible tool to visualise an individual's physiological responses to many of the interventions and approaches used by educational and developmental psychologists (e.g. meditation, mindfulness, guided relaxation, and savouring). For educational and developmental psychologists, the PIP could be used as an objective and tangible measurement tool to demonstrate the efficacy of relaxation exercises. The visual nature of the platform is likely to suit diverse client populations and students of psychology.

While the PIP specifically has a small, yet promising, scientific base and has been found to assist with stress relief, further empirical support can be drawn from the broader biofeedback literature. Kennedy and Parker (2019) conducted a systematic review on biofeedback tools and their efficacy for stress management. They concluded that biofeedback interventions were useful in reducing perceived stress in participants, particularly those in clinical populations. Biofeedback has been found to be particularly effective for people with anxiety and depression (e.g. Schoenberg et al., 2014).

The other major strength of biofeedback tools like the PIP is that they can also serve as a practical example of gamification in psychology. Devices that interact with video games can be engaging and novel for both clients and students of psychology (Vella-Brodrick, 2020). Such tools can be unobtrusive, cost-effective, and used alongside existing objective measures (such as heart-rate measurement). While the evidence-base for these new generation biofeedback devices is still emerging, they hold promise as important self-management tools that could be incorporated into future interventions.

Virtual reality

Virtual reality (VR) is an immersive 3D environment that users can explore and interact with. VR may simulate real environments or develop imaginary environments. As VR technology has advanced, these environments have become incredibly realistic and immersive. VR has a wide range of applications, including business, education, entertainment, and social media. Social media VR is especially pertinent for educational and developmental psychologists.

Some scholars have raised concerns about Facebook virtual reality (VR) and its potential effect on social norms. One way teenagers learn what qualifies as acceptable behaviour is through observational learning. This includes interacting with peers via social media. However, when online social norms differ from offline social norms, there is potential for uncertainty and inappropriate behaviour. Further research is needed to fully understand the relationship between VR use and behaviours that may breach or enhance social norms. Educational and developmental psychologists in the future can expect to have knowledge of approaches and strategies that may mitigate the negative effects of VR. Although relatively new, VR is rapidly advancing as large corporations such as Facebook and Google expand their capabilities. There is likely to be a much greater need for psychological research and interest in the VR space.

Technology is at the intersection of the future of educational and developmental psychology as both a discipline and a practice area. It is not only technology that will shape the field in the future. We have also begun to see emerging trends that may even redefine how we work and who we work with.

Emerging trends in the discipline and practice

Several other factors will affect the future of educational and developmental psychology in Australia and around the world. Emerging trends include evidence-based practice, practice-based evidence, Indigenous psychology, and a focus on transdisciplinary collaborations and prevention and well-being.

According to the APS, evidence-based practice (EBP) "refers to the use of evidence to drive the decision on what processes to implement to solve a psychological problem" (2022c, p. 28). EBP relies on published literature to inform decision-making based on the most current and relevant psychological evidence. However, the APS has also begun to highlight the limitations of EBP. Practising psychologists must consider the bias that is reflected in published literature. Most psychological research reflects Western, educated, industrialised, rich, and democratic populations. Therefore, published literature and EBP are not applicable to every situation. For example, in Australia, published literature may not accurately reflect the needs and experiences of Aboriginal, Torres Strait Islander, or other cultural communities.

An alternative approach that may better address the needs of diverse communities is practice-based evidence (PBE). PBE can be defined as "high-quality scientific evidence that is developed, refined, and implemented first in a variety of real-world settings" (APS, 2022c). PBE considers information from the environmental, social, community, and cultural factors that impact how people perceive and experience the world. The APS recommends that psychology training and practice should incorporate both EBP and PBE.

Another emerging national, but internationally relevant field of psychology is Indigenous psychology. Indigenous psychology focuses on structural factors that can affect an individual's health (APS, 2022c). In Australia, bodies such as the APS and APHRA have recently made formal commitments to embed cultural safety practices when working with Aboriginal and Torres Strait Islander peoples. These policy changes should encourage psychology students, professionals, and organisations to be more aware of ways to work with diverse populations (APS, 2022c).

Jessica Rodaughan, Jardwadjali woman and current Master of Educational and Developmental Psychology Candidate at Monash University, suggests:

> We need to recognise and invest in Indigenous psychology. Indigenous psychologists and mental health practitioners are currently and have for a long time been integrating traditional models of well-being and ways of healing into their practice. These approaches sit largely outside of the mainstream psychology training and service delivery. We all need to embrace this coming together of different knowledges

and ways of working in Psychology, as individuals and at a systemic level. We all have a role to play in actively decolonising our education, our research, and our practice. When working with Aboriginal and Torres Strait Islander people, it is incredibly important to understand colonisation and history. This is a responsibility of the practitioner and not one of the clients to have to teach us. Psychology is dominated by Western ideas and I hope to make psychology a more culturally safe place for Aboriginal and Torres Strait Islander Australians to be empowered in their mental health journeys.

A focus on transdisciplinary collaborations

Educational and developmental psychology is a naturally transdisciplinary field. Our distinctiveness forges connections between professional, learning, and scholarly perspectives, and between various academic communities (Allen, 2021). Transdisciplinary collaborations encourage cooperation and the sharing of knowledge. Traditionally, a practising educational and developmental psychologist might work alongside GPs, paediatricians, occupational therapists, and speech pathologists, but in the future, educational and developmental psychologists may see expansion with other new and existing fields.

One illustrative example is the collaboration between neuroscience and educational and developmental psychology. Developmental neuroscience, which looks at the influence of early life experiences on brain development, and educational neuroscience, which explores brain and genetic bases of learning, are particularly relevant for educational and developmental psychologists (Gilmore et al., 2013). Another example is molecular genetics. Advancements and discoveries in genetic research have major implications for educational and developmental psychology in terms of diagnosis, treatment, and prevention of various disorders (Gilmore et al., 2013).

A greater focus on prevention and well-being

Prevention and early intervention are two essential roles of educational and developmental psychology. As Claire Ting, an educational and developmental psychologist at QUT, points out, educational and developmental psychology has always been at the forefront of positive movements within the Australian psychology profession that look beyond a deficit view and towards human flourishing. Among the many perspectives that are unique to our discipline are our strong focus on attachment, developmental transitions across the lifespan, systemic and contextual influences, positive psychology, a focus on strengths, identity formation, and affirmation of human diversity.

As prevention and early intervention gain more recognition among other professionals, governments, and organisations, educational and developmental psychologists will be called upon to provide their expertise. Associate Professor Louise Mclean of Monash University and past Course Leader of the Master of Educational and Developmental Psychology Course (from 2107 to 2022) says that "well-being is both an outcome and a protective factor across all areas of educational and developmental psychology".

Positive psychology, a contemporary branch of psychology that has emerged over the past two decades, also embraces prevention and early intervention. Positive psychology focuses on strategies to help mitigate negative emotions, cognitions, and behaviours, and foster an individual's overall well-being. (Vella-Brodrick, 2011). One area of positive psychology that will be of note for educational and developmental psychologists is positive education. Positive education aims to cultivate assets such as optimism, empathy, self-efficacy, and resilience among students through school interventions (Vella-Brodrick, 2011). It prioritises holistic development and well-being to prevent psychological distress and mental illness. A growing number of Australian and international schools have adopted positive psychology interventions. For example, anti-bully initiatives, well-being lessons, or exercises to help students identify and develop their strengths (Green, 2011).

Allen et al. (2022) wrote:

A famous quote, often attributed to Desmond Tutu, says, "There comes a point where we need to stop just pulling people out of the river. We need to go upstream and find out why they're falling in." Positive psychology is our invitation to go upstream, by adopting a strength-based approach to provide individuals, groups, and communities with strategies and interventions that promote well-being and prevent mental health problems.

Preventive and proactive approaches like positive education, positive psychology, mental health promotion, and mental health literacy (as some examples) have many obvious implications for the work of educational and developmental psychologists, especially those who work with school systems. Even though it is not a new direction for the field, the idea of promoting the well-being of the populations we work with (as opposed to working with them when things go wrong) may have a greater emphasis in research and practice going forward as people begin to understand the benefits.

New roles for educational and developmental psychologists

Despite common misconceptions, educational and developmental psychology is a richly diverse field that extends far beyond school settings. After discussing predicted changes and future directions of the field, let's imagine a few future careers for educational and developmental psychologists.

1   Climate Change specialist

The ongoing climate crisis has had significant psychosocial implications, including impacts on humans' physical and mental health. Psychologists can help understand human behaviour, motivation, and decision-making concerning climate change and develop strategies to educate people on the importance of pro-environmental behaviour (APS, 2020). Psychologists will also have to help individuals and communities cope with the emotional responses, such as stress and grief, from the threat of climate change. The following exert by Allen (2020, p. 2) shows the significant contributions educational and developmental psychologists have made so far, which shows great promise as to what educational and developmental psychology can offer.

Educational and developmental psychologists have already played important roles in changing the teaching of climate change in schools. While many young people are aware of climate change, many also misunderstand its underlying mechanisms (Thacker & Sinatra, 2019). The complexities of human-induced climate change mean there is no simple catch-all solution for resolving this problem (Lombardi et al., 2013). However, educational psychologists have already contributed widely. These contributions include the development of mental models of climate change using online simulation (Thacker & Sinatra, 2019); examining the role of epistemic beliefs and emotions (Muis et al., 2015); investigating the role of plausibility judgement in climate change beliefs (Lombardi & Sinatra, 2012; Lombardi et al., 2014); considering students' evaluations about climate change (Lombardi et al., 2016); understanding people's willingness to take action (Sinatra et al., 2012); and emphasising the importance of professional development for those who work with students (Beck et al., 2013).

Allen (2020, p. 2)

2 Geropsychologist

As health care and living standards continue to improve, people are living longer than ever, educational and developmental psychologists will be well-equipped to meet the psychological needs of an ageing population. The American Psychological Association recognised geropsychology as a new specialty in 2010. Geropyschologists work specifically with older people and their families. As the world's population ages, geropsychology will be in demand. Geropsychologists address stressors that are common later in life, such as loss of loved ones, retirement, and health conditions. They also address issues such as family relationships, sexuality, and memory (APA, 2016).

Associate Professor, Wendy McKenzie of Monash University is passionate about helping educational and developmental psychologists improve the health and wellbeing of older adults. She offered the following reflection:

As more Australians are living longer there is a rapidly growing need for psychological services to support the health and wellbeing of older adults. Currently, 1 in 6 (16%) Australians are over

65 years of age, with a projected increase to 21% by 2066 (Australian Institute of Health and Welfare (AIHW), 2021). Although most older Australians report being in good health or better (74%), many will experience some level of disability as they age (AIHW, 2021) requiring access to services. In general, the prevalence of mental health issues decreases in later life; however, older adults living in residential aged care are more likely to be diagnosed with a mental health disorder, in particular depression (AIHW, 2021; Davison et al., 2017). One of the most significant health issues facing older Australians is the increased risk of dementia. In 2022 there are over 487,500 people living with dementia, estimated to increase to over 1 million by 2058 (Dementia Australia, 2022).

Just like any stage of life, ageing is a developmental phase with associated physical, cognitive, social, and emotional changes. Educational and developmental psychologists are well-equipped to meet the psychological needs of our ageing population. Promoting better understanding of age-related change is an important part of addressing negative attitudes about the usefulness of psychological interventions for older adults (Davison et al., 2017), including people living with dementia (Cations et al., 2020/2021). The areas of growth for psychologists working with older adults is diverse, including adapting therapeutic interventions to treat depression and anxiety; assessment of and supporting changes associated with cognitive impairment; managing behavioural and psychological symptoms of dementia; providing carer support; health promotion and managing chronic health conditions (Argo, 2020/2021). There are also significant opportunities to promote older adults "ageing well" through psychoeducation and developing adaptive strategies that help older adults adjust to transitions of later life that involve changes to social roles, work, functional ability and living arrangements (Gething et al., 2003).

Geropsychology was recognised as a new speciality by the American Psychological Association in 2010. Development of the Pikes Peak model for training geropsychologists sets out the competencies in knowledge, skills, and attitudes required to provide services specifically to older people and their families (Knight et al., 2009). The historically low numbers of psychologists working with older adults has been attributed to negative stereotypes

Figure 12.2 Considering that the global population is ageing, geropsychology work for educational and developmental psychologists will be more common in the future

Source: Image created by Simone Gindidis and supplied with permission from the College of Educational and Developmental Psychologists National Committee.

and lack of training (Koder & Helmes, 2008). Unless there is a significant increase in the number of psychologists trained to be able to provide psychological services to older adults across a range of contexts there is a real risk these needs will not be met. The Royal Commission into Aged Care Quality and Safety and the COVID-19 pandemic have shone a spotlight on the urgent need to address this workforce shortage (Argo, 2020/2021; Cations et al., 2020/2021). As a result, there have been positive changes in access to psychological services, and in particular for people living in residential aged care (Argo, 2020/2021). Further, with an ageing baby boomer generation it is likely that greater awareness and assertiveness in regard to healthcare will also drive demand for psychological services in later life (Gething et al., 2003). Growing the workforce needed to support the mental health and wellbeing of older Australians will depend on better access to appropriate training and placement opportunities (Davison et al., 2017).

3   Social Media Influencer

Social media can be a great tool for reaching wide audiences, especially audiences of young people. Within the past few years, several psychology professionals have taken to social media to share their expertise with the world. Psychologists cannot provide professional services through social media, but they can help inform and educate followers about important psychological issues.

Tamara Zafiropoulos, a registrar educational and developmental and psychologist uses Instagram to generate awareness about psychology and specifically educational and developmental psychology:

> Social media can be a great tool for reaching wide audiences, especially audiences of young people. Within the past few years, several psychology professionals have taken to social media to share their expertise with the world. Psychologists cannot provide personalised services through social media, but they can educate their followers and help destigmatise conversations about psychological issues. Of course, any psychologists who post on social media must maintain a strict code of ethics, including client privacy and confidentiality.

Psychoeducation forms an important part of the therapeutic work of many psychologists. This skill of providing information about a psychological idea or disorder, and the biopsychosocial functions and implications, can be applied when using social media to many benefits. Increasing the accessibility of evidence-based psychological information to the wider public may increase mental health awareness, reduce the stigma around mental health psychological help-seeking, and allow for the breadth of services offered by psychologists to be more visible and better understood.

At time of publication, there are no specific ethical guidelines for Australian psychologists' use of social media, nevertheless principles from the APS Code of Ethics should be upheld, and psychologists should use social media in a way that does not damage the profession. The Psychology Board of Australia (PsyBA) state that psychologists using social media: comply with confidentiality and privacy obligations, comply with professional obligations defined the PsyBA code of conduct, maintain professional boundaries, communicate professionally and respectfully with or about patients, colleagues, and employers, and do not present information that is false misleading or deceptive. Some psychologists may also use social media to advertise their services or business. While a social media profile can be a great way for a client to learn about you and your services, it is imperative that psychologists do not include testimonials when advertising services nor make claims about professional superiority.

One way to support ethical social media engagement as a psychologist is to ensure you include a "disclosure statement" on your profile. This statement could include the intention of the profile/account (e.g. to advocate for mental health help-seeking), a statement that the information shared is not therapy or a replacement for therapy, and that psychological services cannot be provided on that medium. You might also include links or telephone numbers to services that can provide online/phone-based mental health crisis support relevant to your geographic area.

Finally, content created by psychologists on social media should be informed by research evidence. One may consider including references to the sources cited to inform the content of the post. In line with this, it is recommended that psychologists are mindful of ensuring the content they endorse through liking and/

or commenting on social media posts does not contradict current scientific evidence and literature. Keeping up-to-date with developments in the rapidly moving field of psychology and the world of social media is important for continued ethical and safe engagement online, not only for the psychologist themselves, but also the wider public.

Figure 12.3 It is expected that more educational and developmental psychologists will use social media to communicate messages

4   *HealthTech and EduTech*

The HealthTech industry has seen exponential growth over the past decade; accelerated further by the COVID-19 pandemic. Estimates from analysts vary considerably; however, the consensus is that the industry which includes digital therapeutics, treatment gamification, apps, software and hardware, is valued at billions of dollars and will continue to grow as new technologies become established.

Co-editor and Director of SavvyPsych and GameIQ, Simone Gindidis, reflects on her time as an Educational and Developmental Psychologist at a leading Australian digital therapeutics company:

My passion for marrying a love of technology and gaming with psychology motivated me to undertake a combined Masters and PhD in Educational and Developmental psychology researching the therapeutic use of apps with young people. I started working at a digital therapeutics company not long after – as a side note, if you are seeking an industry role, keep your LinkedIn profile up to date. After my experiences in industry, I can state with absolute certainty that educational and developmental psychologists are perfectly placed to lead the charge in this space.

My role involved working closely with colleagues for whom psychologists outside of a select few research settings are not accustomed to working with: cognitive neuroscientists, front and backend developers, domestic and international marketing teams, a COO, game designers, graphic designers, and animators.

My contributions as an educational and developmental psychologist were multifaceted and in addition to relying on my background and research working with technology, the advanced competencies developed in my psychology training became incredibly valuable: cognitive development across the lifespan, clinical experience navigating family, educational, and healthcare systems, language acquisition, curriculum development, theory, and real-world application of evidence-based assessment and intervention.

Each day was very different. Some days I was working closely with a brilliant cognitive neuroscientist reviewing and changing game design from a scientific and psychological perspective; other days I was making recommendations on voiceover scripts and game instructions informed by learning theory, supervising research students analysing real world game data, developing company-wide strategic clinical plans, researching global reimbursement pathways, and reporting on aspirational product development for different markets. I was incredibly fortunate to learn from a diverse group of professionals and teams, returning the favour where I could by offering presentations on topics including executive function, specific learning disorders, autism, cognitive decline, and the realities of clinical practice.

This experience reinforced the unique relevance of educational and developmental psychologists in HealthTech settings. There is more to psychology than mental health; I firmly believe educational and developmental psychologists offer a developmentally sensitive lens through which to offer services and expertise integral to co-developing digital innovations that are preventative, accessible, and capitalise on the promise of technology to promote learning and wellbeing from cradle to grave. More educational and developmental psychologists need to become involved in HealthTech and EduTech spaces. By contributing a brief reflection of my experiences and ongoing role in these industries, I hope educational and developmental psychologists will seek-out and explore similar opportunities for research and practice. Importantly, I hope educational and developmental psychologists start collaborating more with each other, so we not only contribute to this exponentially important space, but pioneer new solutions for our clients.

We cannot predict what exactly the future of educational and developmental psychology will hold. However, the above text gives a brief overview of some of the challenges and opportunities that future educational and developmental psychologists may encounter.

A New Zealand Perspective

Robyn Stead

Key to working successfully as an Educational Psychologist now and into the future in New Zealand is engaging actively as a treaty partner. New Zealand's foundations are in the Treaty of Waitangi,

Te Tiriti o Waitangi, a document signed by Māori and the Crown defining the relationship between the two. We are fortunate to have a range of highly respected and recognised academics who provide leadership to the profession in this area, Sonja Macfarlane, Angus Macfarlane, and Melinda Webber to name a few. While there is much to be done and we are far from being able to rest on our laurels we have much to be proud of and to celebrate. Future focused work in this area continues to provide opportunities for educational psychologists to improve outcomes for all who seek to learn and progress.

Like Australia the services of educational psychologists are in high demand. Educational Psychologists are registered by the New Zealand Psychologists Board (NZPB) under the relevant legislation, Health Practitioners Competence Assurance Act (HPCA) which was introduced by the government in 2003. In New Zealand, we are registered under an Educational Psychology scope, which is a protected title under the HPCA. There are two universities who are recognised by the NZPB to provide training to registration level, Massey University and Victoria University both of whom run educational and developmental psychology programmes. The types of work undertaken under this scope has at time been the subject of discussion between the NZPB and the professional body that represents educational psychologists in New Zealand, the Institute of Educational and Developmental Psychology, which is a part of the New Zealand Psychological Society. An important undertaking is to share with psychologists registered in other scopes and with the public what an educational psychologist can do. The NZPB is planning on undertaking a review of scopes and an ongoing source of work is preparing to engage with this review pro-actively, so our viewpoint is included.

In Aotearoa, Educational Psychologists are primarily employed by the Ministry of Education in a range of roles across field offices, in leadership and in policy development roles. They can also be found in academia, in Resource Teacher of Learning and Behaviour clusters, Kahui Ako (communities of learning), in child and adolescent mental health, contracting for a range of governmental ministries, and accident compensation corporation along with private practice. In a recent newsletter article, which invited educational psychologists to write about unusual roles we had contributions from a psychologist who provided advice to a children's television creator on content and one who provided assessment for prospective para-Olympians. The job opportunities are wide and varied.

We too are facing a rising tide of need, some of which can be attributed to the difficulties of the past few years and the management of COVID-19 in our community which required children to remain away from school for extended periods of time. Technology has provided us with options to connect with those who receive our services, and many are eager to continue to explore the possibilities while also remaining cautious about the possible negative effects. The future of educational psychology in Aotearoa, New Zealand is bright.

Concluding comments

Aspiring educational and developmental psychologists certainly have a rich and exciting, albeit challenging, future ahead of them. This chapter has provided a glimpse into the current and future state of educational and developmental psychology in Australia and internationally. An expanding research and practice foci, technological advances, and innovations in service delivery that have resulted from the COVID-19 pandemic are important factors that will continue to affect educational and developmental psychology into the future.

Postscript

Welcome to our community. If you have reached this stage of the book, the authors are guessing that you are genuinely interested in becoming an educational and developmental psychologist. As you have seen in this book, educational and developmental psychology represents an area of practice, an academic discipline, and a diverse community. For many of us, educational and developmental psychology is an important part of our professional identity and offers a sense of belonging to a larger local, national, and global network. Take your time to consider the messages in the book and we look forward to meeting you at events, conferences, professional development, or future gatherings.

References

ABS. (2022). *The National Study of Mental Health and Wellbeing 2020–21*. *ABS*. www.abs.gov.au/statistics/health/mental-health/national-study-mental-health-and-wellbeing/latest-release#:~:text=The%202020%2D21%20National%20Study,Diagnostic%20Interview%20(CIDI%203.0)

Allen, K. A. (2020). Climate change, a critical new role for educational and developmental psychologists. *The Educational and Developmental Psychologist*, *37*(1), 1–3. https://doi.org/10.1017/edp.2020.6

Allen, K. A. (2021). The transdisciplinary nature of educational and developmental psychology. *The Educational and Developmental Psychologist*, *38*(1), 1–2. https://doi.org/10.1080/20590776.2021.1956868

Allen, K. A., Frydenberg, E., & Waters, L. (2022, September). Going upstream with positive psychology in our schools. *In Psych*. https://psychology.org.au/for-members/publications/inpsych/2022/vol-44-spring-2022/going-upstream-with-positive-psychology-in-our-sch

American Psychological Association (APA). (2016). *Geropsychology: It's your future*. www.apa.org/pi/aging/resources/geropsychology

Annan, J. (2005). Situational analysis: A framework for evidence-based practice. *School Psychology International*, *26*(2), 131–146.

Argo, A. (2020–2021, December/January). Upsetting the aged-care applecart. *InPsych*, *42*(6), 8–14.

Australian Association for Cognitive Behavioural Therapy (AACBT). (2022). *The AACBT Organisation*. www.aacbt.org.au

Australian Association of Psychologists (AAPi). (2021). *About us*. www.aapi.org.au/Web/Web/About-AAPi/About-AAPi.aspx?hkey=1aacd2e6-5c43-4619-b991-770495e2540a

Australian Association of Psychologists (AAPi). (2022a). *Our story*. www.aapi.org.au/Web/About-AAPi/About-AAPi.aspx

Australian Association of Psychologists (AAPi). (2022b). *Use of social media*. https://aapi.org.au/common/Uploaded%20files/Use%20of%20Social%20Media.pdf

Australian Autism Research Council (AARC). (2018). *A national guideline for the assessment and diagnosis of autism spectrum disorders in Australia.* www.autismcrc.com.au/access/national-guideline

Australian Government. (n.d.). *Study assist. Information for students about government assistance for financing tertiary study.* www.studyassist.gov.au/help-loans/fee-help

Australian Health Practitioner Regulation Authority (AHPRA). (2020). *Guidelines for advertising a regulated health service.* Psychology Board. www.ahpra.gov.au/Resources/Advertising-hub/Advertising-guidelines-and-other-guidance/Advertising-guidelines.aspx

Australian Institute of Health and Welfare (AIHW). (2021). *Older Australians.* www.aihw.gov.au/reports/older-people/older-australians/contents/about

Australian Psychological Society (APS). (2018). *Evidence-based psychological interventions in the treatment of mental disorders.* www.psychology.org.au/getmedia/23c6a11b-2600-4e19-9a1d-6ff9c2f26fae/Evidence-based-psych-interventions.pdf

Australian Psychological Society (APS). (2019, June). *The future of psychology in Australia: A blueprint for better mental health outcomes for all Australians through Medicare.* https://psychology.org.au/getmedia/a1c6fc1f-8356-471c-9247-36832da61299/aps-white-paper-the-future-of-psychology-in-australia-june-2019-final.pdf

Australian Psychological Society (APS). (2020). *Psychology and climate change: Position statement.* https://psychology.org.au/about-us/position-statements/psychology-and-climate-change

Australian Psychological Society (APS). (2022a). *APS college of educational and developmental psychologists.* https://groups.psychology.org.au/cedp/about_us/

Australian Psychological Society (APS). (2022b). *APS colleges and significant dates in the early history of clinical psychology in Australia & internationally.* https://groups.psychology.org.au/GroupContent.aspx?ID=4384

Australian Psychological Society (APS). (2022c). *Evidence-based practice and practice-based evidence in psychology: Position statement.* https://psychology.org.au/about-us/position-statements/evidence-based-practice

Australian Psychological Society (APS). (2022d). *Study pathways.* https://psychology.org.au/training-and-careers/careers-and-studying-psychology/studying-psychology/study-pathways

Australian Psychology Accreditation Council (APAC). (2019). *Evidence guide. Version 1.2.* https://psychologycouncil.org.au/wp-content/uploads/2021/03/APAC-Evidence-guide_v1.2.pdf

Australian Psychology Accreditation Council (APAC). (2022). *About us.* https://psychologycouncil.org.au/about-us/

Beck, A., Sinatra, G. M., & Lombardi, D. (2013). Leveraging higher-education instructors in the climate literacy effort: Factors related to university faculty's propensity to teach climate change. *The International Journal of Climate Change: Impacts and Responses, 4,* 1–17.

Bell, H. D., & McKenzie, V. (2013). Perceptions and realities: The role of school psychologists in Melbourne, Australia. *The Educational and Developmental Psychologist, 30*(1), 54–73. https://doi.org/10.1017/edp.2013.1

Berry Street. (2022, August 9). *Therapeutic services for children, young people and families (take two).* www.berrystreet.org.au/what-we-do/trauma-services/therapeutic-services-for-children-young-people-and-families

Best, P., Manktelow, R., & Taylor, B. (2014). Online communication, social media and adolescent wellbeing: A systematic narrative review. *Children and Youth Services Review, 41,* 27–36. https://doi.org/10.1016/j.childyouth.2014.03.001

Bishop, J., & Chan, I. (2019). Is declining union membership contributing to low wages growth? Research Discussion Paper RDP 2019–02. *Reserve Bank of Australia.* www.rba.gov.au/publications/rdp/2019/2019-02.html#:~:text=We%20find%20that%20changing%20unionisation,as%20union%20membership%20has%20declined.

Booth, P. B., & Jernberg, A. M. (2010). *Theraplay: Helping parents and children build better relationships through attachment – based play* (3rd ed.). Jossey-Bass.

Bravata, D. M., Watts, S. A., Keefer, A. L., Madhusudhan, D. K., Taylor, K. T., Clark, D. M., Nelson, R. S., Cokley, K. O., & Hagg, H. K. (2020). Prevalence, predictors, and treatment of impostor syndrome: A systematic review. *Journal of General Internal Medicine, 35*(4), 1252–1275. https://doi.org/10.1007/s11606-019-05364-1

Buckingham, J. (2020). Systematic phonics instruction belongs in evidence-based reading programs: A response to Bowers. *Educational and Developmental Psychologist, 37*(2), 105–113. https://doi.org/10.1017/edp.2020.12

Cations, M., Low, L.-F., Blair, A., & Koder, D. (2020–2021, December/January). Psychological therapy for people with dementia. *InPsych, 42*(6), 25–29.

Clark, P., Holden, C., Russell, M., & Downs, H. (2021). The impostor phenomenon in mental health professionals: Relationships among compassion fatigue, burnout, and compassion satisfaction. *Contemporary Family Therapy, 44*(2), 185–197. https://doi.org/10.1007/s10591-021-09580-y

Davis, J., Wolff, H.-G., Forret, M. L., & Sullivan, S. E. (2020). Networking via LinkedIn: An examination of usage and career benefits. *Journal of Vocational Behavior, 118,* Article 103396. https://doi.org/10.1016/j.jvb.2020.103396

Davison, T., Koder, D., Helmes, E., Doyle, C., Bhar, S., Mitchell, L., Hunter, C., Knight, B., & Pachana, N. (2017). Brief on the role of psychologists in residential and home care services for older adults. *Australian Psychologist, 52,* 397–405.

Dementia Australia. (2022). *Key facts and statistics.* www.dementia.org.au/statistics

Diamond, E. L., & Whalen, A. (2018). Ethics and social media: Professional considerations for the school psychologist. *Contemporary School Psychology, 23*(4), 351–356. https://doi.org/10.1007/s40688-017-0170-x

DiAngelo, R. (2018). *White fragility: Why it's so hard for white people to talk about racism.* Beacon Press.

Ding, N., & Swalwell, J. (2018). School psychology and supervision in Australia. *The Educational and Developmental Psychologist, 35*(1), 1–17. https://doi.org/10.1017/edp.2018.2

Drude, K., & Messer-Engel, K. (2021). The development of social media guidelines for psychologists and for regulatory use. *Journal of Technology in Behavioral Science, 6,* 388–396. https://doi.org/10.1007/s41347-020-00176-1

Elkins, D. N. (2009). The medical model in psychotherapy: Its limitations and failures. *Journal of Humanistic Psychology, 49*(1), 66–84. https://doi.org/10.1177/0022167807307901

Fisher, K. W., Goswami, U., Geake, J., & the Task Force on the Future of Educational Neuroscience. (2010). The future of educational neuroscience. *Mind, Brain, and Education, 4,* 68–80. https://doi.org/10.1111/j.1751-228X.2010.01086.x

Fletcher, J., Bloor, K., Crossman, C., Thornton, J., Briggs, E., Hawkins, T., Sammut, S., & Cardwell, K. (2010). Profiling the college of educational and developmental psychologists: An examination of demographics, professional practice, attitudes, and professional development preferences. *The Educational and Developmental Psychologist, 27*(1), 1–19. https://doi.org/10.1375/aedp.27.1.1

Freeman, J., & Peisah, C. (2022). Imposter syndrome in doctors beyond training: A narrative review. *Australasian Psychiatry, 30*(1), 49–54. https://doi.org/10.1177/10398562211036121

Gamble, N., & Morris, Z. A. (2014, June). Ethical and competent practice in the online age. *InPsych: The Bulletin of the Australian Psychological Society.* https://psychology.org.au/inpsych/2014/june/gramble

Gething, L., Gridley, H., Browning, C., Helmes, E., Luszcz, M., Turner, J., Ward, L., & Wells, Y. (2003). The role of psychologists in fostering the well-being of older Australians. *Australian Psychologist, 38*(1), 1–10.

Gilmore, L., Fletcher, J., & Hudson, A. (2013). A commentary on the current and future status of educational and developmental psychology in Australia. *The Educational and Developmental Psychologist, 30*(1), 1–12. https://doi.org/10.1017/edp.2013.6

Gindidis, S., Stewart, S., & Roodenburg, J. (2020). Psychologists' motivations for integrating apps into therapy with secondary school-aged young people. *Journal of Psychologists and Counsellors in Schools, 30*(1), 2–12. https://doi.org/10.1017/jgc.2019.22

Green, S. (2011). Positive education: Creating flourishing students, staff and schools. *InPsych, 33*(2).

Grové, C. (2021). Co-developing a mental health and wellbeing Chatbot with and for young people. *Frontiers in Psychiatry, 11*, 606041. https://doi.org/10.3389/fpsyt.2020.606041

Grové, C., Trainer, L., & Rangarajan, R. (2020). *Youth Centred Research Brief Report 1 Co-collaborating with youth as active stakeholders in research (Version 1)*. Monash University. https://doi.org/10.26180/13158170.v1 (['www.monash.edu/youth-booth-exhibition/home'])

Hill, V. (2013). An evolving discipline: Exploring the origins of educational psychology, educational selection, and special education. In C. Arnold & J Hardy (Eds.), *British educational psychology: The first hundred year* (pp. 31–41). British Psychological Society.

Hoare, N., & Luke, J. (2022). Introduction to career development. In T. Machin, T. Machin, C. Jeffries, & N. Hoare (Eds.), *The Australian handbook for careers in psychological science*. University of Southern Queensland.

Interactive Advertising Bureau. (2021). *Online advertising expenditure report – quarter ended March 2021*. https://iabaustralia.com.au/resource/online-advertising-expenditure-report-quarter-ended-march-2021/

Isaac, J. (2018). Why are Australian wages lagging and what can be done about it? *Australian Economic Review, 51*(2), 175–190. https://doi.org/10.1111/1467-8462.12270

Jones, J. L., & Mehr, S. L. (2007). Foundations and assumptions of the Scientist-Practitioner Model. *American Behavioral Scientist, 50*(6), 766–771. https://doi.org/10.1177/0002764206296454

Kennedy, L., & Parker, S. H. (2019). Biofeedback as a stress management tool: A systematic review. *Cognition, Technology & Work, 21*(2), 161–190. https://doi.org/10.1007/s10111-018-0487-x

Knapp, M., McDaid, D., & Parsonage, M. (2011). *Mental health promotion and mental illness prevention: The economic case*. London Department of Health.

Knight, B., Karel, M., Hinrichsen, G., Qualls, S., & Duffy, M. (2009). Pikes peak model for training in professional geropsychology. *The American Psychologist, 64*, 205–214. https://doi.org/10.1037/a0015059

Koder, D., & Helmes, E. (2008). Brief report: Reactions to ageing among Australian psychologists. *Australasian Journal of Ageing, 27*, 212–214. https://doi.org/10.1111/j.1741-6612.2008.00314.x

Langford, P. E. (2005). *Vygotsky's developmental and educational psychology*. Psychology Press.

Larson, L. M., & Suzuki, L. (1992). Development and validation of the Counselling Self-Estimate Inventory. *Journal of Counselling Psychology, 39*(1), 105–120. https://doi.org/10.1037/0022-0167.39.1.105

Lombardi, D., Brandt, C. B., Bickel, E. S., & Burg, C. (2016). Students' evaluations about climate change. *International Journal of Science Education, 38*(8), 1392–1414.

Lombardi, D., Seyranian, V., & Sinatra, G. M. (2014). Source effects and plausibility judgments when reading about climate change. *Discourse Processes*, *51*(1–2), 75–92. https://doi.org/10.1080/0163853X.2013.855049

Lombardi, D., & Sinatra, G. M. (2012). College students' perceptions about the plausibility of human-induced climate change. *Research in Science Education*, *42*(2), 201–217. https://doi.org/10.1007/s11165-010-9196-z

Lombardi, D., Sinatra, G. M., & Nussbaum, E. M. (2013). Plausibility reappraisals and shifts in middle school students' climate change conceptions. *Learning and Instruction*, *27*, 50–62. https://doi.org/10.1016/j.learninstruc.2013.03.001

Macfarlane, S. (2009). Te Pikinga ki Runga: Rising possibilities. *Set: Research Information for Teachers (Wellington)*, *2*.

Mcgillivray, J., Gurtman, C., Boganin, C., & Sheen, J. (2015). Self-practice and self-reflection in training of psychological interventions and therapist skills development: A qualitative meta-synthesis review. *Australian Psychologist*, *50*(6), 434–444. https://doi.org/10.1111/ap.12158

McNamara, J. K., & Willoughby, T. (2010). A longitudinal study of risk-taking behaviour in adolescents with learning disabilities. *Learning Disabilities Research & Practice*, *25*(1), 11–24. https://doi.org/10.1111/j.1540-5826.2009.00297.x

Miller, D. C., & Defina, P. A. (2009). The application of neuroscience to the practice of school neuropsychology. In D. C. Miller (Ed.), *Best practices in school neuropsychology* (pp. 141–157). Wiley.

Muis, K. R., Pekrun, R., Sinatra, G. M., Azevedo, R., Trevors, G., Meier, E., & Heddy, B. C. (2015). The curious case of climate change: Epistemic emotions mediate relations between epistemic beliefs, learning strategies and learning outcomes. *Learning and Instruction*, *39*, 168–183. https://doi.org/10.1016/j.learninstruc.2015.06.003

Muller, J., & Raphael, D. (2021). Does unionization and working under collective agreements promote health? *Health Promotion International*. https://doi.org/10.1093/heapro/daab181

Murphy, P. K., & Benton, S. L. (2010). The new frontier of educational neuropsychology: Unknown opportunities and unfulfilled hopes. *Contemporary Educational Psychology*, *35*(2), 153–155. https://doi.org/10.1016/j.cedpsych.2010.04.006

National Association of School Psychologists (NASP). (2019). *School psychology credentialing fact sheet [handout]*. Author. www.nasponline.org/

National Disability Insurance Scheme Act (2013). *No. 20*. www.legislation.gov.au/Details/C2013A00020

Nissen-Lie, H. A., Monsen, J. T., & Rønnestad, M. H. (2010). Therapist predictors of early patient-rated working alliance: A multilevel approach. *Psychotherapy Research*, *20*(6), 627–646. https://doi.org/10.1080/10503307.2010.497633

Orben, A., & Przybylski, A. K. (2019). The association between adolescent wellbeing and digital technology use. *Nature Human Behaviour*, *3*(2), 173–182. https://doi.org/10.1038/s41562-018-0506-1

Palmer, C. (2021, June 1). How to overcome imposter phenomenon. *Monitor on Psychology*, *52*(4). www.apa.org/monitor/2021/06/cover-impostor-phenomenon

Pappas, S. (2022, January 1). The rise of psychologists. *Monitor on Psychology*, *53*(1). www.apa.org/monitor/2022/01/special-rise-psychologists

Plomin, R., & Walker, S. O. (2003). Genetics and educational psychology. *British Journal of Educational Psychology*, *73*(1), 3–14. https://doi.org/10.1348/000709903762869888

Psychology Board of Australia (PsyBA). (2022a). Guidelines on area of practice endorsements. *Psychology Board*. www.psychologyboard.gov.au/Standards-and-Guidelines/Codes-Guidelines-Policies/Guidelines-area-of-practice-endorsements.aspx

Psychology Board of Australia (PsyBA). (2022b, June). *Registrant data*. www.psychologyboard.gov.au/about/statistics.aspx

Queensland Health. (2021). Health Practitioner Regulation National Law Act 2009. *Queensland Legislation*. www.legislation.qld.gov.au/view/html/inforce/current/act-2009-045

Ramshaw, A. (2022). Social media statistics for Australia. *Genroe Social Media Statistics for Australia*. www.genroe.com/blog/social-media-statistics-australia/13492

Reupert, A., Greenfeld, D., May, F., Berger, E., Morris, Z. A., Allen, K. A., Summers, D., & Wurf, G. (2022). COVID-19 and Australian school psychology: Qualitative perspectives for enhancing future practice. *School Psychology International*, *43*(3), 219–236. https://doi.org/10.1177/01430343221091953

Reupert, A., Schaffer, G. E., von Hagen, A., Allen, K. A., Berger, E., Büttner, G., Power, E. M., Morris, Z., Paradis, P., Fisk, A. K., Summers, D., Wurf, G., & May, F. (2021). The practices of psychologists working in schools during COVID-19: A multi-country investigation. *School Psychology*, *37*(2), 190–201. https://doi.org/10.1037/spq0000450

Schaffer, G. E., Power, E. M., Fisk, A. K., & Trolian, T. L. (2021). Beyond the four walls: The evolution of school psychological services during the COVID-19 outbreak. *Psychology in the Schools*, *58*(7), 1246–1265. https://doi.org/10.1002/pits.22543

Schoenberg, P. L., & David, A. S. (2014). Biofeedback for psychiatric disorders: A systematic review. *Applied Psychophysiology and Biofeedback*, *39*(2), 109–135. https://doi.org/10.1007/s10484-014-9246-9

Schwartz, M. S. (2010). A new improved universally accepted official definition of biofeedback: Where did it come from? Why? Who did it? Who is it for? What's next? *Biofeedback*, *38*(3), 88–90. https://doi.org/10.5298/1081-5937-38.3.88

References

Schweinsberg, A., Mundy, M. E., Dyer, K. R., & Garivaldis, F. (2021). Psychology education and work readiness integration: A call for research in Australia. *Frontiers in Psychology, 12,* Article 623353. https://doi.org/10.3389/fpsyg.2021.623353

Seek. (2022). *How to become a psychologist.* www.seek.com.au/career-advice/role/psychologist

Seligman, M. E. (2011). *Flourish: A visionary new understanding of happiness and wellbeing.* Free Press.

Sinatra, G. M., Kardash, C. M., Taasoobshirazi, G., & Lombardi, D. (2012). Promoting attitude change and expressed willingness to take action toward climate change in college students. *Instructional Science, 40,* 1–17. https://doi.org/10.1007/s11251-011-9166-5

Smith, K. M., Jones, A., & Hunter, E. A. (2021). Navigating the multidimensionality of social media presence: Ethical considerations and recommendations for psychologists. *Ethics & Behavior.* https://doi.org/10.1080/10508422.2021.1977935

Solity, J. E. (2020). Instructional psychology and teaching reading: Ending the reading wars. *Educational and Developmental Psychologist, 37*(2), 123–132. https://doi.org/10.1017/edp.2020.18

Stops, D. (2022). *Educational and developmental.* Australian Psychological Society. https://psychology.org.au/training-and-careers/careers-and-studying-psychology/careers-in-psychology/psychologists-talk-about-careers/educational-and-developmental

Svetaz, M. V., Ireland, M., & Blum, R. (2000). Adolescents with learning disabilities: Risk and protective factors associated with emotional wellbeing: Findings from the National Longitudinal Study of Adolescent Health. *Journal of Adolescent Health, 27*(5), 340–348. https://doi.org/10.1016/S1054-139X(00)00170-1

Swalwell, J., & McLean, L. (2021). Promoting children's social-emotional learning through early education: Piloting the pyramid model in victorian preschools. *Australasian Journal of Special and Inclusive Education.* https://doi.org/10.1017/jsi.2021.15

Tee, E. Y. J., Fernandez, E. F., Li, C. L., & Leong, G. C. (2018). Rethinking undergraduate psychology programs: Examining the level of graduate work readiness. In C. D. Ryff, K. Shigemasu, S. Kuwano, T. Sato, & T. Matsuzawa (Eds.), *Diversity in harmony – insights from psychology: Proceedings of the 31st international congress of psychology* (pp. 358–374). John Wiley & Sons. https://doi.org/10.1002/978119362081.ch19

Thacker, I., & Sinatra, G. M. (2019). Visualizing the greenhouse effect: Restructuring mental models of climate change through a guided online simulation. *Education Sciences, 9*(1). https://doi.org/10.3390/educsci9010014

Tutelman, P. R., Dol, J., Tougas, M. E., & Champters, C. T. (2018). Navigating your social media presence. *Clinical Practice in Pediatric Psychology, 6*(3), 289–298. https://doi.org/10.1037/cpp0000228

Vella-Brodrick, D. A. (2011). Positive psychology: Reflecting on the past and projecting into the future. *InPsych*, *33*(2), 10–13.

Vella-Brodrick, D. A. (2020). Wellbeing education that feels like a TREAT, rather than a treatment plan [Video]. *YouTube*. www.youtube.com/watch?v=u0J8rwCZpus

Vygotsky, L. S. (1978). *Mind and society: The development of higher mental processes*. Harvard University Press.

Wheldall, K., Wheldall, R., Bell, N., & Buckingham, J. (2020). Researching the efficacy of a reading intervention: An object lesson. *Educational and Developmental Psychologist*, *37*(2), 147–151. https://doi.org/10.1017/edp.2020.17

World Health Organisation. (2022). *Adolescent mental health*. www.who.int/news-room/fact-sheets/detail/adolescent-mental-health

Wurf, G. (2018). Culture and personality in international schools: Are trait differences in students' personalities attenuated or amplified? *Intercultural Education*, *29*(3), 418–433. https://doi.org/10.1080/14675986.2018.1438589

About the authors

Kelly-Ann Allen, PhD, FAPS, is Associate Professor and Educational and Developmental Psychologist in the School of Educational Psychology and Counselling in the Faculty of Education, Monash University, and Honorary Principal Fellow at the Centre for Wellbeing Science, University of Melbourne. Dr Allen is Editor-in-Chief of the Educational and Developmental Psychologist and served previously on the National Executive of the College of Educational and Developmental Psychologists (CEDP) where she held multiple roles including Treasurer (2012–2020). The quality of her research has been acknowledged through several awards, including recognition by The Australian's data-science partner, The League of Scholars and independently ranked as Best In Field for her research contributions. Dr Allen is Fellow of the Australian Psychological Society, an honour of esteemed senior psychologists who have made a significant contribution to the profession over a significant period of time. She is also Fellow of the CEDP. Through her teaching into the Master of Educational and Developmental Psychology Course at Monash University, supervision of Graduate Research in the area of educational and developmental psychology and educational and developmental psychology registrars, Dr Allen hopes to support future educational and developmental psychologists and encourage them to join a rewarding profession.

You can find Kelly-Ann on Twitter, Instagram and Facebook @drkellyallen

Chelsea Hyde, MAPS, FCEDP, is Educational and Developmental Psychologist and Senior Lecturer at the University of Melbourne and Course Convenor of the Master of Educational Psychology program. Chelsea is a board-approved supervisor and a member of the College of Educational and Developmental Psychology (CEDP) National Committee. As a teaching specialist and academic-practitioner, Chelsea is committed to the teaching of psychological practice within a scientist-practitioner model, ensuring that best-practice methods underpin education. She has published a number of peer-reviewed publications in the area of adolescent mental health and well-being with a particular interest in supporting students within school settings, and is a regular presenter at both national and international conferences in psychology and education. Chelsea has 15 years of experience working as a school psychologist within Independent and Catholic school systems in Victoria and Queensland across both regional and metropolitan areas. You can find Chelsea on Twitter @drchelseahyde

Emily Berger, PhD, MAPS, is Educational and Developmental Psychologist and Senior Lecturer in the School of Educational Psychology and Counselling in the Faculty of Education, Monash University. She is also Adjunct Senior Research Fellow with the School of Rural Health, Faculty of Medicine, Nursing and Health Sciences, Monash University, and a member of the Australian Psychological Society (APS) and College of Educational and Developmental Psychologists (CEDP). Dr Berger is Registered Educational and Developmental Psychologist and Board-Approved Supervisor with the Psychology Board of Australia. She is an internationally recognised expert in the areas of child and adolescent trauma and trauma-informed interventions, and has published over 90 peer-reviewed journal articles and research reports related to childhood trauma, school mental health, and vulnerable youth. She is passionate about high quality educational psychology research and research translation into school policy and practice. Dr Berger's contribution to the field of educational psychology has been recognised with an award from the APS and invited keynote and community presentations.

Joe Coyne is an Applied Developmental Psychologist who has worked for over 20 years in the area of child and family psychology. He is particularly interested in the developmental processes involved in healthy outcomes and the impacts of parenting and life events on personal trajectories across the lifespan. In recent years, he has been exploring the benefits of incorporating attachment theory and research into contemporary treatment approaches for parents, children, and adults. Of the developmental outcomes that early life impacts, he is particularly interested in how people come to understand and manage their emotions, both individually and in the various relationships of their daily lives. To this end, he is interested in the practice and research related to emotion regulation, mindfulness, and compassion. He is also interested in the life-cycle of professionals in the helping fields and the value of outcome informed practice, science-based service delivery, and deliberate practice. Joe is an accredited therapist, trainer, and supervisor for the Circle of Security Intervention. He is currently the Course Coordinator for Professional Programs (Educational & Developmental and Clinical) at QUT and is endorsed as both a Clinical and Educational & Developmental Psychologist.

Simone Gindidis, PhD, MAPS, FCEDP, FAEDPA, is an Educational and Developmental Psychologist, Board-Approved Supervisor, and Director of SavvyPsych and GameIQ. A former small device and computer technician, she is passionate about the integration of technology with psychological assessments and therapy. Her PhD research evaluated the clinical use of smartphone apps in adolescent therapy and she was the first Clinical Lead at an Australian digital therapeutics company producing serious games for executive function. She works clinically across early childhood, primary, secondary, and community languages schools, in private practice, and as a HealthTech consultant to companies and developers. Simone is as much an energetic advocate for the evidence-based development of ethical, developmentally sensitive, fun, digital solutions as she is about expanding the field of educational and developmental psychology. For this reason she maintains ties to psychology training programs at Universities as a sessional research supervisor and lecturer. Simone currently sits on The Educational and Developmental Psychologist Editorial Board and served on the APS College of Educational and Developmental Psychologists National Committee (2016–2022) in a number of elected and appointed roles. She has recently co-founded the Australian Educational and Developmental Psychology Association, a membership organisation exclusively for Educational and Developmental Psychologists. Her research interests include apps, MHealth, ethics, serious games, ecologically informed technology integration, and digital and professional competency development. You can find Simone on LinkedIn, Twitter @Savvy_Psych, and Instagram @DrSimoneGindidis.

Zoe A. Morris, PhD, MAPS, FCEDP, is Educational and Developmental Psychologist, Board-Approved Supervisor with the Psychology Board of Australia, Course Leader (Acting) for the Master of Educational and Developmental Psychology, and Lecturer in the School of Educational Psychology and Counselling in the Faculty of Education, Monash University. She is passionate about researching, supporting, and shaping the ethical and professional practice of future and current psychologists. Zoe previously worked in public schools as a school psychologist providing counselling, assessment, and intervention to students in both mainstream and specialist settings. Zoe has previously served as an elected member representative on the National Committee of the APS College of Educational and Developmental Psychologists (2016–2019) and as the Krongold Clinic Manager (2017 to 2019) at Monash University – Australia's only university clinic solely focusing on training in Educational and Developmental Psychology. You can find Zoe on Instagram and Twitter @DrZoeMorris.

Camelia Wilkinson, FAPS, FCEDP, is a practising psychologist, a board-approved supervisor, and an endorsed Educational and Developmental Psychologist. She is passionate about the area of Educational and Developmental psychology in which she has been practising, teaching, and supervising (both students and practitioners) for over two decades. That passion is represented by the roles, professional positions, and associations over her career, and reflected in the number of requests from various organisations, universities, and professional bodies for her expertise.

She is a Fellow of the Australian Psychological Society, an honour of esteemed senior psychologist who have made a significant contribution to the profession over a significant period of time. She is a Fellow of the College of Educational and Developmental Psychology, Chair of the College, and Chair of the National Committee.

Camelia is a keen advocate of Educational and Developmental Psychology work and is actively participating in work that helps promote the unique skills and expertise of this profession.

You can find Camelia on Instagram and Facebook @CameliaWilkinson.

Gerald Wurf, FAPS, FCEDP, joined Monash University in 2017 as a Senior Lecturer (Practice) in Educational Psychology and Counselling.

Prior to this, he worked at Charles Sturt University and for the NSW Government as an educational/developmental psychologist. He has provided consultant services to NGOs, Catholic and independent schools in NSW, and international schools in Hong Kong. He is a registered psychologist, board-approved supervisor, and holds endorsement with AHPRA in Educational and Developmental Psychology. Gerald is the immediate past-Chair of the APS College of Educational and Developmental Psychologists. For eight years Gerald worked in Hong Kong including at the University of Hong Kong and at Hong Kong International School. He has had over 30 years' professional experience working with children, young people, and adults with complex learning, behavioural and emotional challenges.

About the illustrator

Kathryn Kallady, MAPS, FCEDP, is Educational and Developmental Psychologist, and Board-Approved Supervisor with the Psychology Board of Australia. Kathryn has worked as Educational and Developmental Psychologist in a number of settings, including public and private schools and public hospital settings. She is currently in private practice providing therapy and neurodevelopmental assessment. Kathryn provides clinical supervision for the Monash Autism & ADHD Genetics and Neurodevelopment (MAGNET) Project.

Kathryn has always engaged in illustration and graphic design and enjoys translating ideas into graphics and pop culture. Kathryn has provided artistic artwork for therapy tools, universities, textbooks, and musicians including Gotye, Tash Parker, and Ben Abraham.

You can find Kathryn on Instagram @psych.babble.bobble

Index

Note: Locators in *italic* indicate figures, in **bold** tables and in ***italic bold*** boxes.

For Product Safety Concerns and Information please contact our EU
representative GPSR@taylorandfrancis.com Taylor & Francis Verlag GmbH,
Kaufingerstraße 24, 80331 München, Germany

Printed and bound by CPI Group (UK) Ltd, Croydon, CR0 4YY
08/06/2025
01896986-0002